The Development of Law
in Frontier California

The Development of Law in Frontier California

Civil Law and Society, 1850-1890

GORDON MORRIS BAKKEN

Contributions in Legal Studies, Number 33

Greenwood Press
Westport, Connecticut • London, England

Library of Congress Cataloging in Publication Data

Bakken, Gordon Morris.
  The development of law in frontier California.

  (Contributions in legal studies, ISSN 0147-1074 ;
no. 33)
  Bibliography: p.
  Includes index.
  1. Civil law—California—History. I. Title.
II. Series.
KFC80.B35   1985   346.794'009   84-25202
ISBN 0-313-24725-0 (lib. bdg.)   347.9406009

Library of Congress Catalog Card Number: 84-25202
ISBN: 0-313-24725-0
ISSN: 0147-1074

First published in 1985

Greenwood Press
A division of Congressional Information Service, Inc.
88 Post Road West
Westport, Connecticut 06881

The paper used in this book complies with the
Permanent Paper Standard issued by the National
Information Standards Organization (Z39.48-1984).

Printed in the United States of America

10 9 8 7 6 5 4 3 2 1

To Angela and Jeffrey

CONTENTS

The Development of Law
in Frontier California

INTRODUCTION

The legal history of California in the period 1850-1890 involves four fundamental topics: the contract-based transactional society, the allocation of natural resources, the public law, and criminal law. This is the first of four volumes that will explore certain fundamental questions about law and society in nineteenth-century California and America.

The writing of this legal history has been fraught with problems. There are no state legal histories. The models do not come easily to mind, but there are certain clear guideposts to follow. First, contract law dominated the nineteenth-century legal scene. The transactional society in its broadest context has its history.[1] Second, contract law was court law. Judges decided more about its contours than did legislators in the nineteenth century. Third, contract existed within a marketplace environment. Contract and its ramifications must be a focus for any state legal history. From contract, other areas of law emerge. These will be the topical foci of the chapters. Fourth, by late century a new branch of law, tort, emerged to challenge the dominance of contract. Its development must be explained. All of this involves formal law. Further, law was a critical reality for people in frontier California. Law was an experience of people, not just lawyers.

California in the period 1850-1890 was a state filled with people and opportunity. The gold rush resulted in a frontier becoming peopled at a fantastic rate. The legislature gave those people law and public policy in law. Courts received cases under that law, adjudicated disputes, and gave public policy in law. Lawyers, who joined the rush for gold and clients, gave their clients guidance, brought their grievances to court, and pondered the public policy. Californians conducted business, forged transactions, and experienced the reality of law at arm's length. The legal history of California is then a history of people and law and law and people. It is the tale of people experiencing law. Whether the law they experienced emanated from an autonomous legal system or not is a question historians must ask.

Another question historians have asked is whether appellate judges in the nineteenth century were instrumentalists or formalists when they made their decisions.[2] When courts confronted a comprehensive and complete set of decisions, making the legal question "settled," the formalist deferred to the precedents, considering the law a static and closed system. The instrumentalist questioned whether any question could be "settled," considering law to be a framework in need of craftsmanlike finishing. Law was organic. The formalist saw the general scope of judicial creativity to be narrow. The instrumentalist saw the need for growth and change to demand judicial craftsmanship. In other cases courts found common law or state statute on point; formalists declared the "found" law, and instrumentalists made law by elaboration in light of changed circumstances. Formalists wanted judicial decisions that were harmonious and consistent with existing wants or interests derived from social or economic facts consistent with "public policy." Formalists found law in books. Instrumentalists focused upon "law in action." Formalists found this law in authoritative treatises, appellate opinions, and unitary conceptions drawing the sources together into a principled whole. Instrumentalists found law in facts, impact, and context. Historians, like the jurists they study, often fall into the same modes of analysis and tend to see law as falling into one construct or the other. A historiographic consensus has emerged, finding both modes of analysis existed concurrently. Whether either construct or the consensus position has evidentiary validity in California is another matter of inquiry for this volume.[3]

Legislators were another category of people that experienced law. They created a statutory context for Californians. They gave notice of threats and the actualities of punishment for deviance. Statutes provided incentives, rewards, and inducements of all kinds. Legislative language also provided symbol. It stated a "public policy." To give an institutional reality to the symbols, the law provided for continuous official supervision, if needed. The grants, denials, or revocations of benefits were rationing devices allocating the society's energy and asset. The law facilitated transactions. It created conditions for exchange including legal tender, weights and measures, and forms for exchange. Law recognized the incidents of the ownership of private property and provided institutional means for declaring that ownership to the world. Statutes also created public facilities for communication and transportation, aiding the transactional society. The law created and nurtured the court system that provided a forum for dispute resolution and for public action to direct persons to action. The California Supreme Court often directed the legislature to act to remedy a policy slip of the statutory pen.

Lawyers also experienced law in California. Attorneys, like people from all walks of life, joined the rush to find gold. Most found it mining the transactional society rather than panning the streams. They represented clients in court. They drafted documents, wrote letters, and mediated disputes. Lawyers also acted on their own account, building up their fortunes from their fees in land and lucre. What did they see in California's legal institutions? Was the law an autonomous system? Was it clear, certain, and predictable? What were the principles they operated on in their business of experiencing law? This is the stuff of legal history on the lawyer's level.

The stuff of life for the layman was law in his day-to-day transactions. Law was vast reality in most facets of the human enterprise. People made agreements. Some committed those agreements to writing. A select few thousand pursued disputes to appellate finality. Thousands of others did business without lawyers or judges, but with law. Their contracts, leases, mortgages, promissory notes, and letters attest to their reliance on law to channel their behavior. They were people of all kinds. David Jacks was a prominent Monterey County pioneer who built an empire in land, wheat, sheep, and enterprise. He also left a half million documents behind for historians to ponder. Jacks was a winner in the nineteenth-century transactional society. Julia Barber was a trusting lender of money. She left her name on an appellate case. In the end, she lost her money and the case. Both experienced law and with thousands of others were the players in the frontier society.

Another question we must address is the role of law in that society. How did it function? Was it the cement that bound the frontier society together and formed channels for the economic behavior of its citizens? Was it something that functioned smoothly, or was there trouble, dysfunction?

Finally, the question of California's peripheralness in American legal development must be addressed. Was the law distinctive in the flow of national legal events? Was it part of regional developments? Did the stages and rates of industrialization, agribusiness, and natural resource exploitation impact the period and subject variations in California law? In this volume private law is the stuff for analysis. It was a law for people in their environment and their times.

This sounds like a tall order, and I hope that the chapters that follow will give meaning and some answers to the questions raised. Getting to this point has taken a great deal of time, several grants, and the encouragement of many. In 1969 Warren Beck guided me to the subject, and Ray Billington encouraged my inquiry. Along the way Doyce Nunis, Jr., John P. Reid, Willard Hurst, and Jackson K. Putnam provided suggestions and comfort amidst travail. The National Endowment for the Humanities, the American Bar Foundation, and the American Council for Learned Societies made generous grants in support of this research. My wife, Erika, tolerated, for a while at least, the thousands of note cards, case summaries, and computer printouts that periodically decorated the floor of my study. My children, Angela and Jeff, became accustomed to the clutter and the response of "writing a book" when they asked what I was doing at odd hours. To all--my thanks and appreciation for toleration and encouragement.

Finally, gentle reader, I must beg your indulgence. The style of this book is my own and is eccentric. No two chapters are structured alike. Some are long; others are short. I am fond of words, which is the curse of an English major turned historian. This tendency to seek art in language rather than precision has brought some degree of reservation from my colleagues in law schools. But from a fellow western historian, the greatest compliment I can remember: "Gordon, you're the only legal historian I can understand." Here again a problem: whether to write for lawyers or historians. Law was the people's experience in the nineteenth century. Perhaps I have written for them.

Finally, my thanks to journal editors who have given permission to reprint parts of the following: "The Growth of Chattel Credit Law in Frontier California, 1850-1890," 57 *Southern California Quarterly* 109-27 (Summer 1975); "Admiralty Law in Nineteenth Century California," 58 *Southern California Quarterly* 499-514 (Winter 1976); "The Development of Landlord and Tenant Law in Frontier California, 1850-1865," 21 *The Pacific Historian* 374-84 (Winter 1977); "The Development of the Law of Tort in Frontier California, 1850-1890,"

60 *Southern California Quarterly* 405-19 (Winter 1978); "Law and Legal Tender in California and the West," 62 *Southern California Quarterly* 239-59 (Fall 1980); "The Development of Mortgage Law in Frontier California, 1850-1890: Part 1, 1850-1866," 63 *Southern California Quarterly* 45-61 (Spring 1981); "The Development of Mortgage Law in Frontier California, 1850-1890: Part 2, 1867-1880," 63 *Southern California Quarterly* 137-55 (Summer 1981); "The Development of Mortgage Law in Frontier California, 1850-1890: Part 3, 1881-1890," 63 *Southern California Quarterly* 232-61 (Fall 1981).

The errors of fact and interpretation are, of course, my responsibility.

1

CALIFORNIA CONTRACT LAW

Contract law in California involved nearly all the relationships of people during the period 1850-1890. It was the law that regulated much of human behavior whether institutionally or interpersonally. The formal law found in books described contract law as coextensive with the universe of enforceable agreements and all allowable terms of all possible agreements.[1] As Theophilus Parsons said in 1853, "Almost the whole procedure of human life implies, or, rather, is the continual fulfillment of contracts."[2] Of particular concern to lawmakers across the nation and in California was the building, extending, and implementing of the marketplace. The market took on legal definition mainly in the law of contract.[3] Contract gave dealers in the marketplace the security and certainty in their transactions necessary for creating a market and enforcing its expectations. The commercial community needed certainty and predictability in the law to structure transactions.[4] The society needed contract law to structure daily life and society's sometime turbulent affairs. On a professional level, lawyers needed certainty and security in the contract law to advise their clients. Since contract law was primarily court law in the nineteenth century, the bar looked to the appellate courts for the principles that would guide the marketplace. The contract law of California was the law for the people in socioeconomic relationships, for merchants dealing in the marketplace, for lawyers dealing with clients, and for appellate judges confronting people in trouble with each other, with the economy, with their lawyers, and with the law. For the judges sitting as the Supreme Court, it also was a dealing with the collective legal experience of the country, with the lawyers that wrestled with that law and each other to gain the day, and with the facts of a frontier marketplace and society seeking resolution in an institutional forum. What emerged in the period 1850-1890 was both a textbook picture of contract law--hornbook law for hornbook facts, and a mystery--a puzzle of omission on the part of the California Supreme Court.

The puzzle to contemporary attorney and client alike was the case without citation. As would be expected in appellate court reports, the California Supreme Court did annotate their opinions, but the judges failed to do so in 39.93 percent of the 288 cases involved in this study of contract law. Polonius-like counsel for the victor as well as the vanquished had to seek direction by indirection, or at least look to cases of similitude in the darkling mirror of the *California Reports* when the decision reached print. Some cases contained rules that the justices thought too clear to require citation. Justice Joseph G. Baldwin declared that "the law does not presume from the rendering of the wife's services in such cases, that a contract had been made by her with her husband, either alone or when associated in business with another, to pay her for the services."[5] When the case involved the services of a "doctor" (not a graduate of "a legally constituted medical institute"), Baldwin announced that "the contract" once made "by the Board of Supervisors" was not within their power "to abrogate it by rescinding the order under which the plaintiff was appointed, or abolishing the office. This has been often decided."[6] Chief Justice Stephen J. Field found the law equally clear for the services of a ship's steward. "The law is well settled," Field wrote, "that where a contract for service is made for a fixed period, if the employer discharge the servant before its termination without good cause, he is still liable and the servant may recover the stipulated wages."[7] Baldwin thought a parol evidence question "so plain a proposition" that it was "unnecessary to adduce authorities."[8] The action of courts of equity to Justice Joseph B. Crockett was so clear that "it [was] unnecessary to cite authorities."[9] Abel Stearns learned that he had a duty to prepare a deed of conveyance. Justice William T. Wallace also informed Don Abel that "the English rule, by which the purchaser is required to prepare the necessary conveyance, had its origin in circumstances peculiar to land titles in England, and is believed never to have obtained in any of the United States, except, perhaps, in the State of Arkansas."[10] Although Wallace cited nothing for his legal history of the rule, counsel had a rule.

The California Supreme Court also issued opinions from Olympus without telling counsel that the rule was obvious. In *Schwalm v. Holmes* (1875), the Court issued this two-sentence opinion: "The contract recited in the answer is not illegal, as being in restraint of trade. The Court erred in sustaining the demurrer to the answer."[11] Fortunately, counsel could refer to the argument made by the prevailing attorneys and their citations for ammunition in future litigation. *Packard v. Bird* (1870) was another similar declaration of public policy. The case was one of both frontier transactional intrigue and judicial divination. Isaac Bird sold land to John Chapman in 1864 and gave John a bond for a deed. Bird's creditor, one Mr. Cottle, swooped down on the transaction and attached the land then being possessed, sowed, and claimed by Chapman. An execution sale took place, with Cottle buying and assigning to Benjamin Packard. Ben's wheeling and dealing got him the sheriff's deed, but not Bird's, so Ben sued. Before trial the transactions became as cluttered as a crow's nest. The Bird-Chapman transaction involved Bird taking Chapman's note for $3,197.50 and $702.50 cash. Bird then borrowed $4,000 from Chapman and gave him a note secured by a mortgage. Chapman then surrendered this note to C. T. Bird, who was also security for Chapman's wife, Hannah, to the extent of $2,000 in a divorce suit against him. Hannah then sued Isaac Bird on the $4,000 note to foreclose the mortgage, claiming that John had assigned the note to her. Isaac negotiated a settlement by which Cottle, with the knowledge of Packard, was to receive $500 to release the land from attachment, with Bird permitted to buy it without Cottle participating in the execution sale. But Cottle played John for a pigeon and bid in and bought the property. He then assigned it to Packard. With the deceit doubled, the whole matter proceeded to trial and finally to the Supreme Court. Chief Justice Augustus L. Rhodes gave the case three paragraphs. He focused upon the agreement between Bird and Cottle that Cottle would not bid at the sale, but would allow Bird to purchase Chapman's interest in the land. Rhodes found that "the direct effect of that branch of the agreement, was to prevent bidding at the sale under the execution; and it cannot be doubted that such an agreement is contrary to public policy and therefore void."[12] Deprived of the perch, Bird lost all, and attorneys were left with the sure and certain hope that the precedent case cited by prevailing counsel as *Stevenson v. Steinburg,* in the *Sacramento Union,* July 26, 1867, was correctly reported by the newspaper.

On occasion the Supreme Court decided questions of marketplace understandings without reference to general principle. In *Guernsey v. West Coast Lumber Company* (1890), the Court found that "the size of lumber usually required in the market" was a term without "much exactness" and that there "was considerable difference in the size of the boards sawed at the same time from the same log." After deciding not to decide what merchantable lumber was as a matter of law or practice, the Court was able to decide that the real problem was that the "price of lumber had fallen below the contract price at the time of the refusal to go on with the contract."[13] The Court did decide what "graders' rejection" meant in the wool business. Without fear or footnote, the Court decided that the wool merchant had a duty to grade "fleece by fleece" rather than to have "the graders . . . rip the sack open from one end to the other."[14] Although precedent may not have been as useful as the practice of the local market, the Court's methodology in these cases was not as clear as it could have been for the education of the bar.

The Court also construed terms in contract without revealing the rules of construction that they favored. Joseph G. Baldwin ruled that 18 days was a "reasonable time for repairing [a turpentine] distillery" that had burned.[15] Baldwin disagreed with a district court interpretation of a contract, declaring that "we do not so construe it."[16] The Court found other sections of the contract to give it a different meaning. In construing a "long written contract," in *Wallace v. Maples* (1887), the Court found two articles to be independent covenants that were complied with although other covenants were not fulfilled, giving the defendant a right to the wheat claimed in the case.[17] In a 14-line decision, the Court looked at a drover's contract and told the parties that "as we construe the contract, it was not within the contemplation of the parties that the defendant was to charge interest on the money to be advanced by him."[18] Although the contracts were susceptible to these interpretations, the concepts applied in arriving at the conclusions were not as readily clear as they could have been to the casual professional reader.

Lawyers could, of course, resort to the head notes of the cases to see if the reporter gleaned principles from the opinion. This was dangerous, however, as the head note and the holding in the case did not always match.[19] The reporter's summary of points and authorities was useful, but not always included in the official reports. When the Court, in a case like *Dameron J. McRaven v. James P. Dameron* (1889), cited "a number of decisions of this court" without giving a single citation, and the reporter did not include a summary of points and authorities, the bar could determine neither the first nor the last point of the contending sides.[20] Some cases did involve elemental procedural problems that were clear to the Court and the bar without citation. Witness the case of *Christian Hoffman v.*

George Remnant (1887). The reporter did not include the contributions of
Charles B. Younger and J. M. Lesser, attorneys for the appellant, or Warren
Olney and Joseph H. Skirm, lawyers for the respondent. The Court did not
cite a single case, statute, or ruling, but it left Hoffman with a tale of
common lawyer knowledge that "to allow a defendant in an ordinary action
of ejectment to set up matters which do not constitute a defense, but are
intended merely as the foundation for a money judgment against plaintiff,
would be to sanction something unknown to the principles and rules of
pleading and practice."[21]   The citationless decision could have some
directive force for the bar.

On occasion it was the failure of the bar to make a case that aroused the
ire of the Supreme Court, but the failure of counsel to argue well did not
compel the Court to cite any precedent for its holding. Witness the case of
Buckingham v. Waters (1859), involving the question of whether good will
was a vendible commodity in the purchase of a drayage firm. Justice
Joseph G. Baldwin hauled plaintiff's counsel, Caleb Burbank, over the
jurisprudential coals on argument that good will was not a vendible
commodity and then pointed out his "fatal" pleading error.[22] In another
citationless opinion, Baldwin simply pointed out to counsel that his answer
was defective.[23] Another lawyer lost before the Supreme Court because he
failed to allege damages.[24] In 1862 the Court curtly stated that "the other
points do not seem to be well taken, nor are they stated with sufficient
particularity to entitle them to much consideration."[25] Appellate practice
was not all the justices would have liked to see.

The Court also provided counsel with practical advice, without citation,
on how to write contracts and file lawsuits. In *Brown v. Pforr* (1869), the
Court told brokers to protect themselves against clients who wanted to
revoke before complete performance with specific language in their
contracts. It was "a very easy matter for the broker to protect himself,"
the Court stated, but "if he does not insert a covenant to that effect in his
contract, the Courts cannot do it for him."[26] The Court also told
contractors that the San Rafael and San Quentin Railroad Company practice
of inserting a clause limiting extra work to that ordered in writing was a
good one "for the protection of the company against doubtful claims."[27] In
1861 Justice Joseph Baldwin told the parties in an 11-line opinion that "this
matter seems to be rather in the nature of a tort, than a matter showing a
violation of contract on the part of the plaintiff."[28] In *Hewlett v. Owens*
(1875), the Court informed counsel that he could not maintain replevin
against the defendants but would have to sue on the contract.[29]
California's bar sometimes needed the sage advice of the justices to perfect
the frontier practice.

Although the California bar may not have been clear on the source of
appellate opinion and was in need of judicial advice regarding practice, the
conduct of business in California was rooted in a faith in the efficacy of
contract. That faith was a simple one. Frank Clough wrote to his mother in
1883 as follows:

> I am sorry that Hicks and McCutchens will not put any water
> on their wheat. They agreed to irregate their land. I propose
> to hold them to their agreement. Mr. Hicks is mistaken about
> the hay. The agreement was that we were to have all the hay
> on the Eustus and his own place. He reserved nothing by
> the pasture near his house and a certain portion of the fruit.

I don't recollect whether he reserved all the fruit or not.
The agreement will tell.[30]

Frank saw in the contract something that could be used to enforce the
promise. The promise was contained in the "agreement." Contract was
a basic institution, and promise was a fundamental part of that institution.[31]

As would be expected in nineteenth-century America and California, land
transactions were a substantial portion of the work of the California
Supreme Court in contract cases.[32] California case law involved the
problems of getting land, developing land, and selling land. Land was a
commodity to be traded. This was particularly true of urban land. San
Francisco real estate was a hot commodity in the 1850s, as was Los Angeles
land in the 1880s.

The rapidity of transactions often resulted in the formalities being
overlooked or delayed to the disappointment of one of the parties. In *Hoen
v. Simmons* (1850), the buyer made an oral agreement to buy a lot in San
Francisco for $5,000 and paid $1,000 down. The parties agreed to have a
written contract drafted, but before the seller signed he went to Oregon and
the buyer proceeded to erect a building on the lot. When the seller
returned, he refused to perform, and the Court refused specific performance
of the verbal agreement because the buyer had not "fully complied with the
substance of all the provisions."[33] Another buyer found that without a
covenant to have the seller evict the squatters swarming over his San
Francisco lot in 1850, he had the sole responsibility.[34] Another buyer, in
Salmon v. Hoffman (1852), found that the Court required complete
performance regardless of title or other considerations. Henry Fisher was
attorney-in-fact for the heirs of James Scott to sell 12 50-vara (Mexican
land grant measure equal to 32.9927 inches) lots in San Francisco. Francis
Salmon, acting as attorney-in-fact for his sister Mary Catherine Salmon,
went angling for the property and landed it for $34,000 with $1,000 paid to
bind the deal. Three weeks later another $9,000 changed hands and Francis
executed notes and mortgages. Five months later and one month before the
next payment of $12,000 was due, Francis asked Henry to obtain
conveyances of the lots to a third party. The heirs, suspecting something
fishy, tendered the conveyances on demand for the $24,000 balance. Francis
refused and sued. The Court firmly stated that the heirs had acted properly
and noted that "it is but a just precaution on his part, that he should
withhold the title until the purchase-money is fully paid; and the law will
not deprive him of the only security which he has."[35] Buyers had to fulfill
the terms of their contracts before they could trawl for subsequent buyers
and profits. Finally, buyers had to be certain of the formalities of the
contract. Justice David S. Terry stated that under Mexican law, the
contract had to "contain at least the names of the parties, the things sold,
the date of the transfer, and the price paid."[36] Although the trading in land
in the 1850s and 1880s was feverish, the buyer and seller had to set their
expectations to writing with some specificity.

The most basic of the formalities was the expression of offer and
acceptance. The Court looked for an offer by one party and assent by the
other party. If one party failed to sign an agreement, then the party signing
was not bound.[37] However, when the Central Pacific Railroad Company
distributed a circular inviting people to settle on its land, make
improvements, and apply for purchase rights, it had made an offer that any
party could accept by complying with the terms of the circular.[38] Even

with offer and acceptance, there had to be mutuality, a two-sidedness to the bargain. The California Court would deny enforcement to agreements that it regarded too vague in marketplace terms, assuming that no dealer would buy or sell on a mere guess.[39] The contract also had to evidence something of value passing in the transaction as consideration.[40] These hornbook rules found frequent citation in the decisions of the California Supreme Court.

The Court also had to construe or interpret the contract language or the actions of the parties to determine their intent regarding a transaction in real estate. Draftsmanship was a problem at times. For example, in *Burnett v. Kullack* (1888), Chief Justice Niles Searls reviewed a transaction involving 43.5 acres in Carpenteria and stated that "a glance at the agreement shows that it was loosely and inarticulately drawn" and as a result was "too indefinite and uncertain to support a judgment for specific performance."[41] Absent sloppy draftsmanship, the Court applied traditional concepts to give the contract the construction most closely approximating the intended meaning of the parties.

A major role of the Supreme Court was enforcing contracts in land. The Court used the doctrine of specific performance to judicially order the transference of title. In other cases, the Court looked at whether a party had substantially performed under a contract sufficient to order the enforcement of a contract. For example, in *Emeline Wallace v. T. W. Maples* (1889), Wallace owned five tracts of land in Tulare County and contracted with Maples regarding a leasehold of four and the sale of one. The contract was typical of bootstrap improvement arrangements. Wallace agreed to convey one tract to T. W.'s wife for $5,840 and certain improvements plus taxes and water assessments on the other four tracts. Maples was to plow the four tracts, plant certain crops and trees, pay the taxes, and pay the water company bills. Maples got rentfree land for four years. Wallace got improved land after four years without any capital investment. If all went well, Maples would have had his profits sufficient to buy the fifth tract at a stipulated price. But all did not go well and when the four years were up, Maples had not plowed all the land and had not paid all the taxes. He refused to vacate. Wallace sued in ejectment, and the case appeared before the Supreme Court. The Court found that there was sufficient evidence to sustain the ruling of the trial judge (despite a contrary jury finding) that T. W. had not performed and ejected him from the land, leaving Emeline with the land, some trees, and the unpaid bills.[42] Although T. W. had been left up a tree by a drought, the constriction of credit in 1887, and farm commodity price fluctuations, the Court found that his lack of performance was without excuse and put the parties back in a position outlined by the promises they had made in 1884.

The Court also confronted questions of constitutional law in real estate transaction cases. In *Dentzel v. Waldie* (1866), counsel questioned the constitutionality of the retrospective application of an 1863 statute allowing married women to make powers of attorney. Chief Justice Silas Sanderson reviewed the works of Chancellor Kent and adopted the distinction for remedial statutes. Then he observed that "statutes which operate to divest vested rights, or in other words, which take the property of one citizen and, without compensation or his consent, bestow it upon another, are opposed to natural right and subversive of any government founded upon fixed laws."[43] Given this substantive due process of law proposition based on eighteenth-century vested rights theory, Sanderson nonetheless found another distinction. Statutes that do not touch any title acquired under a deed and operate to confirm rather than impair contracts are constitutional. In that the statute was remedial and confirmed contracts, the Court found it constitutional and thereby lifted another disability of married women in the marketplace. *Floyd v. Blanding* (1879) presented the Court with the classic question of creative destruction, when water lot warehouse owners in San Francisco made a constitutional challenge to a Board of State Harbor Commissioners' plan to build a sea wall limiting their business and profits. After reviewing "the grave question presented on this appeal" and the great constitutional law cases of the Marshall Court, the Court decided that the state did have the police power to alter the waterfront line for the commercial advantage of the state at the expense of the warehouse owners' profits. Interestingly, the Court also found that the warehouse owners had failed to prove that they had any contract with the state and would have failed on that defect alone.[44]

While the judicial forum for dispute resolution was a part of the contract law history of California land transactions, the negotiation process handled by the parties and their lawyers was very much a part of the day-to-day business of trading in real estate. John D. Bicknell's Los Angeles law practice in the 1870s and 1880s continually involved negotiating property transactions and compromises to settle litigation. The most frequent motivation cited for settlement was the avoidance of lawsuits and the rapid perfection of title to the property.[45] The tradability of the commodity was important to the dealers in the marketplace.

Lawyers played a major role in facilitating this trading in land. Beyond their roles as advocates in the judicial arena and negotiators in the office, lawyers were active participants in the trade on their own account and for their clients. Bicknell and another Los Angeles attorney, Jackson A. Graves, had numerous clients who used their services as brokers as well as superintendents of their real estate interests. For major clients like General William S. Rosecrans, Bicknell received regular salarylike monthly payments. For others, the arrangement was on a transaction basis. One client, Henry Gleason, wrote Bicknell from Salinas City that "in raising that money don't forget to raise the amount of your fee also as I don't think it right that I should give you so much trouble without some recompense."[46] Lawyers did not forget that the fee was the thing.

For many of the people who were engaged in trades in California, the written contract was the thing. People wrote contracts to build fences, butcher meat, carry and deliver picket fencing material, cultivate vineyards, build roads, erect quartz mills, bore tunnels into mountains, fabricate pumps, tend cattle, breed stock, build flumes, tailor clothes, manage ranches, dig wells, paint buildings, build buildings, and cook meals.[47] But contracts did not always work out as expected. Laurence Sinclair was herder foreman for David Jacks, a prominent Monterey County landowner, and in 1879 reported problems with herders quitting or refusing to accept greenbacks for wages. To make matters worse, the work was not going all that well either. Sinclair wrote that

> the hot days that came after castrating them [lambs] was rather hard on them. They lay down under the shades near all the time wherever they could find shades to go under. I hope the worst is past this is the 9th day since the last of them was castrated and that is said to be the worst part. The maggots got into a few of the cuts. We use turpentine and that killed them. There are no swelling shown itself as yet.[48]

Although a contract relationship came to smart, others turned to lawyers to heal the wounds. J. M. Griffith turned to the Los Angeles firm of Graves and O'Melveny when the construction of a common wall with the Young Men's Christian Association went afoul of expectations.[49] On occasion, these festering relationships went all the way to the California Supreme Court.

In construction cases, the California Supreme Court followed long-established precedents and frequently told the parties to write better contracts and the lawyers to follow the norms of practice. The parties sometimes altered material aspects of a construction agreement orally. If that oral agreement was executed, then the Court enforced it.[50] If the contract required written alterations, the Court enforced the contract.[51] Acceptance of a structure by the owner or agent bound him to pay the general contractor.[52] If one of the parties wanted a warranty in the contract or special conditions, the language should have been put in the agreement.[53] When lawyers failed in their craft, the Court bluntly told them that "the complaint is radically defective," the defense of unworkmanlike construction must be put in the answer, and the contract or an explanation for its loss had to be put into the bill of exceptions.[54]

In employment cases, the Court had little sympathy for parties that did not keep their promise or that did not like the terms and conditions of the agreement. If the parties had stipulated for a specific wage in writing, then the prevailing wage rate "was a matter of no consequence."[55] If the parties had agreed that labor would be performed for a specific length of time, breach of the promise to work for the whole term barred the laborer from suing for wages based on work performed. To do otherwise would "encourage an infraction of contracts for frivolous causes."[56] If a custom plower agreed to till 1,280 acres for two dollars per acre, with a stipulation that payment was conditioned upon plowing all 1,280 acres, and the entrepreneur tilled only 750 acres, then the breach of the promise relieved the landowner from making any payments.[57] However, if the landowner-employer denied the laborer some rights, then the employee could maintain an action for the reasonable value of work done.[58] Yet, when conditions dramatically altered the expectations of the parties, the Court found services to be rendered under reasonable, not absurd, conditions. A cattle owner who agreed to have a landowner pasture no less than 3,000 head of cattle was not required to pay for residual grazing fees when 134 of the first 717 head delivered starved or drowned.[59]

The short-term personal services contract business involved oral agreements or employment agency placement and used the general understandings of contract law. Sam Kee's Chinese contract labor service forms stipulated that the servant had to work "sufficient time to earn the above amount (agency fee)."[60] Although employees might abandon their positions, the principals in the employment agency transaction maintained a business relationship predicated upon the promise to provide labor.

Lawyers and doctors also brought their claims for professional services to the Supreme Court. One doctor prevailed against Yuba County on an employment contract, but Dr. F. E. J. Canney lost his claim for $11,000 against the South Pacific Coast Railroad Company because the promise to pay for professional services had been made to the injured passengers the doctor treated rather than to the doctor. The simple legal fact that no promise had been communicated to the doctor left the physician with a remedy against the patients if he could find them.[61]

Lawyers normally had written contracts that they enforced against recalcitrant clients. Those contracts involved the prosecution of cases involving title to land. In *Mathewson v. Fitch* (1863), the California Supreme Court cleared the way for contingency fee agreements, an arrangement that attorneys and clients needed as bootstrap financing, whereby the lawyer devoted his time and money to the suit in return for an interest in the land.[62] Despite the language in *Mathewson*, the Court repeated on two occasions that it was not against public policy for lawyers and land title seekers to make contracts containing contingency fees in lands confirmed to the client.[63] Lawyers also wrote contracts that provided for contingency fees in land in domestic disputes. One such case also involved malpractice. In 1869 San Joaquin County attorneys Budd and Dudley sued their clients M. J. and L. J. Drais. When they lost, J. M. Hogan, the Draises' lawyer, filed for a new trial. After the new trial had been denied, M. J. and L. J. discovered that Hogan's failure to file an appeal resulted in their being out of pocket $2,884.92. They did what came naturally and sued their attorney for malpractice. Hogan immediately secured the services of Budd and Dudley to represent him against the intended ravages of the Draises and their attorney, David S. Terry. At trial Hogan lost and appealed. The Supreme Court found Hogan's failure to appeal "inexcusable," particularly in light of the fact that "the complaint of Budd and Dudley, upon which the judgment against Lucinda Drais was founded, was radically defective, and wholly insufficient to support that judgment." Hogan lost. Budd and Dudley still had their $2,844.92 for their services from the loving couple.[64]

Lawyers also lost supposed fees for other reasons. In *Houghton v. Clarke* (1889), the attorneys agreed to take land as fees if they won a title dispute. They lost in the California Supreme Court and then demanded a greater share of the land to take the case further in the system. The land title disputant refused to make a new contract on these terms and settled the dispute out of court. The attorneys sued their client. The Supreme Court rebuffed them, stating sarcastically that "it is manifest that if the attorneys refused to render further service, they cannot claim that they were prevented from rendering them, or complain that the defendant took them at their word."[65]

The attorney that used third parties to procure clients in return for a percentage of the fees violated public policy. The reason was that "such a practice would tend to increase the amounts demanded for professional services. In such a case an attorney would be induced to demand a larger sum for his services as he would have to divide such sum with a third party."[66] Clear violations of the public trust in the profession brought stern language of disgust.

Real estate brokers in California suffered from a different legal malady. As brokers in Wisconsin had experienced in the nineteenth century, so too their California brethren suffered from the ambiguities of the trade and the law.[67] In 1869 the California Supreme Court decided that real estate brokerage contracts were contracts of employment and not within the Statute of Frauds requiring that they be in writing.[68] That same year the justices told brokers that they needed written contracts to protect their interests:

> The rule that in this class of contracts the principal may revoke at any time before complete performance by the broker, unless he has expressly otherwise agreed, may be a harsh rule, as suggested by counsel; but if it is, it would seem to be a very

easy matter for the broker to protect himself against it. At all events, if he does not insert a covenant to that effect in this contract, the Courts cannot do it for him.[69]

Regardless of a written contract, the law presumed that credit terms in any sale would be "reasonable and such as was usual and customary on sales of real estate in that vicinity."[70] Further, the broker was entitled to his commission when he produced a buyer, unless the contract provided otherwise.[71] But the broker had to be wary. In 1869 the Court also decided that if a broker took real estate as part of the fee for services, then the agreement was within the Statute of Frauds and had to be in writing.[72] Property of decedents had to be liquidated in accordance with the Probate Code.[73] Finally, to settle the question of whether the agreements had to be in writing or not, the legislature decided according to Civil Code section 1624, passed in 1872, by requiring brokerage contracts to be in writing. Thereafter, real estate brokers that asked the Court for their fees got the answer of "no recovery."[74] By the 1880s the brokers had moved from the bargaining mode of behavior on a case-to-case basis regarding terms and conditions of employment to a regularized form-bound practice. The law aided this transition and provided protection to those who followed its strictures.

Lumbermerchants and contractors generated two periods of feverish appellate opinion that corresponded to two periods of rapid growth in California--the 1850s and the 1880s. Lumber was a critical ingredient in the construction of the cities and towns that instantly sprung from the soil and quartz. Lumber was the stuff of barns, fences, square set timbering, flumes, and much of what made up California's farming, mining, and mercantile enterprise.[75] The appellate cases reflected the realities of the problems of the trade.

Cases involving the sale of livestock also fell into the same two main time periods. These cases often contained problems of attaching creditors, claims that the sales were fraudulent to avoid creditors, and legal questions regarding the nature of delivery of the livestock. Entrepreneurs put third parties in charge of cattle and sheep to share in the future profits arising from the increase in the herds. People bought and sold livestock in the marketplace. When market conditions soured, attaching creditors had the sheriff at the corral selling the livestock to satisfy the debts. So livestock owners "sold" their livestock to friends and relatives at reasonable prices, and the stock disappeared into the hills. The California Supreme Court looked for the legal ingredients of the transaction, and if they were present, found that a sale had occurred and the creditors would have to look for other assets to attach.[76] Economic hard times created the environment that generated the transactions in these cases, but the Court used a formalistic approach in solving these as well as other problems involving the sale of livestock. Dealers used the formal mechanisms of contract to forge their livestock transactions and enterprises. They struck deals and committed them to writing, exchanging livestock, money, and a "bill of sale" or receipt.[77] In good times and in bad, the actors in the marketplace used the regularity of contract formality to give them certainty in their transactions.[78]

When products reached market, the parties often asked the Court to rule on the issues of product quality. Sheep ranchers found that affirmations regarding the quality of wool constituted a warranty that the wool be in a merchantable condition, not containing "the sweepings of the corral, and burs, dirt and sand."[79] The term "graders' rejection" meant that the merchant had the duty to grade "fleece by fleece" rather than "rip[ping] the sack open from one end to the other."[80] An agreement to sell apricots implied a warranty of quality and merchantability.[81]

The Court also had to construe the contract terms. The buyer controlled the terms of a requirements contract when he accepted a certain number of pounds of grapes.[82] Despite the fact that "the parties could not very well have made their contract more indefinite," the Court found that a canner had to pay for every load of fruit delivered rather than pay at the end of the season.[83] A contract for all the fruit produced from a particular plot of ground obligated the buyer to purchase all of the crop regardless of quality.[84] If the buyer had wanted the seller to warranty the quality of the crop, he should have put the requirement in the contract. The fruit packer also assumed the risk of shrinkage during shipment and would have to write better contracts to avoid the loss.[85] Similarly, if a winemaker had wanted a particular grape grower to continue to produce the fruit of the vine and not to have the option to assign his contract, he should have so stated in the contract.[86] The Court clearly emphasized the freedom to and of contract in these cases and called upon the parties to make explicit the particulars of the trade if they wanted judicial enforcement.

Agricultural dealers in hay seldom wrote their contracts with particularity. Grass was an important commodity for the sheep and cattle ranchers. They often bought and sold rights to grass for graze and hay.[87] The appellate reports contain few cases involving hay, owing to the informal manner of the transactions, the low value per unit of the commodity, and the low level of risk involved in the transaction. When the haystack burned down after part payment, but before the buyer could haul it away, then the buyer got excited enough to pursue the matter to the Supreme Court. But to no avail. The part payment constituted delivery, and the buyer was then at risk.[88]

The risk in the cereal grain trade was much greater. Farmers had to worry about the weather, prices, shipping, grain bags, insurance rates, and commissions before the age of home computers. They struck deals on the street, by letter, and by telegram. David Jacks committed his 1874 crop of wheat for shipment to Isaac Friedlander on a "verbal understanding." Friedlander set the understanding to writing that same day.[89] Issues of freight, shipments by rail, storage, and marine insurance found finality in contract terms. Those issues could be set out on a sheet of yellow, legal-length, lined paper as William John Connor did with David Jacks at Salinas City on September 27, 1876.[90] The issue of merchantability could be decided by a 100-ton sample for the buyer or the mere presence of excessive barley in the brass kettle.[91]

Price fluctuation and greed were the motive forces behind the parties who litigated their claims before the California Supreme Court. *Ruiz v. Norton* (1854) contained all the casebook elements. José, Francisco, and Manuel Ruiz signed a contract with commission merchants on December 22, 1852, to deliver 2,000 bags of rice to Joshua Norton and Company. They delivered, and Norton paid $2,000 on account, in turn selling to third parties on the wharf. But San Francisco prices were not stable in the 1850s.[92] The price of rice fell over 30 percent, and the defendants refused to pay the balance of $23,000. The Ruizes went to court and won in the district court. Norton and Company appealed and won because the Ruizes' attorney had failed to allege and prove that the rice was in a "sound" condition when delivered. The Ruizes went back to the district court and made the proper allegations and offerings of proof, but the district judge granted a motion of nonsuit based on the Supreme Court's decision. Justice Solomon Heydenfeldt in delivering the Court's opinion had discussed the merchantability issue, the distinctions of general and special cargoes, the action on a *quantum valebant* (a common-law action of assumpsit for goods sold and delivered based on an implied promise to pay what the goods were reasonably worth), whether an agent or a principal had standing to sue, and the like. Perhaps the district court judge thought the opinion so extensive that the plaintiff could not prevail. Perhaps the district judge could not tell what the precise grounding was for the opinion. On the second appeal to the Supreme Court, it was clear. Heydenfeldt stated the Court's decision in one sentence and then concluded the opinion with the observation that "upon this decision we see no reason why the District Court should have granted a nonsuit upon the proof proposed."[93] *Crosby v. Watkins* (1859) also involved price. The buyer and seller agreed that the buyer would pay two and one-half cents per pound for wheat to be delivered on demand. The price of wheat rose to four cents per pound, and the seller refused to deliver. The buyer sued and won, recovering damages equal to the difference between the contract price and the actual market price. The Court cited *Ruiz* as precedent despite the fact that the *Ruiz* Court did not discuss damages. The Court also cited *Parsons on Contracts*, which did give guidance on the issue.[94] The Court aided counsel in *Utter and Calden v. Chapman* (1872) as they had in *Ruiz*. The second time the case was up on appeal, Justice Joseph Crockett stated that "the correct interpretation of our decision on the former appeal is that the plaintiffs are entitled to recover only the actual loss which they suffered from the breach of the contract." Crockett then gave counsel the rule: If a profit were realized in the contract period exceeding the contract profit, then the Court would award nominal damages only.[95] Although the Court applied known rules apportioning damages, the fact of commercial life in the grain trade was that when you were without money and the commodity, the delay of the legal process could spell economic disaster. To the Ruizes of the grain trade, the fact that they could prove that their product was sound was little comfort with $2,000 in hand and lawyers to pay.

The Court was no less tolerant of the fool in the marketplace. *Hawkins v. Hawkins* (1875) applied formalistic rules to a transaction despite unusual circumstances. A. C. Hawkins had his crop of wheat in sacks waiting for profit north and south of Putah Creek in Solano County. Duane Ballard and Isaac R. Hall were friendly neighborhood commission merchants from San Francisco who employed V. Hawkins as their agent in Solano County to buy the golden grain. V. Hawkins told A. C. that he would buy his north-field wheat for $27.00 and his south-field wheat for $27.50 per ton. A. C. and V. Hawkins told Hall of their agreement, and Hall drafted a contract that offered $1.175 and $1.27 per ton. A. C. signed the contract after hearing representations that it was just like the oral agreement. A. C., believing the deal was wired, delivered the wheat, received payment, receipted for the payment, and started home. Although "illiterate and scarcely able to read writing," the hammer dropped for Hawkins when he discovered that he was $1,463.62 short. He demanded payment, and when refused, he sued. The Court gave him a four-sentence opinion concluding that

> the care and diligence of a prudent man in the transaction of his business would demand an examination of the instrument before

signing, either by himself or by someone for him in whom he had a right to place confidence. The fact that the plaintiff was illiterate, and could read manuscript only with difficulty, did not render this precaution less necessary.[96]

As formalism, the opinion stood for the proposition that dealers in the marketplace were responsible for the contracts they signed.

In the world of merchandise, dealers were concerned about price, binding agreements, and the law. Fong Wo and Company of Downieville wanted to know "what [is] the price of opium." Yu Wo and Company of San Francisco quoted $160 per 100 vials, but warned that "opium will be higher."[97] The price of "montery pine cones" was a matter of concern in San Francisco.[98] One thousand dollars in gold was offered for butter in the *Yreka Journal* if the dairyman could deliver it to the Black Bear Mine.[99] John Center bought a steam engine for a woolen factory at Mission Dolores in 1860 for the price of $3,200 with cash down and progress payments provided in the agreement.[100] David Jacks struck a deal with Hopkins and Huntington, irrigation pipe merchants in San Francisco, in October 1879, but found that a week later the merchants' memory of the agreement had faded with the rapid appreciation of the price of the pipe. Jacks' agent by the bay, Robert McElroy, advised that "I would go without the whole rather than buy any from a firm that would play me so mean a trick."[101] The market rather than the law seemed a solution. For John D. Bicknell, an attorney, the law was a problem as he interpreted a San Bernardino County ordinance to the Southern Pacific Company:

> While we lawyers guess at the meaning of the law or ordinance unfortunately the court has the last guess and may possibly guess the other way. I deem it much safer for the company, however, to deliver the trees and take up the controversy with the Commissioner [of the Board of Horticulture].[102]

Significantly, Bicknell thought it more important for the railroad to abide by its contract to deliver trees than to obey the quarantine ordinance. The promise was the thing.

The Supreme Court busied itself with questions of delivery and the nature of the promise in cases involving the sale of merchandise. Sales had to include some act of actual possession accompanied by good faith.[103] The California Statute of Frauds in its fifteenth section required that a sale be "accompanied by an immediate delivery, and be followed by an actual and continued possession of the property sold." The object of the statute, Justice Peter H. Burnett stated in *Steward v. Scannell* (1857), was "the prevention of fraudulent sales of goods." The statute took "away from the parties the means of carrying out their fraudulent intent, and remove[d] the temptation."[104] Delivery was the issue when the sheriff was at the door with a creditor's attachment; the Court reiterated the doctrine that the possession had to be open and notorious.[105]

The merchants often conducted day-to-day sales on a cash-and-credit basis. Dan Collins tended a general store and was a liquor dealer in Grass Valley. He sold on a cash-and-credit basis. Customers received loans and gave notes. His business practices were regular on this procedure and dutifully recorded.[106] L. B. Clark's Smartsville store operated on a similar basis with cash-and-credit sales, but Clark also allowed customers to labor for their groceries. Barney Leary worked seven days for $3.50 per day in 1864 for his groceries. C. A. Inskepp paid off his tab with sweat in 1865 at the same daily rate. High-volume customers like the Squaw Creek Tunnel Company gave promissory notes for their provisions.[107] Over-the-counter sales were often on credit, but the means of repayment varied.

Although the bulk of consumer goods passed across the counter without legal challenge, the Court decided a variety of issues of warranty and delivery regarding manufactured goods. The Court also decided, despite the ingenuity of counsel, that certain commodities like firewood were not manufactured goods.[108] *Hoult v. Baldwin* (1885) presented the Court with more difficult questions. Los Angeles County farmer Baldwin bought a harvesting machine from the San Joaquin County (Stockton) manufacturer. The railroad dutifully delivered the magnificent engine of enterprise, but after moving 40 feet from the iron horse, the great engine broke its tillerpost and crunched to a halt. The manufacturer replaced the broken part with a "new casting," but, alas, it too broke. Baldwin offered to return the cripple and pay the freight to boot. The manufacturer refused and produced a new casting with a stronger tillerpost. Baldwin refused to pay for his header and separator, and the manufacturer sued. The jury came in for the hometown employer. The Supreme Court found the warranty stated in the Civil Code requiring the harvesting machine to be "reasonably fit for that purpose" and "free from any latent defect . . . arising from the process of manufacture." Further, the Court found that the trial court erred in its instructions and sent the matter back for trial.[109] Four years later the case was back again. This time the jury was rightly instructed, but they again found no breach of any warranty. Justice John D. Works found absolutely no evidence to sustain the verdict and reversed again.[110] The law was clear. The jury would not see that law with equal certainty. In other cases, parties would sell hay presses, five-stamp batteries, and steam boilers with the rapidity a harvester could not muster. They did so just ahead of attaching creditors. The Court applied familiar rules on delivery and possession to decide the cases.[111]

Entrepreneurs made contracts to finalize business ventures of many types. They pledged their money, goods, and time to the ventures. In 1853 Isaiah Churchill Woods agreed to advance his money to Cohen and Company to conduct a storage business in San Francisco in the North Point dock warehouse. Cohen agreed to give the business "all the necessary and proper personal attention for its successful prosecution."[112] Ventures grand were reduced to writing as were the modest. In 1886 David Jacks paid $300 for license to produce "Eureka Preventative for Black-leg in Cattle," with his interest to be represented by a deed to the property right in the formula.[113] Whether great or small, enterprise was the thing of the period. John D. Bicknell expressed it well:

> The longer I live the more profound respect I have for a successful business man. Men may command armies and be honored as great generals; they may be prominent in politics and be applauded by admiring citizens, but for a man to start out in life poor and make an even-handed fight in a busy world and pay his honest debts, support for his family and save enough to build a block possesses more of the qualities that go to make up a man than any of the other classes mentioned above. It is something, in my opinion, in this busy, rattling and wicked world for a man to accumulate and keep a fortune.[114]

Transactions were the stuff of business of the period.

But all in life and business did not go smoothly. When entrepreneurs disagreed, they occasionally pursued their discord all the way to the California Supreme Court. In the feverish days of 1849, a small group of men put together the New York Union Mining Company, pledged their lives and resources to venture, and departed New York for the diggings. All was very carefully set out in writing. Upon arrival in California, the company broke up and several of its members, Peter Von Schmidt included, found themselves expelled. Peter and Julius Von Schmidt, Thomas Holman, and Lewis Newman sued. Justice Nathaniel Bennett, in delivering the Court's decision, first dispensed with a procedural problem of concern due to California's Mexican heritage. The plaintiffs argued that the villainous dissolvers had not used the Mexican "conciliacion" procedures prior to disgorging the plaintiffs. Bennett devoted seven pages of the *1850 Reports* to a discussion of the procedure and observed that

> since the acquisition of California by the Americans, the proceeding of conciliacion has, in all cases, been deemed a useless formality by the greater portion of the members of the bar, by the courts and by the people; that it has, in fact, passed into disuse and become obsolete.[115]

Bennett concluded that this extensive analysis was provided "in order that the profession may understand, that the objection for the want of conciliatory measures, is . . . disposed of now, and, as we sincerely hope, forever."[116]

The plaintiffs raised another procedural point and asked that the proceedings include all the members of the company. Bennett dismissed the objection to a defect of parties, observing that

> from the nature of the enterprise which was the object of the formation of the company, from the condition of the country and the ever changing locations of people engaged in operations in the gold mines of California, it would be, if not utterly impracticable, productive of manifest inconvenience and oppressive delays, to require that all the members of the association should be brought into court before it would proceed to administer justice between any of them.[117]

Gold-rush litigation had to forego all the procedural niceties to achieve rapid judicial attention.

Bennett then turned to the factual problems. Did Von Schmidt's fellow argonauts abandon the cause in violation of their agreement? Yes, they went to the digging and then returned to San Francisco to reap great profits despite their promise "to devote" their "entire time and energies to promote the common interest." Von Schmidt did not use due diligence regarding his responsibility for three gold-washing machines and had $200 deducted from his share of the company proceeds. In that "the successful prosecution of gold mining at the present time, under such an organization . . . appear[ed] . . . to be an impracticability and a delusion," the Court ordered the dissolution of the company.[118] The lure of profits in San Francisco did not stop the enterprise deserters from going to law to recover scraps from the shattered dream of golden wealth. Their abandonment (Von Schmidt excepted) of their promise and the enterprise forfeited their investment in accordance with the contract.

Enterprise also faltered and found its failures before the bench for other reasons. Some parties failed to act in time when time was important.[119] Others did not have the capacity or authority to make the business deal.[120] Illegality and fraud clouded other business arrangements that appeared in the appellate reports. Two of interest were both cases of proper instructions to juries and seemingly contrary appellate results. In *Forbes v. McDonald* (1880), the Court found the instructions to the jury proper but the verdict contrary to the instructions, leaving one party with a worthless promissory note for his trouble.[121] In *Newell v. Desmond* (1887), the Court found the instructions to be proper and allowed the verdict to stand despite the fact that the goods in question did not exist at the time of the transfer.[122] *Forbes* involved illegality as a judicially defined concept, and *Newell* questioned the sufficiency of delivery to avoid the sheriff's execution sale. Despite the distinctions, the Court demonstrated judicial restraint in the latter case.

Restraint of another kind, restraint of trade, gave the California Supreme Court ample opportunity for judicial lawmaking. The public policy issues in this branch of sales cases were not always clear. Arthur L. Corbin observed in 1962 that

> although all branches of law are in constant evolutionary change, and although that change is always determined by prevailing economic notions, political events, societal mores and business practices, the field entitled restraint of trade and commerce is one in which economic notions are most confused and uncertain, political events are portentous and ill-directed, societal mores are suffering the tests of battle, and business practices and interest have developed round about great combinations and international cartels and systems of interrelated patents.[123]

The cases usually arose from the sale of a business with an agreement not to compete or form contracts limiting competition or establishing marketing areas. In *California Steam Navigation v. Wright* (1856 and 1857), the Court found an explicit agreement not to compete with the steamer *West Point* for three years with a $15,000 forfeiture clause. Justice Peter Burnett found the "language . . . too specific, definite, and certain to be mistaken" and to control with the finding of a breach of the condition. Such a contract was clearly enforceable and damages controlled by the promise in the contract.[124]

A decade later the Court found a similar contract to be in restraint of trade despite the fact that the restraint did not impair the public convenience. In 1864 the California Steam Navigation Company (CSNC) sold the steamer *New World* to the Oregon Steam Navigation Company (OSNC) with a condition in the contract that the OSNC not use the *New World* on any of the routes of the CSNC for a period of ten years. The contract also contained a $75,000 forfeiture clause. In 1867 the OSNC sold the *New World* to Henry Winsor. Henry and fellow entrepreneurs executed a bond to the OSNC for the observance of the condition. Winsor sold the *New World* to Calvin Hale three weeks later without the condition in the bill of sale. Hale was one of the entrepreneurs who made the bond to the OSNC. Two days before Thanksgiving, the bondsmen, excepting Hale, conveyed the *New World* to George Wright and Duncan Finch without the condition in the bill of sale. Wright and Finch knew the condition. James Ryder bought the *New World* from Wright and Finch on July 16, 1868, to establish a passenger and freight business between San Francisco and Vallejo. One of the conditions of the sale was that after execution and delivery of the bill of sale and tender of possession, Ryder was to pay $22,000 down and give a note for $41,000. Wright made delivery on August 5, and Ryder accepted delivery and the bill of sale but refused to pay. Five days later Ryder offered to return the *New World*. Ryder learned of the covenant in the San Francisco newspapers in a notice published jointly by the CSNC and OSNC threatening legal action. In September, Wright sued Ryder on the contract. Wright won a default judgment as Ryder went off to rent something more reputable. On appeal attorneys appeared for the OSNC. They attacked the English precedents. The Supreme Courts of Mississippi, Massachusetts, and New York had allowed agreements contrary to the strict English rule. The American rule, they declared, was to allow such contracts unless the public was injured by the restraint. Opposing counsel countered with state cases receiving the English rule and English cases. They also argued that the covenant was too broad, having the practical result of making the *New World* useless to the owners and public until May 1867. The attorneys on both sides presented a fundamentally formalistic case to the Court.

The Court, by Justice Joseph B. Crockett, brushed instrumentalism aside and embraced formalism, handing the steamboat monopoly a minor defeat. Crockett found the "general principles [to be] well settled." The English rule was that "private citizens should not be allowed, even by their own voluntary contracts, to restrain themselves unreasonably from the prosecution of trades, callings, or professions."[125] The exception was when the result did not place unreasonable restrictions on the trade or did not impair the public interest. Courts had used spacial concepts holding statewide restraint to be unreasonable. Despite such a territorial restriction, the transaction involved the sale of personalty and the liberty of the owner to dispose of that property under specific conditions. Crockett found the argument that the owner could destroy the property a mere nuisance, declaring that the Court had grave doubts whether

> in this age of abundant capital and active competition in all avenues of commerce, the withdrawal of a single boat from our navigable waters could be deemed an appreciable restraint upon trade, or result in the slightest inconvenience to the public.[126]

In fact, the sale of a single sloop or schooner under the same condition would result in injury to the public that "would be scarcely appreciable." But Crockett analogized that the sale of such an inconsequential vessel was like the agreement of a single carpenter or mason not to practice his trade. Hence, Crockett stated that

> we would be bound by a long line of adjudications in England and America to hold the contract void, as in restraint of trade. The reasoning on which their decision rests applies to the sale of a single boat as fully as to the case of a single tradesman; and we feel constrained, in deference to these decisions, to hold the contract in this case to be void.[127]

The steamboat monopoly, born in the unprofitable frenzy of competition in 1854, now had one of its chief weapons sunk. But in April 1869, the CSNC was purchased by the Central Pacific Railroad Company, bringing the capital to bear to torpedo the remaining independents.[128]

Another irony of the *California Steam Navigation* case was the fact that counsel had brought an even more restrictive covenant before the Court with "Winsor and others," but the Court did not need to decide whether it was valid in the *California Steam Navigation* case. The U. S. Supreme Court made that decision in 1873 and found that it was valid.[129] Further, one of the cases cited by the *California Steam Navigation* Court was a New York case, *Dunlop v. Gregory* (1851). That case purported to state that contracts in total restraint of trade were invalid where the agreement was stateside. Reading the case, however, one must conclude that it supported the proposition that the sale or lease of property may contain a covenant not to compete with the property sold or leased.[130] The California Supreme Court's formalism was apparently a tool to instrumentally hamstring the steamboat monopoly. It failed in the marketplace.

The *California Steam Navigation* precedent galloped through the appellate reports. In 1870 the Court struck down a purchase by plaintiff More of the M. Bonnet and Company asphaltum roofing and pavement laying concern because it contained a covenant restraining Bonnet from pursuing the trade in "the City and County of San Francisco, or the State of California." The contract was void because the covenant related "to the whole State."[131] Bonnet had $750 under his hat and $1,250 more in More's notes plus his business to boot. Philemon Prost had three of the $250 notes More gave Bonnet. Unable to collect from More, Philemon went to court and found that the illegality of the transaction barred recovery. Bonnet then had Phil's money and More had less than he started with in the marketplace, having lawyer fees in two appellate cases to cover.[132] *Prost v. More* paved the way for the Court's decision in *Callahan v. Donnolly* (1872). T. C. Donnolly sold his "Donnolly's Yeast Powder" business to the plaintiff with the covenant not to compete in the yeast business in the state of California. Donnolly, being a rising capitalist, entered the yeast business again and Callahan sued. The Court cited *California Steam Navigation* and *Prost* and refused to enforce the illegal bargain, noting, however, that if the restriction were territorially reasonable, the Court might enforce the covenant.[133] In *Schwalm v. Holmes* (1875), counsel cited *California Steam Navigation* and *Prost* for the proposition that "unless the restriction in the contract [was] limited to a city or county," it was void. The contract in question restricted sales of lime to a single party. The Court decided, in a three-sentence opinion, that the contract was enforceable.[134] Finally, the *Prost* and New York precedents provided the Court with ammunition to blast a combination to splinters. In *Santa Clara Valley Mill and Lumber Company v. Isaac Hayes* (1888), the plaintiff bought lumber from the defendant with a covenant not to sell lumber to any other parties in four counties. The object was to give the Santa Clara Valley Mill and Lumber Company (SCVM&L) a monopoly and drive up prices. The parties fortified their agreement with a $20 per 1,000 feet forfeiture clause. When Hayes sold to others, SCVM&L assaulted his position in court. Because the sole object of the contract was monopoly, Hayes gained the victory and planted the jurisprudential flag of illegality firmly on Mount Suribachi for all entrepreneurs to see.[135] Monopoly was clearly not welcome within the confines of contract law in frontier California.

The exchange of promissory notes and other financial instruments was more a part of frontier trade. Money was scarce and promissory notes circulated as currency in the frontier economy. John Hume wrote to his sister Jane from Placerville on February 28, 1858, that "we have no paper currency; a bank bill is seldom seen, and is of no possible use. I have not seen one for years."[136] Cash flow, accounts receivable, and time lag on receipts and payments were daily problems for mercantile concerns in California of the 1850s.[137] Letters of credit and drafts on accounts were common throughout the period.[138] When these credit or finance relations went sour, some made their way to the California Supreme Court. Some cases involved procedural issues under the Practice Act, others endorsement, and others statutory construction.[139] The Court promoted the negotiability of the promissory note and its utility.

The problem for the creditor was not negotiability but collection. California became notorious as a haven for debtors. Bankruptcy laws were lenient. Many people followed the wisdom of the old adage that "many a clever fellow had been ruined by paying his debts" and followed the legal path to insolvency.[140] In addition to bankruptcy, the Statute of Limitations provided a shield against collection if the creditor tarried in pursuit of capital.[141] Other defendants who "came to the United States as absconding debtors" and "assumed fictitious names for the purpose of more successfully eluding the vigilence of their creditors" failed to avoid the creditor, but found shelter in the California Civil Code because the statute did not authorize attachment unless the underlying debt was incurred in California or contained an express stipulation that it be paid in California.[142] California was clearly a state of opportunity for a fresh start, but we will return to this theme in later chapters with more detail.

Another debt that the legal system would not provide assistance in collecting was the wager. The case of first impression was *William E. Johnston v. P. H. Russell* (1869). On September 8, 1868, Bill loaned P. H. $850 and P. H. gave Bill his note for the loan. On September 28, Bill made a bet that Seymour would beat Grant in the presidential election. Russell was the stakeholder and put up $500 on the note to cover the bet on Johnston's behalf. Filled with the venturous spirit, Johnston bet another man $200 that Horatio would triumph. Russell was again the stakeholder and put up another $100 on the note and held another $100 from Bill and the third-party Grant supporter. Russell made the same bet with a third man that day and put up his horse, Consternation, against the wagerer's horse, Young Jack, with both parties depositing $250 with Russell for nondelivery after the people had spoken. Russell used $250 on the note to guarantee the delivery of Consternation. On November 3, the people cast their lot with Grant, and 20 days later Johnston repudiated all bets and gave Russell a written order not to pay. Russell paid. Johnston tried to collect on the note and pursued the matter to the California Supreme Court. The Court found that there was "no statute in this State upon the subject of wagers" and that the justices had to resort to "the principles of common law."[143] The Court found that wagers on public elections were against public policy. Chancellor Kent had so stated. Further, if the election had occurred, the parties could not repudiate their bets or recover from the stakeholder. Such was the New York rule. In that this was a case of first impression, the Court stated that "we are at liberty to adopt the rule, which, in our judgment, best promotes good morals, and subserves the public policy, upon which all rules upon this subject are supposed to be founded."[144] The Court found the New York rule to be "founded upon the better morality" and common sense.[145] The opinion was filled with instrumentalist orientation to buoy the adoption of the formalistic New York rule. Further, the link of public policy and good morals was overt, and the language of the opinion filled with theology of repentance and forgiveness. When the Court again faced a similar case in 1880, it was ready to fire with similar language. In *Gridley v. Dorn* (1880), the Court stated:

> If, notwithstanding the evil tendency of betting on races, parties will engage in it, they must rely upon the honor and good faith of their adversaries, and not look to the courts for relief in the event of its breach.[146]

Wagering contracts had no place in the Court's morality or law of California.

One group of California entrepreneurs, building contractors, gambled with their capital every time they made a contract with a public entity. The state questioned the capacity of its subdivisions to make certain contracts.[147] Cities avoided paying contractors because they lacked the capacity to make certain types of contracts.[148] Counties avoided paying contracts for work completed in cases like *Murphy v. Napa County* (1862), where the contractor repaired a bridge at the request of the board of supervisors, but statute required that such contracts be let by the road overseer.[149] Counties also avoided liability if a printer foolishly printed the delinquent tax list for the county board of supervisors rather than for the tax collector.[150] Road contractors in San Francisco were afflicted with a similar legal malady, collecting from property owners for work authorized by the city. The state legislature authorized the city to let contracts for street grading and improvements, with the payment coming out of the pockets of the abutting property owners. In *Emry v. San Francisco Gas Company* (1865), the Supreme Court spent 32 pages finding the act constitutional "to discuss the question in this case for the last time."[151] The Court decided that the method of determining the amount owed the contract belonged to legislative discretion and not the judiciary. As might be expected, the *Emry* decision did not prevent counsel from bringing the issue back to the Court. One case concluded on its third trip to the Supreme Court for a job completed 19 years prior to final disposition.[152] Clearly, those contracting with the public required more circumspection and legal advice in the process of negotiation than others in the private marketplace in California.

Many property owners covered another risk in the cities, fire, with insurance as it became available. Fires, particularly in early San Francisco, had a devastating impact upon business.[153] Wood frame construction, dangerous heating systems, and the lack of safe chimneys created high risks in the crowded instant cities of frontier California. McLean and Fowler, agents for the Pacific Insurance Company of San Francisco, wrote to Roger S. Day in Folsom in 1860 and 1861 regarding fire insurance. The fire risk in "frame Hotels in the country" was one The Hartford did not like, so they "divided the risk and placed it in two different companies." They also explained that the rate was due to "the number of stoves and there being no chimneys."[154] Although premiums followed risk, the California Supreme Court followed a formalistic path in eastern, particularly New York, precedent.[155]

Contract law in California contained a degree of risk whether in court or on the street. The formalistic approach dominated appellate opinion, but instrumentalism was also present. On the street, a man's promise was a bond of performance enforceable in the courts. Jackson A. Graves put it well in 1883: "Freman will hold us to the strict letter of our contract. If we don't sell enough land to pay him $5,000 by April 5th, up goes our whistle."[156] David Jacks of Monterey was another man who enforced his contracts. Edward Berwick was correct when he wrote to Jacks in 1887: "As I understand your character, in business you have insisted on a strict fulfillment of contracts; and, like all businessmen, have looked to your own interests; at the same time your almsgiving and benefactions are more or less known to all dwellers in Monterey."[157] If that bond were broken, then the legal system was a weapon as well as a means of enforcement. Delay and costs were always factors in court. In 1872 A. W. Cook of Mohawk Valley wrote to his lawyer, John D. Goodwin in Quincy, that expectations had gone awry:

> We thought he was perfectly satisfied as we told him we would pay him all we possibly could when we cleaned up. But instead he went off to Quincy, sued and attached everything. . . . Since he has acted so mean we want to give him all the trouble we possibly can.[158]

Cook's adversary, Thompson, took advantage of his legal rights, and Cook sought to take advantage of his procedural leverage.

California's contract law was in the mainstream of American legal history. The Supreme Court found frontier conditions to be critical, particularly in the rush of transactions on the mining frontier. Despite the unusual circumstances of California's frontier marketplace, the broad principles of contract law ramified through the structure of legal institutions to the dealers in the marketplace. When cast in the frames of a frontier marketplace seeking stability, the law was the cement that coagulated the aggregates into a workable mass. The Supreme Court was not always the skillful mason any more than the lawyers and dealers that operated in the building enterprise. The expectations of a transaction-based marketplace were realized, but not without the trowel marks of many a master and journeyman.

2
LANDLORD AND TENANT LAW

California's lawmakers also provided a statutory framework and a common law for landlords and tenants. The legislature in 1850 enacted a statute for forcible entries and unlawful detainer that afforded landlords the strong arm of the law to oust holdover tenants. Subsequently, statute provided a specific appeal process for tenants as well as statutory procedures for the recovery of waste and tenant injury to property.[1] The California Supreme Court in the period 1850-1865 construed the statutes in numerous cases, attempting to implement legislative intent. What the statutes and case law did not deal with readily was the bane of many a landowner: the squatters. But the landowner used the law of landlord and tenant as a tool to deal with the problem.

Although the California Supreme Court was molding law, landowners were leasing their interests to tenants in an equally judicious manner, but paid more attention to the marketplace than the law. In the frenzy of urban speculation, rents were "reconed by the month" and "paid monthly in advance."[2] Similarly, leaseholds were of short duration, commercial property renting for rarely more than a year.[3] In more stable times, the terms of commercial leases lengthened and the complexity of the relationship increased. Rents rose with demand and followed the periodic demise of business community fortunes. The *San Francisco Daily Herald* reported on December 5, 1853, that

> it has long been supposed that rents in the city should have fallen
> materially before this time. Such, however, does not appear to
> be the case. Some idea of the value of property on Montgomery
> Street may be found from the fact that an office with a front of
> but ten feet is now renting at four hundred dollars a month, and
> would bring five hundred."[4]

Another element, particularly in San Francisco, gave landlords reason for renting: squatters. A. M. Van Nostrand rented two lots to Rodman Price: "The only consideration is to be the erection of a fence and the ejectment of all squatters."[5] Tenants could protect property while using it.

The interests of landlords in California's rural areas were little different; market conditions controlled relationships. When the prices of agricultural products were down or proximity to markets distant, landlords often rented for nominal sums plus certain improvements. On May 22, 1851, William Potter leased Potter's Ranch in Butte County to Samuel Norris for a ten-year term for $50 per year, but Norris paid the real estate taxes.[6] David Jacks, of Monterey, leased 25 acres in the Canada Honda to Thomas Allen on July 13, 1864, for six years at $31.50 per year, but waived the rent in return for a rail fence.[7] Similarly, John Bidwell rented 190 acres to Rufus C. Rose in 1860 for 10 months and 25 days for the payment of taxes, planting 100 fruit tress, caring for 40 apple and 60 other fruit trees, and fencing all the trees.[8]

While improvements imparted increased value to land, clear title was, of course, necessary to any marketability. Rural landowners, like their San Francisco counterparts, put tenants on the land to fend off squatters. When landowners like David Jacks found squatters on his land, he had them sign leases.[9] Jacks believed that the California Supreme Court would confirm that a tenant under a lease could not contest the landlord's title.

In addition to leases to protect title, Jacks also wrote leases to induce improvements and sales. He and D. R. Ashley leased Salinas Valley farm land to Hardy Thompson in 1860 for 75 cents per month for a year with an option to buy or lease at market rates at the end of the year. For better lands, Jacks leased for $75 for six months and $100 for the second six months payable at the end of the term. These leases financed the tenant by allowing capital to be devoted to the crop and evidenced bargaining on the amount and timing of rent payments.[10] The marketplace had a marked influence on the rural leasing practices.

The California Supreme Court gave legal sanction to the landowner's practice of putting tenants on the land to bar their contesting title to the property. In *Tewksbury v. Magraff* (1867), a divided Court held that a tenant could not dispute a landlord's title during the term of tenancy unless the tenancy had been repudiated, possession was openly adverse, and the Statute of Limitations had run in the claimant's favor.[11] Justice Silas W. Sanderson grounded the majority's position on a substantial number of New England precedents. Sanderson also set out the exceptions, all properly supported by case law. Justice Lorenzo Sawyer dissented. He maintained that the exceptions went too far. In particular, if a tenant was in possession prior to signing a lease, the tenant could dispute the landlord's title before surrendering possession of the property. Sawyer stated the objection to the exception because he did "not find the exception so broadly stated anywhere in the books--either by the elementary writers or in the reports."[12] In other words, the squatters that David Jacks had sign leases could contest his title in court, but the tenants he brought onto the adjacent tract could not unless they surrendered possession.

Justice Sanderson replied to Sawyer's dissent in *Franklin v. Merida* (1868). Not only was the principle well supported by case law, Sanderson boasted, but also justice supported the rule. Building one hypothetical example on another, he concluded that Sawyer's reasoning "on the score of logic . . . if it proves anything, proves too much." Further, cases argued to be contrary to *Tewksbury* were, in fact, "entirely consistent with it." After an extensive review of the case law, Sanderson concluded that *Tewksbury* was rightly decided. Chief Justice Sawyer dissented again, but only in three terse sentences.

The process of decision was important. Neither Sanderson nor Sawyer deviated from the formalistic approach of basing decision on case law. Precedent rather than policy reasoning controlled in the debate. The Court continued this approach as the question came up again and again. In *Johnson v. Chely* (1872), Chief Justice William T. Wallace adhered to precedent but eased closer to Sawyer as he tied prior possession to deceptive inducement to sign a lease as relieving the tenant of estoppel and allowing title to be contested.[13] It became clear, however, that possession alone was sufficient, but when the landlord produced the lease, the burden of proof shifted to the tenant to show paramount title.[14]

Regardless of the state of the law, squatters were a problem through the 1870s. Archie Fraim wrote from Salinas City to David Jacks on October 23, 1871, that R. T. Buell had given him a "riten Guarantie" that read as follows:

> Know all Men by these Presents that I, R. T. Buell do hereby announce myself as an unwilling Tenant in the Rancho Known as the Souse to Rancho and Leased to David Jacks and owing to things from the beginning Deprived of all rights in said Rancho by Squatters shall not molest Archibald Fraim in anything He may sec fit to do on said Rancho. In other words, if He chuses to Squat on said Rancho, I shall deam It none of my Business. R. T. Buell.[15]

Fraim then stated that when Buell's lease expired, "I shall be verry Happy to become your Tenant." Trespassers also could give landlords and tenants headaches. One of Jacks' stubble tenants (sheep grazing) found "a large band of sheep running" on his leased lands and sent word to the owner. The answer he gave "by way of his herder was that he had the place rented and we might all go to Hell. I shall expect an answer to this tomorrow."[16] Although the Supreme Court in *Franklin v. Merida* rightly reflected that the rule of estoppel provided a shield for the landlord against the tenant, the realities of squatters evidencing possession for third parties, coercing other squatters or tenants off a landlord's property, and snatching the value of land from beneath a tenant's sheep were neither before the Court nor part of the analysis of the policy considerations. Sanderson made clear that the public policy was "designed merely as a shield for the protection of the landlord, and not as a sword for the destruction of the tenant."[17] The tenant should not be made to pay the rent he had contracted for to a landlord without title, as well as the market value of the use of the land to the owner with title. The realities of the scramble for title in early California could not be found in eastern precedents.

The problem was one of many dimensions. Owners of real estate needed law to protect their interests in quiet enjoyment of their property. This included ejecting squatters as well as holdover tenants. The legislature had provided the Forcible Entry and Unlawful Detainer Act, but as earlier cases had demonstrated, the statute required precise handling. Frontier counsel had to know the law and apply it precisely to protect their land-owning clients.

The record of counsel was checkered. In *Hodgkins v. Jordan*, (1873) the landowner had been in possession of his San Joaquin Valley farm since 1857. He had fenced it and cultivated it. Suddenly, in September 1864, a squatter erected "a small board tenement." The landowner went to the courts for help, but because counsel did not allege and offer to prove "wrongful detention of the premises by force," the suit was thrown out in 1866.[18] In a more genteel setting, a landlord and a tenant faced off at the Geyser Springs Resort Hotel complex in Sonoma County. In 1862 Mary Polack purchased the 640 acres along Sulphur Creek and erected a hotel to minister to the ailments of mankind with mineral spring treatments. James Shafer leased the hotel for 1866, 1867, 1868, and 1869 on one-year leases. The fourth lease expired on the final tick of the 1869 clock. But 1869 was a hard year for resort owners, and the creditors came to hound Shafer. His hotel furniture was attached in November, and Shafer turned over the hotel keys to the sheriff so that a keeper could be put in possession. Shafer also failed to pay the rent. Mary's husband acted with characteristic dispatch and gave a man named Susenbeth a one-year lease beginning January 1, 1870, and power of attorney to enter and take possession of the hotel for the Polacks. Susenbeth went to the hotel on December 29 and arranged to get possession to save the attached hotel furniture.

On New Year's Eve, the Geyser Springs Hotel had visitors. Susenbeth must have been elated to see customers so soon and in such troubled times. The first "guest" signed in as James Shafer. Seven hours later, Thomas W. Moore and Horace Templeton signed in and joined Shafer. Jim introduced them to the proprietor as his lawyers. Then more of Shafer's friends arrived, Clinton Gurnee and William S. Chapman. All occupied rooms and took supper. At ten they all gathered in the parlor. Gurnee then announced that he owned the land. Susenbeth and Gurnee both found the other's presence embarrassing, but they smiled and went to bed, Susenbeth hoping for better news in 1870. On January 2, Shafer demanded the key to Susenbeth's room; he refused and locked himself inside. The New Year's Eve guests then broke down the door and hauled all of the room's furniture belonging to the Polacks into the front yard. The fearless five then gave Susenbeth the option of acknowledging that he was dispossessed and putting the furniture back. He took it. On January 5, Susenbeth had had enough and left the pungent odors of Sulphur Creek for clearer air. The Polacks demanded possession and sued. Unfortunately, the Polacks were nonsuited and thrown out at the trial court. The New Year's Eve surprise party then became a nightmare.

Reaching the Supreme Court three years later, the Polacks could do no better. Their attorney had framed the first five counts of the complaint under the Forcible Entry and Unlawful Detainer Act of 1866 and the sixth count under the Landlord and Tenant Act of 1863. In that the entry was "peaceable," the first statute was of no avail. In that the forcible ouster on Susenbeth was accomplished on January 2, 1870, and Susenbeth was the tenant at that time, "the forcible entry . . . was an injury of which he alone would complain."[19] The complaint failed. Polack's attorney obviously had not read the statute or *Hodgkins*, or had failed to recognize that an action of ejectment was available. Other appellate cases evidence the fact that the landlords gave defective notices demanding possession or failed to demand rent due in a timely manner. These foibles of landlords were, interestingly, pursued by their attorneys all the way to the California Supreme Court rather than remedied prior to litigation.[20] After the lapse of years and the expense of litigation and lost rent, the landlords then could give proper notice or their lawyers pursue ejectment.

There was a gap between the declared purpose of the statute and counsel's ability to use the law. As Justice Augustus L. Rhodes so aptly stated in *Brawley v. Risdon Iron Works* (1869), "The purpose of the Act, like that of the earlier Acts upon the same subject, [was] to secure a speedy, if not a summary, restitution of the premises to the party who [had] been deprived of the possession."[21]   But if the statute were not followed precisely, the statutory remedy was worthless and common law was the last resort, whether at Sulphur Creek or in downtown San Francisco.[22]

One of the reasons for strict judicial construction of the statutes was the legislative policy of remedies for landlords. Double and triple rents were available under statute, but the California Supreme Court clearly favored tenants in requiring strict compliance with the statute. As Chief Justice Robert F. Morrison clearly stated in *Iburg v. Fitch* (1881), "The section [was] highly penal in its character, and the landlord seeking to avail himself of its harsh terms must bring himself within its provisions."[23] The other factor favoring tenants was the inertia of the legal system that could delay the process for years.

Since law was not always a trusty ally, landlords and counsel either drafted around the problems or used marketplace devices to ensure a degree of security and certainty in their leases. For example, John D. Goodwin, a Quincy lawyer, had tenants of questionable business reputation post bonds not only to vacate at the end of the lease but also for the rent itself.[24] David Jacks had tenants covenant to pay rent, a not uncommon lease clause, and make promissory notes. If they did not pay rent on time, Jacks got notes for penalties as well as interest.[25] Jacks also had third parties sign guarantees for rent and rent past due.[26]

Another common leasehold agreement was to accept improvements to the land in lieu of cash rent. This type of agreement benefited the landlord by the tenants giving notice of title by occupation and by increasing the value of the property. Hence, in 1864 David Jacks leased 25 acres to Thomas Allen for six years for $31.50 per year, but "instead of the rent above mentioned for the first year the said Allen shall fence said land with a good substantial fence made of redwood or cypress posts and pine rails."[27] Although rents might reflect the market value of land, it is clear that landlords designed fencing provisions to establish notice of possession and title. Even when the rent was as high as $250 per year, Jacks wrote in fencing provisions.[28] The converse also was true. If the land were virtually worthless for rental purposes, then the fencing provision was included along with "clearing the land and grubbing out roots" as consideration for a short-term lease of marginal lands.[29] However, if evidences of possession were existent on the land, then Jacks would allow a tenant to improve upon his handiwork. He offered Henry A. Grant a field and a house for a year for "putting in a floor, doors, and windows and a good chimney into the house in which the said Grant now resides."[30] The practice was little different in southern California. Jackson A. Graves, a Los Angeles attorney and founding partner in the powerful O'Melveny firm, reported to his client Thomas Bell that a prospective tenant had offered $1,200 per year in rent plus planting 100 acres of alfalfa and erecting a fence, house, and outhouse in return for a five-year lease.[31] Graves also put tenants on land for Bell to protect water rights. In 1880 he reported to have leased the Leo Felio for $1,000 per year to a responsible sheepman who had agreed to put in 100 acres of crop and irrigate it "so as to protect your water rights."[32]

Taking a share of the crop was another common means for a landlord to receive a profit from the land. It was, of course, a gamble on the weather and the skill of the tenant. David Jacks took that gamble throughout the period. He gave Gabriel Delonay a three-year lease in 1866 on 200 acres in Monterey County for one-third of all crops plus "a substantial fence."[33] Henry Olds leased land in 1872 for one-fifth of the crop the first year and one-fourth the second. Olds had to deliver the crop to the storehouse at the railroad junction. Jacks retained all rights to the straw and stubble, but if the first season were dry, Olds owed only two dollars rent.[34] In 1876 David Sniveley agreed to one-third of the crop in return for an eight-month lease and Jacks' furnishing the sacks for his portion of the wheat.[35] Charles McFadden rented land three years later for the same percentage of the crop with hay in bales and grain in his sacks.[36] That same year, Jacks rented 24 acres of the Point Pinos Rancho to Ah Jim and Ah Kong for one year at $2.50 per acre. However, the tenants covenanted to raise five acres of beets, which Jacks agreed to buy at two dollars per ton. Jim and Kong agreed to feed them to Jacks' cattle for 50 cents per ton. In return, no rent would be charged for the five acres.[37] One hundred acres of the El Alisal Rancho in Monterey County went for one dollar per acre and one-fourth of the wheat and barley "delivered in new bags to the Salinas City railroad warehouse" in 1881.[38] Although cropping agreements were common devices precedent to a tenant's occupation of the land, the drought of the early 1870s drove some cash renters into cropping agreements as well as interest assessments on unpaid rent.[39]

Drought among other causes resulted in loss for tenant and landlord alike. John Iverson wrote David Jacks from Salinas City on June 2, 1871, that his "crops on your ranche is almost an entire failure and as per agreement I am released from paying full rent."[40] In 1887 Mrs. J. J. Collins Gondonin, a farm machinery dealer, wrote to Mrs. Jacks asking for a delay in paying the rent because "business [was] very dull in this part of the country for the last three years, owing to the drought." Four months later, she wrote again from Lodi asking for another delay until the insurance money arrived to compensate them for the fire that wiped out the business.[41]

Disaster for tenants took many forms. Mrs. William H. Harrison wrote to Jacks from Santa Ana in 1890 that the reason the rent was not paid was that "for three years we have had sickness added to sickness." Worse yet, her husband was then in Pueblo, Colorado, and she had been the breadwinner "until my own health entirely failed."[42] Jacks carried her on the books as he had in years past, merely filing the yearly tale of woe. But Jacks was not always so patient. William B. Unruh wrote Jacks from the Santa Anita ranch on August 27, 1880, that although the rent was due in November and had not been paid, he "thought it no more than right and just in view of the labor and money [he] had already lost [that Jacks should allow] us to go away unmolested," excepting, of course, the "20 or 25 tons of hay" Jacks had attached.[43] Importantly, Unruh inquired whether Jacks would be satisfied with the hay. Unruh assumed that he owed Jacks, and he would pay eventually. His respect for private property extended to a moral obligation to "settle accounts." Other tenants did not have as strong a moral fiber. C. T. Tomie warned Jacks in 1880 that one of his tenants was not attending to business and was "drunk most of the time." Hence, Jacks should "make a formal demand for what is due now, and not let it go till too late."[44] But Jacks had a 30-year track record of carrying tenants year after year, reluctant to go to law but always willing to accept notes or assess interest on past due rents.[45] This reluctance to go to law also was reflected in G. D. Hines' 1884 letter to J. W. Jenks, a Quincy attorney, regarding his tenant. Hines stated that he had "no desire to give him any trouble or expense, and . . . deprecated the necessity of any legal process to recover the amount" then 15 months overdue.[46] Many landlords favored the marketplace and moral obligation as allies in gaining their profits.

The marketplace in rental property was periodically strong as would-be tenants hounded agricultural landlords in search of tillable soil. They, like D. O. Hein, wanted to make a "liberal offer you cannot refuse." To Hein in 1874, that was one-fourth the crop and a portion of the sacks.[47] Others, like Isaac Holcomb of Portland, Oregon, wanted to "rent on reasonable terms" with an option to buy for "part cash, taking the balance on time."[48] Many sheep ranchers wanted only temporary tenancy strictly to graze their sheep on the stubble left after the wheat harvest.[49] Stubble was of such great value that David Jacks commonly reserved rights in it. For example, Anton Gigling's 1880 lease for three years, seven months, and six days called for one-third of all crops in bags or bales at Castroville, but

> immediately upon the harvest being made, the said party of the first part shall have full and exclusive use of all the stubble--the land to be used by said Jacks or his assigns to consume the stubble, each year until rain shall have fallen sufficient to plow the ground, but not to be used by him later than the 8th day of November each year. Said Gigling shall have the first privilege of purchasing the stubble of said Jacks at current rates, to be paid by said Gigling as soon as the crops are removed and in case said lessee shall need for his own use straw for the purpose of maintaining his stock he may without let or hinderance of said Jacks appropriate, haul, and stack so much thereof as may be necessary for such purpose, free of charge.[50]

Jacks advertised his land in the newspapers and commonly had heavy demand from farmers and sheep ranchers.[51]

A high-volume traffic in tillable land, pasture, and stubble required a high-volume production of leases. Landlords of the first two decades scrawled the appropriate recitations across paper to bind their tenants, but the process was tedious and subject to transcription error. One lease was dutifully copied from a prior instrument. After the Civil War and more particularly by 1870, legal stationers in San Francisco produced form leases by the ream. Landlords had only to fill in the blanks.[52] Once the form became part of leasing practice, practitioners' ability to write leases atrophied. One of David Jacks' agents reported in 1880 that because he "had no lease to copy from," he had not written "any lease" at all.[53] Regardless of the existence of forms, landlords and tenants still had to negotiate terms and conditions. Landlords still had to sufficiently describe the property leased.

These negotiations were conducted in a marketplace for land and buildings. From time to time, David Jacks even had to use "a little diplomacy" for stubble rental.[54] When renting a hotel, Jacks' tenant bargained for reduced rental in return for a clause allowing Jacks to sell the property during the term of the lease.[55] Jacks and George F. Bodfish dickered over rent, pastures, fences, and the like over the years.[56]

The conclusion of negotiations was always a lease or the severance of the dialogue. Significantly, tenants wanted a lease in hand before they entered upon the landlord's property. George Bodfish wanted a simple dairy farm lease before he started farming in 1879.[57] W. P. L. Winham wrote to David Jacks the next year that the Bodger brothers were ready to move onto Jacks' ranch and that:

they are ready to pay the first half year's rent, but they refuse
to move or pay til they get their lease. Please make the lease
and other papers and send to me or direct--the kind of lease you
want, or send me blanks--but don't delay this any longer--it is
necessary and very proper that it should be attended to and not
forgotten.[58]

In 1886 John Bauman wrote Jacks from Soledad, "[I] beg you to send my
lease soon as I want to start in grubbin and clearing up the land and heuwling
menour in the field bout [I] don't like to start in untill I have my lease in
hand."[59] The tenant clearly wanted the lease to protect his interests by
making clear the conditions under which he entered the land. More
basically, nineteenth-century Californians respected private property and
did not want to enter upon another's land without an agreement to do so.[60]
This respect for private property must, of course, be recognized in the
context of a half-century of problems with squatters.

On occasion, when the lease was in hand, the landlord or the tenant
resorted to the legal system to enforce his agreements. Frequently, the
courts had to decide whether the tenant had agreed to pay the taxes on the
property. The justices of the California Supreme Court applied
common-law standards of interpretation in reading covenants to pay taxes.
Frequently, they found "express stipulations" in the lease requiring the
payment of taxes and assessments by the tenant.[61] Unfortunately for some
property owners, the property had been sold for taxes before the legal
process could extract compliance with a covenant to pay taxes.[62] The
covenant to pay taxes was common in the first two decades. William
Potter's ten-year lease of the Rio Chico in Butte County in 1851 to Samuel
Norris called for a rent of $50 per year plus a covenant that the tenant pay
all taxes.[63] David Jacks commonly had the tenant pay real estate taxes
and assessments, but the economic collapse of the 1870s and the rising
incidence of delinquent tax notices resulted in a change of position to pay
the taxes himself.[64]

Another covenant commonly found in leases that received judicial
attention was the one on improvements to the property. Early practice was
to lease for nominal cash rent plus a fence, a house, an outhouse, and the
like. On occasion, landlords would covenant to purchase all improvements
at a "reasonable price."[65] Such a covenant was more likely on urban land
than rural as the expectations as well as the costs of capital improvements
were substantially different.[66] However, residential property leases
sometimes put the entire burden of improvements on the tenant for the
benefit of the landlord. So it was with a Sacramento brick house, the
Supreme Court declared in *Gett v. McManus* (1873) after reading the
lease.[67] Further, when a tenant erected a building, in law a fixture, it
became part of the realty, and unless the tenant reserved rights to the
fixture such as compensation at "a reasonable price," the building belonged
to the landlord.[68]

When faced with questions about building or repairing structures,
the Court looked to the lease for the essence of obligation. In *Cowell v.
Lumley* (1870), the Court found a five-year lease made in 1863 for a San
Francisco water lot "capped and piled." The tenant covenanted to construct
a building on the pilings, which he did. Unfortunately, the building burned to
the water in 1866, and the landlord sued to force the tenant to rebuild. The
Court, citing *Beach v. Farish* (1854), held that absent an express covenant
to rebuild, a tenant "was bound to build but once."[69] Similarly, the Court
would not imply any covenant requiring a landlord to repair property

excepting certain dangerous defects in the property.[70] The landlord's duty to repair, even in statute, existed only when the premises "had become unfit for occupation" and then only "within a reasonable time after notice from the lessee."[71] After notice the landlord could repair, but could not make alterations of the premises without the express consent of the tenant.[72]

Beach v. Farish also played a significant role in molding the law where the building itself was destroyed. In *Beach* the Court told the parties to deal with the probable eventualities in the lease. Time did not change their position. If a house were destroyed by a flood of water from a man-made embankment, the tenant's covenant to repair excepting "the elements or the acts of Providence" did not insulate him from liability to repair. As the embankment was the handiwork of man and not nature, the exception to the covenant did not cover the situation.[73] On the other hand, if a house were destroyed and the tenant did not covenant to repair, "no action can be maintained . . . for rent accruing subsequent to the destruction of the building." So said Justice Royal T. Sprague in *Ainsworth v. Ritt* (1869),[74] citing Taylor on *Landlord and Tenant* as well as Ohio and Massachusetts cases. *Beach* immediately faded and covenants proliferated. However, in *Erenberg v. Peters* (1884), the building burned and the tenant continued to be liable for rent because he failed to get the landlord's alleged promise to rebuild in writing.[75] For the provident attorney scanning the reports, *Erenberg* did little good, as the Court failed to cite a single case as precedent. The best advice was to cover all probabilities by contract.

The problems of periodic flood and fire leaving tenants in the street were minor in comparison with cases of personal injury. When excavations next to San Francisco's Sumner House resulted in its collapse killing the tenant, the Court went directly to the lease and, finding no covenant to repair or maintain the premise in a habitable condition, decided that no liability for the landlord existed.[76] Further, the landlord was not liable to third parties for injuries arising from the negligent use of the property unless the landlord contributed to the hazardous condition.[77] The Court applied some of the same reasoning it did to industrial employers in insulating landlords from liability for personal injury.

The covenant to repair also bound subtenants, making them jointly and severably liable under the lease. The Court in *Coburn v. Goodall* (1887) saw "no hardship in this rule."[78] Many landlords tried to avoid the problem by inserting covenants against subleasing in their leases.[79] Without the covenant, many tenants turned their entrepreneurial skills to subletting land. A. P. Hendon of Santa Cruz wrote David Jacks on March 3, 1879, that he should not be concerned about the delay in the rent payment because "lease Renters become landlords--sub-leasing":

> I expected to have had $1,000 or $1,200 for you by the first of this month but matters have been delayed. I suppose I will know whether I get it or not tomorrow or the next day. I suppose from your last letter that you would like to have it. I sold seven of my cows the first of last month for $280. This will pay all that I owe outside of what I owe you. I will write as soon as I find out whether I get the money. I am aware that the above sum will not pay you all that I owe you but I want you to wait on me for the rent. I will have about four acres of potatoes . . . I have rented three acres of my land to the Chinese for $150 per annum.

Two of the houses are rented for $13.00 so the rents will come to $25 per month. I am growing chickens now but in about six weeks I shall turn my attention to something else.[80]

Jim Kee was even more proficient in putting his countrymen on the land.[81] But Jim and his brother Chung were good tenants, improving the land and paying the rent within a year of it coming due or signing notes for it. Jim's plea was about the same year after year:

I can't see you come to measures the wood. The wood is 15 1/2 cord. I am sell. The rant. I not rich. I please you wait to next years. I am pay you all.[82]

Jacks would then carry him for another year, having placed another promissory note in the account book.

When landlords wished to dispossess their delinquent tenants, they often found it difficult to fully comply with statute. Nonetheless, they still attempted to draft around notice requirements.[83] Normally, the landlord went to a lawyer and had a notice to quit or pay rent drafted. Then the sheriff served the notice, with the landlord paying a fee.[84] After the termination of the lease, some landlords like David Jacks went so far as to have tenants acknowledge that they did not want to renew their lease, that they had surrendered possession, and that they had taken all personal property with them.[85] As we have seen, the California Supreme Court strictly construed statutory requirements for notice. Further, the Court relied on New York precedent in statutory construction cases, for many provisions "were taken literally from the statutes of New York."[86] The prudent counselor could look to the Empire State for guidance in appellate practice.

However, the landlord's problems were greater than statutory compliance. Too often, counsel failed to practice effectively what the law required. The case of *Easton v. O'Reilly* (1883) was a monument to the nineteenth-century practice of law. On January 20, 1874, Easton's attorney filed an action of ejectment against the defendants, Burr and O'Reilly. The defendants answered. On March 8, 1875, the plaintiff filed an amended complaint including three other defendants. On August 9, 1878, a second amended complaint added more defendants. However, it was clear that O'Reilly was not a proper party as he was not in possession. Henry Jones, who was in possession, was not made a party. Burr, being out of possession, was not joined with his tenant Jones. The mistake regarding O'Reilly was repeated in both the first and second amended complaints. Although the plaintiff prevailed, he did so nine years after commencing suit.[87] On occasion, the Court was critical of both counsel and the trial bench for pleading and/or appellate advocacy.[88]

But the California Supreme Court was little better in its judicial product. In the period 1880-1890, 24 percent of its landlord and tenant decisions were handed down without citing a single case or statute. Other cases cited a statute or some section of a treatise. Hence, the careful practitioner could expect little help from fully a quarter of the decisions in the decade. The decade of the 1870s was not immune from the practice. In *Clark v. Clark* (1875), the Court decided to grant specific performance of a verbal agreement in neat outline form without a single citation gracing its decree.[89] Patrick Clark, the defendant, was the tenant of Almer Clark, the plaintiff, from October 1871 to October 1872. Patrick had a bad crop that year and went to Almer to get another year on the land. They dickered over the matter until November 8, 1872, when Patrick and John Dake called on Almer to finalize an agreement. The tenant's proposal was for one year, an option to renew for two more years, and $600 annual rent. After presenting the proposal, Dake handed the landlord a lease to sign. Almer refused, but accepted the rent money in advance and agreed to visit the office of F. W. Shattuck, an attorney, the next day. So on November 9, they visited Counselor Shattuck, but he was too busy to draw up the lease. Shattuck did take careful notes and promised prompt expedition. Patrick then received a rent receipt and gave John Dake power of attorney. Dake and a compatriot, John Himebach, then entered the land and started farming. The next year, Almer called on Dake for the rent. That was September 30, 1873. John Dake told Almer he would pay when it was due. Almer then stated that he would not receive it and wanted the land. On October 4, Dake tendered the rent, and Almer refused it. On October 23, Patrick appeared with a lease for Almer to sign, but Almer refused. Almer then sued, and the trial court awarded him the land. Patrick and both Johns appealed.

Chief Justice William T. Wallace brushed the whole matter aside in four inches of print. The terms of the lease were sufficiently specific to warrant specific performance. Dake's entry was no violation of the terms of the lease Shattuck was instructed to draft, but failed to scrawl. The tender of the second year's rent was well-made. Specific performance must be granted. Almer was left without a written lease for a term of at least two years for a rent unstipulated in writing. All of this was set down without case law, treatise, statute, or reasoning. A practicing attorney reading the reports could only conclude, as Jackson A. Graves did in 1890, that the Court was "eccentric."

The California Supreme Court, despite its frequent abstinence from *stare decisis*, formalism, or instrumentalism, did construct some doctrine on eastern precedent as well as commercial practice. For example, in *California Conference v. Seitz* (1887), the justices looked to Massachusetts precedents, "the intentions of businessmen," and "the practical construction" of the parties.[90] In deciding what constituted a breach of the covenant of quiet enjoyment, the Court used New York, New Hampshire, and North Carolina precedents for guidance.[91] When deciding upon the nature of fixtures, the Court relied upon the experience and reasoning of New York, Kansas, and New Hampshire justices.[92]

Further, the Court did evidence the traditional deference to precedent from time to time. Justice James D. Thornton eloquently recited the traditional language in *Thompson v. Felton* (1880). Despite the fact that a prior case was wrongly decided and defied precedent across the nation, Thornton supported its application because

> this decision, however erroneous, under numerous decisions of the Supreme Court of this State constitutes the law of the case in all of its stages. To this we must yield. I have long had much doubt as to the propriety of this rule concerning the law of the case, but it has been too long settled to be now disturbed.[93]

Was that a statement counsel could take to the bar?

When counsel stood back from the bar in 1890, the cases revealed only subtle changes in results. While landlords had won 61.905 percent of the cases up to 1865, they won 61.417 percent after the war. The subject

matter of the cases changed somewhat. From 1850 to 1865, urban land
and/or structure cases constituted 73.407 percent of the appellate cases.
For the period 1866-1890, they amounted to 61.8 percent, reflecting both
the boom in agriculture and the continuing problems of tenancy, particularly
in San Francisco.[94] The percentage of commercial structures involved in
litigation dropped from 34.694 to 29.4 percent, reflecting the regularization
of leasing practices. What counsel could glean from the statistics and the
cases was not a seamless web of jurisprudence. It was a developing law of
landlord and tenant fractured by frequent and confusing legislation, case law
of varying quality and precision, and practice of varying quality. Focusing
upon that practice, a lawyer was best advised to obtain the best Bancroft
blank forms, check the property descriptions at the recorder's office, and
insert language as necessary in the sure and certain hope that tenants would
abide by it.[95]

California's law, like eastern landlord and tenant law, described a
developing relationship of changing socioeconomic circumstances. The law's
development and squatter or tenant "revolts" were not part of the identical
circumstances. Landlords and tenants experienced law at arm's length on a
regular periodic basis. Squatters questioned the underlying title great and
small. Law was the resort of most frontier Californians. The law played a
major, if varying, role in the socioeconomic development of California.
Most importantly, it gave landlords, tenants, and their attorneys
mechanisms to structure their relationships. The frontier flavor in these
relationships was of the times more than of the law.

3
REAL ESTATE MORTGAGE LAW

The development of the law of mortgage in California reflected the tensions of lawmaking amid rapid social and economic change. Mortgage law development was critical for the new state because of the need for investment capital, the security of interests in land, and the stability of investment without mature banking institutions. The legislature and Supreme Court labored to create a mortgage law to enable transactions in a frontier marketplace.

There were several different types of mortgage instruments. The common mortgage was a deed or conveyance of land by a borrower to a lender followed or preceded by a description of a debt, commonly a promissory note, included in or attached to the mortgage instrument. A second type of mortgage was the trust deed. Here the borrower conveyed the land to a third party, not the lender, in trust for the benefit of the holder of the note that represented the mortgage debt. Finally, an equitable mortgage was any written instrument demonstrating the intent of the parties that real estate be held as security for the payment of a debt.

Not only did California lawmakers have a variety of mortgage instruments to deal with, but they were aware of a substantial history of mortgage law developed amidst the pull and haul of creditor-debtor antagonism. Much of mortgage law had been developed by courts of equity in the colonial period,[1] and a costly and complicated system of equitable foreclosure had evolved, giving the debtor a right to redeem his land.[2] Skillful lawyers drafted mortgage instruments around this "equity" and created the trust deed by which the debtor agreed, in advance, that if he defaulted, the trustee could sell his land without going to court. Legislators, however, urged on by debtors caught in the crush of a boom-and-bust economy, enacted statutes to protect debtors. New York passed a statute in 1820 giving debtors a year of grace in response to the panic of 1819.[3] Illinois legislators passed a one-year redemption statute in 1841 spurred on by the panic of 1837.[4] The Illinois statute applied to existing as well as future mortgages.

The U. S. Supreme Court struck down the Illinois statute in *Bronson v. Kinzie* (1843).[5] Chief Justice Roger B. Taney held the statute unconstitutional as an impairment of the obligation of contracts, but explained that the legislature could alter the remedy so long as the modification of the legal remedy or the method of enforcing the mortgage did not impair the terms of the mortgage itself.[6] The decision in *Bronson*, while establishing that a legislature could impose a redemption right on future mortgages, also served notice on legislatures that the courts would intervene to curb legislative excesses favoring debtors.[7]

Again, in the 1850s, states tampered with mortgage law amid economic stress. Debtors, particularly farmers, agitated for government loans, cheap mortgage money, tough rules on foreclosure, and easy rules on redemption.[8] Laws such as Wisconsin's 1858 statute stripping the notes and mortgages of negotiability were struck down by state courts.[9] The tensions between legislators sympathetic to debtor interests and the courts, which tended to adhere to constitutional law doctrines, were part of California's legal context for lawmaking.

The California Supreme Court's approach to the redemption issues was, in the early cases, to apply rules of construction beneficial to the statute. In *Kent and Cahoon v. Laffan* (1852), Justice Solomon Heydenfeldt applied the rule of construction to the California Practice Act, section 229. The statute provided that upon a sale of real property, when the estate was less than a leasehold of a two-year unexpired term, the sale should be absolute. In all other cases, the real estate was subject to the redemption. The mortgage in question was made subsequent to the redemption act. Heydenfeldt found the act "sufficiently comprehensive to include within its design, sales of real estate under decrees of foreclosure of mortgages." Heydenfeldt rejected any technical reading of the act and concluded that "it [was] safest to look to the obvious policy of the law and to maintain such policy against a mere hesitation, caused by the inapt language of the act."[10] Heydenfeldt also had occasion to declare law on redemption in *Benham v. Rowe* (1852). There he concluded that "where a power of sale [was] contained in a mortgage, and under a sale by virtue of such power, the mortgage [became] the purchaser, the equity of redemption still attache[d] to the property in favor of the mortgager."[11]

The problems of the first years of statehood also were the problems of rapid development. The facts of *Woodworth v. Guzman* (1850) illustrate the frenzy of San Francisco in 1849. The defendant, Guzman, bought city property on June 17, 1849, from Samuel Brannan. Brannan, in the haste of the transaction, made the deed on property on Montgomery Street instead of Washington Street and gave Guzman a receipt for part payment. Guzman then borrowed $3,000 on the property from Brannan, giving him a mortgage on the property. Subsequently, Guzman mortgaged the property again, this time to a Mr. Rynders for $7,000. Foreclosure followed, and the trial court gave the Brannan mortgage priority over the Rynders mortgage. On appeal, Justice Nathaniel Bennett rejected Rynders' claim that Brannan's mortgage, being unrecorded, should not receive priority in foreclosure. Bennett noted that it was "settled in the states, where statutes requiring mortgages to be recorded are in force, that if a subsequent mortgagee has notice of the existence of a prior unrecorded mortgage, he takes his lien subject to the lien of the first mortgage."[12] Rynders had such notice. Further, Bennett declared, "we think the same rule applie[d] under the Mexican system." Even if it did not, "we are not aware that there was any officer in San Francisco, who according to Mexican law, was authorized to record mortgages."[13] The public policy was to prevent imposition upon subsequent purchasers and mortgagees, in good faith and without notice of prior incumbrance. Here, Rynders had notice, and the protection of law was unavailable.

The Court in *Woodworth* set policy in tune with general national legal experience. That policy protected dealers in the marketplace in their expectations, even expectations in the rough-and-tumble speculation of rapid urbanization amid a gold rush. The legislature aided this policy by providing dealers with a recording statute in 1850. The legislature also provided for conveyances and mortgages of real estate.[14] In 1851 the legislature provided that a judgment debtor could redeem his real property by paying the purchaser the amount of his purchase plus 18 percent and any taxes, assessment, or creditors' liens within six months after sale.[15]

As *Woodworth* demonstrated, speculation in land was prevalent, trading sharp, and litigation common. In July 1852 Cave Johnson Couts accurately reported to Abel Stearns in Los Angeles that "speculations in land is rife-plenty of sellers and as many purchasers."[16] Money was dear and mortgages short term. John Center bought a downtown San Francisco lot for $1,000 down, a six-week note for $1,000 at three percent per month, and a five-month note for $2,500 at three percent per month due August 1, 1851.[17] Speculation in Los Angeles city land was fierce, but at moderate prices. Benjamin D. Wilson acquired numerous city lots in 1853 and 1854 for $300 to $4,500 each, with interest ranging from two to five percent per month, for terms ranging from 18 days to six months.[18] Phineas Banning, founder of Wilmington, built up substantial interests in wharves, warehouses, and lumberyards through rapid trading in swamp lands, railroad leases, lumberyard leases, and tax title purchases.[19]

Speculation in agricultural land was equally sharp; interest rates were high, and mortgages were short term.[20] Abel Stearns frequently loaned money on southern California land at two percent per month for six months to one year.[21] Frequently, Stearns foreclosed on mortgages and became the owner of numerous ranchos. Litigation also was very much a part of his dealings.[22] In most transactions in the 1850s, time was of the essence in the turbulent dealings in land and money at high interest.[23] But profits were equally high in the first flush years of statehood, and dealers were quite willing to assume the risk of unconscionable interest rates, inflated prices, and short-term notes.[24]

The torrid pace of business often made dealers less mindful of the formalities of their transactions. Mortgages took a great variety of forms. Some were printed forms with the appropriate blanks completed. Others were handwritten. Some were entitled "indentures." Others were described as a "contract and deed of mortgage."[25] A deed and promissory note often evidenced a mortgage. Some were two separate documents; others were incorporated in a single paper.[26] In a more formal format, deeds of trust could detail many aspects of a transaction. In 1864 Abel Stearns transferred cattle, horses, mines, and water rights to Henry Davis Bacon as trustee on a three-year trust deed for several ranches on a $150,000 transaction carrying 18 percent interest.[27] Complex transactions could also be overly simple, such as "sheep raising, being in lieu of interest" or promises to execute notes without simultaneous execution.[28] Some dealers struck out one form of legal action on default on a document and substituted another.[29] Lawmakers had to bring some regularity to preserve the expectations of the parties.

The California Supreme Court had an early and surprisingly prolonged problem of legally defining a mortgage. Justice Heydenfeldt declared in *Godeffroy v. Caldwell* (1852) that "mortgages at the present day, are considered as mere securities for the payment of money, and no breach of their conditions can possibly vest the title in the mortgagee."[30] Justice David S. Terry repeated Heydenfeldt in *Sherwood v. Dunbar* (1856).[31] Chief Justice Peter H. Burnett repeated the principle at great length in *Belloc v. Rogers* (1858).[32] Justice Stephen J. Field felt compelled, in *McMillan v. Richards* (1858), to embark upon a 16-page disquisition on the subject.[33] Field cited *Godeffroy v. Caldwell*[34] and Chancellor Kent, concluding that "in truth, the original character of mortgages has undergone a change. They have ceased to be conveyances, except in form."[35] Field's extensive scholarship and detailed declaration of law quieted counsel on the subject, but justices did, from time to time, repeat the Field litany. The legal character of California mortgages was established.

The California Supreme Court also had to deal with whether a mortgage existed. The justices had little sympathy for sloppy draftsmanship and clever argument.[36] As Justice Joseph G. Baldwin warned in 1859, careful research on title and liens was necessary to avoid some subsequent reverse, which he called "one of the unfortunate blunders common to all speculation."[37] Another critical question was the admissibility of parol evidence (verbal evidence). The problem arose from the often irregular transactions in property. A deed in the hands of a party would indicate nothing more than fee ownership. A deed and promissory note could evidence a mortgage or unrelated transactions. To clarify the situation, testimony under oath could supply needed information. However, parol evidence was not always considered desirable or reliable.

Stephen J. Field first approached the issue as an advocate. In *Lee v. Evans* (1857), Field argued, for the appellant, that English and American decisions held that such evidence was admissible in cases of fraud, accident, or mistake, but there was a conflict of authority on whether it could be admitted in the absence of special circumstances. Field based his argument on Kent's *Commentaries*, opinions by Joseph Story, and numerous cases.[38]

The Court, by Justice Burnett, rejected Field's argument, Burnett painstakingly reviewing Field's cited cases as well as Kent's *Commentaries*. He distinguished some precedents involving fraud, accident, or mistake as not legally on point and others on the basis of fact. After such review, Burnett concluded that "with the utmost deference for authorities so high, I must confess I could never see the reason upon which these decisions rest."[39] Burnett's vision was clearer on viewing the terms of California statute. The clear language would not permit Field's reasoning. Further, Burnett was concerned about the role of the Court.

In statutory interpretation, Burnett rejected what he considered an invitation to make law. To revise statute, Burnett claimed, exceeded the Court's authority.[40] He concluded that the Court's constitutional authority was limited, and only the legislature could make the change.

But Burnett was not satisfied to leave the issue alone. He embarked upon a subterranean undermining of cited authorities, reconciling the statutory language and the admission of parol evidence. On a U. S. Supreme Court opinion of Justice John McLean that had been joined by Joseph Story, Burnett tunneled in and retorted that he could not "understand the force of this explanation."[41] Similarly, Burnett could not "see the reason of the distinction" in an opinion by Chief Justice John Bannister Gibson of Pennsylvania. But dredging up dissents seemingly silted over by time, Burnett declared that "we think the strict rule the true one."[42] Field's argument was seemingly buried under the tailings of Burnett's labors.

Rebuffed on parol evidence, Field nonetheless won the case and ultimately made the rule. After seven pages of argument on Field's position, Burnett acknowledged in two sentences that Field's opposition had failed to deny facts alleged in Field's pleading, resulting in a mortgage being admitted as a matter of law. On October 13, 1857, Field joined the Court and set about unearthing his parol evidence rule. In *Pierce v. Robinson* (1859), he wrote the opinion for the Court overruling *Lee v. Evans*, in part holding that parol was admissible in equity to show that a deed, absolute on its face, was intended as a mortgage.[43] Field's opinion clearly established California law. In 1865 Justice Lorenzo Sawyer could safely say that "it is now settled in this State that parol evidence is admissible to show that a deed absolute on its face was intended to be a mortgage."[44] Field's position was California's. It was a position well suited to California's frontier condition.

The California Supreme Court also decided doctrinal questions of conditional sales contracts and mortgages containing the power of sale. Both types of transactions exhibited the turbulence of the era and the desire to promote the rapid, certain, and conclusive sale of property upon the default of a debtor. In *Hickox v. Lowe* (1858), Chief Justice Field distinguished the mortgage from a conditional sale in deciding a case involving a conveyance and an agreement to reconvey. Field repeated the well-known fact that a mortgage was mere security for a debt and noted that "the relation of creditor and debtor must exist between . . . [the] parties."[45] If the debt was extinguished by the conveyance, the agreement to reconvey was an independent contract. If doubt existed, then the court would find a mortgage.[46] In *Fogarty v. Sawyer* (1861), Field again stated California law with clarity. He declared that there was "nothing in the law of mortgages in this State which prevents the mortgagor from investing the mortgagee with a power to sell the premise upon default in the payment of the debt secured."[47] This was a critical holding because it allowed dealers to write mortgage instruments with strong default language and upon default to sell without resort to statutory procedures. Further, when sold in accordance with mortgage contract language, good title would pass to the purchaser.[48] It was only a single step to the trust deed by putting the trustee in the place of the mortgagee.[49] The ingenuity of draftsmen and dealers was directed at avoiding the more cumbersome statutory foreclosure procedures.

In construing the statutory foreclosure procedures and the Statute of Limitations, the Court favored bringing debtor and creditor into the judicial foreclosure proceedings unless the creditor had been sitting on his rights. In *Guy v. Ide* (1856), Justice Heydenfeldt rejected the English rule providing for the appointment of a receiver of rents and profits and declared that the statute forbade the recovery of the mortgaged estate except by foreclosure.[50] Despite language in the mortgage instrument, the Court required statutory procedures. In *Cormerias v. Ganella* (1863), Chief Justice Edwin B. Crocker noted that the mortgage instrument contained language vesting a power of the sale in the mortgage "according to law." Crocker observed that "the clause [was] evidently copied from some form in a State having laws regulating such sales." In that the California statute required a judicial proceeding, the Court held that the statutory procedure be followed. "In that way," Crocker maintained, "there is no doubt of the right of the mortgagor, or parties holding under him, to redeem the property within six months after the sale."[51] The case evidenced both the frontier nature of legal documents adopted from other jurisdictions rather than drafted for California law and the willingness of the Court to require the statutory procedure. Not only was redemption involved, however, but more fundamental rights were at stake. Due process was a definite consideration. As the Court asserted in *Skinner* v. *Buck* (1865), the statute "does not propose to relieve mortgagees from the constitutional necessity of giving all persons whose interests they may seek to compromise by foreclosure decrees a chance to be heard."[52] The justices gave the Statute of Limitations similar application. In *Grattan* v. *Wiggins* (1863), Chief Justice Crocker rejected English statutory applications and declared that California's Statute of Limitations applied to the subject matter of the lawsuit regardless of the form of action or the type of court in which the suit was being tried.[53] In *Low* v. *Allen* (1864), the Court observed that a mortgage contract was "manifestly one of the written contracts" described by the statute limiting actions for four years from accrual. The Court found the facts presented to be "within the mischiefs against which the Statute of Limitations was intended to guard."[54] The Court was loath to allow untimely lawsuits in times of rapid frontier transactions.

In accordance with the foreclosure statute, when the trial court had rendered judgment in favor of the creditor, the creditor could have the property sold by the sheriff at auction.[55] The statute required the posting of notice of sale for 20 days and publication in the newspaper for the period of one week "in a newspaper in the county if there be one." The sheriff could be penalized $500 for failure to publish such notice. Sales were at auction to the highest bidder. Upon sale, the sheriff issued a certificate of sale that was to state whether the property was subject to redemption. The sheriff also filed duplicates of the certificates with the county recorder. The property could be redeemed six months after sale by the judgment debtor or a creditor having a judgment against the property or a mortgage. Redemption required payment to the purchaser at the sheriff's sale of the purchase price plus 18 percent interest plus assessments or taxes plus interest. If the sheriff's sale purchaser was a creditor, redemption required the amount of the prior creditor's lien plus interest. If a creditor redeemed the property, other creditors had 60 days in which to redeem from him with six percent interest added on. This 60-day window could be exercised again and again by all subsequent creditors until the last had redeemed or the 60-day period had passed without a redemption. Notice of these redemptions was to be given to the sheriff when the six-month or 60-day term had duly expired; the last redemptioner was entitled to a sheriff's deed. The process was slow and, being subject to redemption for a lengthy period of time, costly.[56] Creditors obtained possession of property but, because of redemption interests, were seldom free to rapidly sell their property.

The Supreme Court did provide creditors with assistance in enforcing their rights. The Court ruled that fixtures could pass by sheriff's deed. In arriving at the position, Chief Justice Field applied familiar property law concepts and precedents.[57] If the purchaser had a sheriff's deed in hand, but the occupier of the premises refused to vacate, then the Court held that a writ of assistance was an appropriate remedy.[58] Although providing the creditor with the sheriff's strong arm of the law in sale and dispossession, the Court construed the statute strictly. In *Heyman* v. *Babcock* (1866), the Court voided a sheriff's sale where both the creditor and sheriff had failed to follow the statute.[59] The Court favored the statutory proceedings and carefully protected creditor and debtor interests within the terms of the law.

Similarly, the Court protected the statutory and equitable rights of debtors to redeem their interest in the real estate. Even where the power of sale was contained in the mortgage, if the creditor became purchaser, the equity of redemption still attached to the property. The Court construed statutory language beneficially, considering redemption to be a remedial legislative act. If interpretative questions arose, then the Court attempted to balance interests and retain for the debtor the opportunity to completely fulfill his obligation. This was made difficult by failures of legislative craftsmanship, but the Court construed language to save it and make the statutory system workable.[60] The antagonism frequently experienced in other states was not overtly evident, excepting the Court's open distaste for unskillful draftsmanship of early statutes.

Despite foreclosure proceedings, the lender had a variety of hurdles to vault. If a woman were involved in a transaction, then creditors could easily be hamstrung by common-law doctrines concerning capacity or spiked by a homestead exemption. Whenever a married woman signed the note and mortgage without her husband, the creditor had no contract. The woman lacked legal capacity to make a contract. The Supreme Court was unwilling to unilaterally alter this doctrine. Justice Heydenfeldt stated in 1855 that a married woman "has no power to make a contract is a doctrine of law which this Court has no power to disturb."[61] The burden of inquiry was upon the creditor or purchaser. As Justice Sawyer pointed out in *Ramsdell v. Fuller and Summers* (1865), the fact of a woman's name on a deed "afforded to all persons seeking to acquire title under it a clue to the title, which they were bound to pursue, or suffer the consequences." The presumption of the law was that she was not married and could pass title, "but she may be married, and her deed may not pass title." The fact of marital status had to be determined by the creditor-purchaser, "or omit to do so at their peril."[62] Creditors could be left with a worthless deed and an uncollectible promissory note if not diligent.

Creditors also had to be cognizant of the $5,000 homestead exemption from execution for debt. The Supreme Court construed the statute favorably to debtors to find a homestead. In *Moss v. Wainer and Wife* (1858), Chief Justice Field held that the fact that the debtors were driven from their ranch by Indians, their buildings burned, their cattle stolen, and their lives preserved only by a hasty retreat to San Diego did not constitute an abandonment of their homestead.[63] Similarly, in *Lies v. De Diablar* (1859), Justice Baldwin declared that "adultery or abandonment by the wife did not divest the property of the character of the homestead."[64] But the Court would not brook the deliberate manipulation of creditors to evade a mortgage. Chief Justice Hugh C. Murray forcefully stated that the Court would not "lend its aid to do an injustice and assist a party in escaping from a just liability which he has contracted."[65] Despite the Court's stern warning, the creditor of the family farm or ranch had a particular limitation in getting from the blocks to the finish line without an occasional stumble.

Although a creditor could control, to a degree, the problems of a married woman's property and the homestead exemption, hard times and bankruptcy were not so easily avoided. Bankruptcy did not release the lien of the mortgage, but did operate to limit the creditor's recovery to the proceeds of the mortgaged premises.[66] A debtor could mortgage property and not have the mortgage be declared an assignment for benefit of creditors to avoid the statutory distribution of assets.[67] Nonetheless, bankruptcy stood as yet another statutory mechanism altering creditor expectations.

Creditors often grounded their expectations in the priority of their interest in real estate. But in the turbulent speculation of frontier transactions, whether a creditor had a first, second, or sixtieth mortgage on a single piece of California terra was often a question only a court could answer. The questions of priority came to the Supreme Court with statehood. In *Woodworth v. Guzman* (1850), the Court held that notice to a subsequent creditor of a prior unrecorded mortgage gave priority to the first in time.[68] The legislature's efforts to give creditors notice of mortgages and other liens were insufficient. As Chief Justice Murray lamented in *Rose v. Munie* (1854), "Not only is the Mechanics' Lien Law defective but also the Recording Act itself, and it may be safely said, that no provision is made for recording a numerous class of liens." Without compulsory recording of mortgages, the Court relied upon common law, which did not require recording and recording did not impart notice. All had the duty of "ascertaining all outstanding titles or incumbrances against the estate."[69] With knowledge of prior incumbrances, creditors, of course, loaned money at the risk of the value of the property being insufficient to satisfy all debts. With the recording of mortgages, secret liens were less likely and creditor risks reduced by reference to the county recorder's mortgage book.[70]

The fact situations of the cases portray the vitality and variety of mortgage transactions of the period. Of the 144 cases studied for the period 1850-1865, 118 had identifiable demographic facts set out in the appellate reports. Forty-four percent involved property in urban areas. Nineteen percent concerned commercial properties, while canals represented nine percent and mines seven percent of the cases. Cases concerning the family farm or ranch and the great ranchos constituted the remainder. The cases coming before the Supreme Court were those of an urban frontier and of an exploitative era. The monetary stakes involved were also significant. Ninety-seven of the cases had monetary values contained in the report. These ranged from $202.65 on a mine to $120,000.00 on a San Francisco office building. The average values per year indicate that significant economic stakes came before the bench for decision.[71]

The Supreme Court decided 58 percent of its cases in favor of creditors. Had the lender-plaintiffs been more careful in drafting documents, securing a wife's signature, searching title, or prosecuting foreclosure in a timely manner, the percentage of creditor holdings would have been much higher. The Court was making an overt effort to protect creditor expectations, preserve statutory procedures, and maintain the debtor's statutory recourse of redemption. The justices attempted to rationalize the legal system to these ends while according the legislature's statutory pronouncements appropriate deference.

The Court's methodology was significant, given the turbulent frontier nature of transactions. If statute would provide a means to resolve creditor-debtor problems, then the Court would defer. If statute were inadequate, then the Court would rely upon common law. Whenever common law was not clearly applicable to California's frontier condition, the Court would make law for the state in tune with its needs. This methodology was instrumentalist in character and reflected a means-end mode of analysis focusing upon expected consequences.[72] Given the turbulent, sharp, and varied nature of frontier transactions, the judicial style suited the situation. However, the justices, particularly Chief Justice Field, were very careful to extensively review precedents and ground decisions in both law and public policy.[73] The work of the Court in this period laid the foundation for the extensive litigation that would follow in the remainder of the century.

The period 1867-1880 was one of boom and bust, speculation, monopolies in land and transportation, and the stabilization of financial institutions. It also was a period of constitution making. In this context the California Supreme Court and legislature continued the efforts to foster the mortgage money market.

The availability of money at interest on real estate became critical to California in this period because of the expansion of wheat production and the first real estate boom in the state's history.[74] Many large landholders subdivided their lands and sold them to small farmers.[75] Concurrently, Dr. Hugh J. Glenn and Isaac Friedlander bought up huge tracts of land in the Sacramento and San Joaquin valleys and then planted wheat.[76] In the Salinas Valley, David Jacks combined vast holdings in wheat with cattle, sheep, mustard, lumber, cord wood, nursery trees, and cashmere goats.[77] The real estate and wheat boom had repercussions in the handling trade, mercantile interests, and the railroad industry. For example, Phineas Banning bought up swamp lands, leased land to railroads and lumber companies, and purchased tax titles to further his interests in the port of Wilmington.[78] David Jacks helped develop the Monterey harbor and promoted a narrow-gauge railroad to get his crops to harbor. Economic expansion, of course, impacted other sectors. Demand increased. H. T. Holmes of the Pacific Glassworks, San Francisco, sent a plea to David Jacks in Monterey on May 16, 1866: "You must try and send us more sand as the Glassworks have taken all you have sent . . . and we have a great many outside orders which we have not been able to fill."[79] Although the fever of speculation reverberated across the state, the small farmer's desire for a family farm was ever present. D. W. Lawton said it to David Jacks in September 1873 when he asked for a $500 loan on his 40-acre farm: "I feel like making a great effort to secure what I think every family ought to have--a home."[80] Under such conditions, the pressures for land financing would be constant.

The clarity of the transaction increased somewhat in the period. Printed form deeds and promissory notes avoided some problems.[81] The A. L. Bancroft Company of San Francisco, among others, supplied dealers with form number 1072, "Mortgage," which recited appropriate language and allowed the lender to fill in the details.[82] But dealers did not always have forms, and transactions could be relatively informal on small mortgages.[83] Some experienced dealers in land still did not make clear distinctions between mortgages and deeds of trust.[84] However, the vast majority of dealers avoided warranty deeds because of title problems. George Hansen, writing to Matthew Keller on May 12, 1877, stated the California situation clearly:

The purchaser wants a warranty deed. We have a kind of warranty deed from Judge Widney and the title is otherwise perfect and there is no reason, why we should not give a warranty deed except the <u>general</u> <u>habit</u> of the country to give bargain and sale deeds, <u>based</u> <u>on</u> <u>the</u> <u>fear</u> <u>of</u> <u>blackmailing</u>.[85]

With titles so subject to litigation, no dealer in land dared venture liability on the title, and even if lenders might want greater security of title, it was not generally to be had in the period.

The Supreme Court often reiterated the definition of a mortgage and pondered the intent of parties using a deed as part of a transaction. As Justice A. L. Rhodes cautioned in *Henley v. Hotaling* (1871), "To convert the deed into a mortgage, the evidence ought to be so clear as to leave no doubt that the real intention . . . was to execute a mortgage."[86] Justice Joseph B. Crockett restated the familiar rule making a transaction a mortgage: "The fact whether or not, notwithstanding the conveyance, there [was] a subsisting, continuing debt from the grantor to the grantee" rendered the transaction a mortgage.[87] If the consideration for the conveyance was a preexisting debt, then a mortgage existed. Often the justices looked to the instrument of the transaction. As Justice Rhodes stated in *Hellman v. Howard* (1872), "The term 'deed' will in its largest sense include a mortgage . . . but it is manifest from the context, that the term was used in that instrument in a more limited sense."[88] Although issues of interpreting the intent of parties would be expected before the California courts, the reiteration of well-known legal rules indicates a degree of uncertainty on the Court and more likely in the legal profession.[89] One necessary task, therefore, was the consolidation of legal principles established by the Supreme Court in the preceding 15 years. But, on occasion, the justices could not agree among themselves whether certain basic principles should apply.[90] The uncertainty of the Court and legal profession would be a factor in the marketplace.

The legislature attempted to lend a degree of certainty to transactions by statutes for conveyancing and out-of-state acknowledgments.[91, 92] Further, solons required county recorders to prepare an index of sales of real estate sold under execution.[93] The legislature also gave purchasers at the sheriff's sale greater certainty by declaring that conveyance recorded after a foreclosure action was commenced did not impart notice.[94] The courts followed the traditional path of enforcing the statute and making careful inquiry of personal knowledge of unrecorded mortgages in deciding cases.[95]

Foreclosure of a mortgage with the subsequent redemption period and sheriff's sale was not always the result of debtor's default. Refinancing the original debt or continuing it for an additional term of years was a means of avoiding foreclosure. Debtors often asked, "What will be the prospects to let the mortgage run another year if I keep the interest paid up?"[96] Others wanted to refinance to make improvements.[97] Large-scale dealers in land and businessmen regularly refinanced to consolidate debts, lower interest, create liquid capital, or speculate further in land.[98] Debtors also made partial payment to avoid foreclosure. As Isaias Hellman told Matthew Keller in 1879, with the creditor having half the mortgage money in hand and a promise of the rest being forthcoming in his ear, "he will not push the balance."[99] Creditors, of course, had the heavy hand of the law if payment was ultimately not forthcoming. In fact, creditors could use the threat of foreclosure to spur fiscal responsibility in debtors. James A. Clayton of San Jose asked his client David Jacks to give him such leverage in 1879. "You had better write me a letter I can show him--stating that you want the money or more security and ordering me to commence suit if not settled," Clayton wrote.[100] Not surprisingly, Clayton was able to report, two weeks later, that the debtor had obtained the money from an Oakland bank.[101] But when the loan fell through, Clayton ruminated that "if you could spare the money it would be good policy to let them have it at the same rate (10% per year)."[102] Jacks could and did. But where the debtor had not demonstrated a basis for extending further credit or time, foreclosure could result.[103] After the action and the sheriff's sale, the debtor could redeem his property upon payment to the lender. The creditor was normally forced to rent the premises for the period.[104] Although the legal system gave the creditor the force of the law to protect his interest, informal settlement was always available.

Some debtors opted to sell out rather than to continue in their relationship with the creditor. Depression, crop failures, bad judgment, and a high debt service often combined to motivate the debtor to look for other means of employment. J. M. Soto pondered his situation and wrote to David Jacks in 1870 that he had "been figuring the interest on my debt and I do not feel very encouraged: because what I make with the people that owe me is not even one half of what I pay: therefore I want to offer you all my ranch at $18 per acre with all improvements."[105] The other option for the debtor was bankruptcy. Interestingly, creditors sometimes found that under certain circumstances, bankruptcy could yield more than a foreclosure.[106]

The Supreme Court enforced mortgages and their foreclosure, attempting to avoid the legal conclusion that the creditor was without remedy. For example, in *Himmelmann v. Fitzpatrick* (1875), the justices steered clear of the conclusion that the plaintiff was without recourse for refusing the debtor's tender of payment.[107] Himmelmann had loaned $1,100 on December 1, 1868, for one year at two percent per month. Fitzpatrick and his wife had given him a mortgage on San Francisco real estate. On April 1, 1871, Fitzpatrick made a tender of $1,567.20, then due; but Himmelmann refused to take it. Rather he filed an action of foreclosure on May 3, 1873. The trial court found for him in the amount of $2,991.46 including $250.00 attorney's fees. The mortgage contained a clause requiring 20 percent of the amount due as attorney's fees. The trial court found the 20 percent to be a penalty and held that only reasonable attorney's fees could be allowed. The Supreme Court agreed. Following a precedent case of nearly 16 years standing, the Court reiterated that "it would be very harsh to hold that the debt is lost--the general effect of losing the security--by a mere refusal at a particular moment to receive it."[108] The California Civil Code, section 1504, further stopped the running of interest at the time of tender. The attorney's fee issue also was affirmed, but had been dealt with by the legislature. In 1874 the legislature had passed "an act to abolish attorney's fees, and other charges, in foreclosure suits," leaving to the courts rather than the creditor the setting of a reasonable attorney's fee.[109]

The Homestead Act of 1860 continued to be a concern to lenders.[110] Section 2 of that act declared void any mortgage on the homestead portion of property. In *Sears v. Dixon* (1867), the Supreme Court left the unwary plaintiff with a decision and no money. The defendant had applied to the lender for $1,000. The lender, doing the prudent thing, "referred the matter to his lawyer, who advised him that a mortgage on the homestead . . . would be ineffectual to secure the payment of the money."[111] The lender refused the loan. But the defendant proposed, and the lender accepted, a transaction whereby the defendant conveyed the land by deed, the lender leased-back to the debtor at a "rent" equivalent to interest on the $1,000, the lender covenanted to reconvey upon payment of $1,000 plus "rent," and the defendant-debtor covenanted to pay $1,000 plus "rent" on or before the expiration of the lease. Of course, the debtor stopped the payment of the rent, and the prudent lender conveyed the land to a third party, now the plaintiff. Citing extensive precedent from Massachusetts and California as well as Chief Justice John Marshall, the Court found that a mortgage existed and, in that it was on a homestead, the mortgage was void. Lenders and third-party purchasers of land clearly heard the signal.[112]

But the naiveté of lenders and the ingenuity of debtors were unlimited. In *Barber v. Babel* (1868), the debtors, Frederick Babel and wife, executed a note and mortgage to Julia Barber in 1860.[113] In 1861 the Babels filed their homestead declaration. In 1865 Frederick, applying his sly tongue and quick wit, induced Julia to take a new note and mortgage and surrender the first. She did so and entered a discharge and satisfaction on the record. Fred even went so far as to swear that no homestead declaration had been filed. Mrs. Babel uncharacteristically remained mute on the homestead declaration and refused to sign the second note and mortgage. As fate would have it, the debtors stopped paying and the lender sued.

Chief Justice Lorenzo Sawyer met the issues head on in his analysis. The legislature had clearly stated that a husband could not divest the wife of her homestead interests without her concurrent act. Even more certainly, the second mortgage, not being executed by the wife, was invalid. Unfortunately for poor Julia, any action on the first mortgage was barred by the Statute of Limitations, and Sawyer concluded that with the husband having been discharged in insolvency from the debt in question, there was and could be no personal judgment against him, and as the action to foreclose the mortgage failed, there was nothing left.[114] Julia was, as Sawyer put it, "not the first in the business world to find herself a victim of misplaced confidence."[115] Perhaps also Julia was not sufficiently suspicious of Babel's many tongues.

Fate occasionally worked in favor of lenders. In *Parry v. Kelley* (1877), the husband's unfortunate demise left the lender with a mortgage lien he otherwise would have been deprived of by law.[116] In 1872 the Kelleys purchased a lot in Oakland with community funds, but solely in the name of the wife, Seraph, a physician. George Parry loaned Mr. Kelley some money, and the good doctor gave Parry a mortgage on the lot, telling him that the property was "bought with money she had earned in the practice of medicine." In 1875 Mr. Kelley passed away, and Mr. Parry brought an action to foreclose the mortgage. To no one's surprise, the doctor denied the validity of the mortgage Mrs. Kelley signed. The trial court agreed with poor Mrs. Kelley, but George Parry appealed.

The Supreme Court reasoned around the Civil Code, section 167, language that stated that "the property of the community is not liable for contracts of the wife made after marriage, unless secured by a pledge or mortgage thereof executed by the husband." First, the Civil Code also gave the wife the capacity to give the mortgage. Clearly, the mortgage stood "on the same footing as a mortgage made by any other person on property to which he had, at the time, no title."[117] Second, another Civil Code section provided for after acquired title to inure to the benefit of the mortgagee. Finally, in that the husband died intestate, the wife was entitled to the lot and thereby the mortgagee to his mortgage foreclosure. Had the husband willed his interest to his children or not so conveniently passed on, the lender, Parry, would have been without his security.

Debtors also claimed duress to avoid paying. Duress did not render a deed void, but did make it voidable. In *Connecticut Life Insurance v. McCormick* (1873), the defendant's wife attempted to set up the defense of duress to have declared void a one-year-old mortgage. The Court found that she had signed the deed over to avoid the criminal prosecution of her husband for embezzlement. The Court found no evidence of notice to Connecticut Life "of the alleged compulsion under which the mortgage was executed."[118]

Intrafamily transactions could also make less certain titles to land. In the case of *Bernal v. Gelim* (1867), the husband and wife entered the land in 1846, mortgaged it in 1851, and conveyed it to their children without the wife acknowledging the transfer to pass her separate property. Default and foreclosure followed. Then the sheriff sold the property in 1852. Twelve years later the children reached the age of majority and dutifully conveyed to their beloved mother in 1865. To no one's surprise, she sued, and the Court found the sheriff's sale void and put dear mother into possession under the 1865 conveyance.[119]

Lenders on land had to proceed with great care whenever a married couple was involved in the transaction. As the cases demonstrated, without a careful and professional search of the title and a transaction of some exactitude, the lender had some concern for an actual return on his money. The certainty that law should lend to transactions was existent, but creditors had to proceed only after close scrutiny of the title to land and the transaction itself.

Another unsettling case was *Simpson v. Castle* (1878).[120] The Court struck at the heart of one of Stephen J. Field's significant pronouncements on mortgage law, *McMillan v. Richards* (1858). The facts of the case were not unusual; the legal background was complex. The defendant-creditor had loaned money on land and had received a mortgage. The debtor defaulted. The creditor foreclosed. Castle bought the premises at the sheriff's foreclosure sale for less than the amount of the judgment. The sheriff issued the usual certificate to Castle and reported the deficiency to the Court. A judgment was duly docketed. The six-month term for redemption began to run, and during this term the debtor conveyed the premises to Simpson. Being careful of his rights, Simpson made the redemption payment to the sheriff, and the sheriff issued a certificate of redemption to Simpson. Castle then sued out an execution on the judgment for the deficiency on the property, and the sheriff stood poised to sell it again for the deficiency. Here the saga took a new twist. To the dismay of the creditor, Simpson sued to enjoin the sale. The trial court sustained the defendant's demurrer and ordered the sale. So it had been for 20 years in California.

The law for 20 years had been based on *McMillan* and statute. The Practice Act of 1851 had provided for the six-month term of redemption in which a judgment debtor or a redemptioner could pay the purchaser the amount of the purchase plus 18 percent interest "and if the purchaser be also a creditor, having a lien prior to that of the redemptioner, the amount with interest." Stephen J. Field interpreted the language to mean that neither the judgment debtor nor a redemptioner could redeem without paying the deficiency. In reaction to Field's holding in *McMillan*, the legislature embarked on antideficiency legislating. First, in 1859, the legislature amended the Practice Act by adding "after the sale of any real estate, the judgment under which such sale was had shall cease to be a lien on such real estate." Then, in 1860, the legislators honed their language to greater sharpness. They added that "if the purchaser be also a creditor having a prior lien to that of the redemptioner other than the judgment under which such purchase was made," the amount of such lien, with interest, shall also be paid. The legislative intent was simply to cut off creditors from continuing liens against property and to practically free debtors from their incumbrances. The public policy interests were similar to those of bankruptcy legislation. The Supreme Court in *Simpson* recognized this policy grounding, struck *McMillan*'s effect, and denied

Castle his execution sale. Simpson "took title free from the pretended lien of the judgment for the deficiency."[121]

The impact of the decision on creditors was multiple. First, the redemption period rendered most land useful only for tenants during the six-month period. As W. H. Clark informed David Jacks in 1879, with the default of the debtor and the contemplation of foreclosure, only tenancy was functional:

> The workingmen have a written lease from Jolly to cover all the time of redemption at $3 per month. The proper way to get at it if it can be done now will be to have a receiver appointed by the Court to take charge of the property and rents.[122]

With deficiency judgments unavailable against the property, lenders had to be sure of sufficient security, resulting in a lower percentage of the property being financed and at higher interest rates. Although interest rates had been higher in the 1850s and 1860s, the interest of the late 1870s was greater cause for concern as economic distress befell many. Bankruptcy as well as deficiency resulted. But some creditors like David Jacks allowed late payments and even extended the time of redemption.[123] California's experience was not one exclusively of rapacious creditors and pitiful debtors caught in the vise of low prices, drought, and debt.

But depression and high interest forced many into insolvency. Speculation was clearly a factor. As Henry D. Bacon complained to Samuel Barlow in 1879, "The loan is for a year and in the meantime sales must be made of property to meet it. The mortgage is for $27,000. How soon I am fast come to grief."[124] Bankruptcy proceedings and assignments for the benefit of creditors closely followed overextension, depression, and drought.[125] Bankruptcy was another alternative to foreclosure of a mortgage. In 1878 David Jacks received such an option from T. Wood, the assignee in bankruptcy for Peter Heron. Wood told Jacks that he knew of "no objections to Peter Heron getting his discharge [in bankruptcy] and presume he will sometime in January. If you wish the mortgaged property to be sold I can go on and it will not cost as much as for you to foreclose the mortgage."[126] The costs might be less, but the creditor could generally receive only his proportional share of the debtor's assets.

As creditor and debtor struggled to protect their respective interests under California law, the California Supreme Court had a concurrent struggle with statutory construction. *Odd Fellows Savings Bank v. Banton* (1873) sorely tested judicial analysis.[127] On January 13, 1873, the defendant Banton executed and delivered a mortgage to another defendant named Hammett. The mortgage was recorded on February 15 in the San Francisco County Recorder's Office. On February 7, 1873, Banton executed and delivered another mortgage to another defendant, Kingsbury. This mortgage was recorded on February 12. On February 10, the industrious Banton executed a third mortgage to the Odd Fellows Savings Bank. The mortgage was recorded on the same day. Hammett was a resident of Portland, Kingsbury of Sacramento, and the bank a local. All these creditors took mortgages in good faith and without notice of the other mortgages. The whole affair became a case, of course, when Mr. Mortgagor, Banton, failed to pay. The sole question for the Court was the priority of the three mortgages.

The statutory scheme of things was less than clear. One section of the Civil Code provided that every conveyance of real estate from the time filed gave constructive notice of its contents to subsequent purchasers. Another section held that first-recorded conveyances voided subsequent conveyances of the same property. It was apparent "that the Legislature intended that all . . . conveyances . . . should be filed for record in the proper Recorder's Office," and until so filed should be void as against all persons who subsequently, without notice, in good faith, and for valuable consideration, might acquire any interest therein either as purchasers or incumbrances.[128] Elsewhere in the Civil Code, the legislature provided that mortgages be recorded in books kept exclusively for real estate mortgages. Further, the mortgagee was allowed one day for every 20 miles of distance between his residence and the county recorder's office to record. More importantly, during this period of time, the mortgage was legally considered recorded. This time allowance acknowledged the problems of frontier transportation and attempted to protect nonresident investors. Here Hammett was 683 miles and Kingsbury 117 miles away. Naturally all claimed to have priority.

The Court recognized that a statutory conflict existed. Justice Isaac S. Belcher went directly to the California Political Code, sections 4480 and 4481, which provided that the statutes must be construed as though they were parts of the same statute and that the provision of each title in the code must prevail for all matters arising from the subject matter of the title. Hence, in that one title covered "transfers," another "liens," and another "mortgages of real property," the matter of recording mortgages of real estate would fall under transfers rather than liens, and more clearly mortgages of real estate than mortgages in general. The only result possible, then, was that former statutes prevailed against the mileage statutes, and Odd Fellows' filing first had the first priority. To creditors the ruling was clear. The rush to the recorder's office was imperative. For the Court, the decision was one to make the system workable and more certain, although certain by judicial opinion.

Legislative waffling also confused a mortgagee's rights when the mortgagor passed away. In *Hibernia Savings and Loan Society v. Hayes* (1880), the Court noted three different statutory procedural provisions between the time the mortgage was executed in 1872 and the time the bank started foreclosure proceedings in 1875.[129] When the mortgage was executed in March 1872, the presentation of all claims for allowance to the representative of the estate of the deceased mortgagor was necessary. The mortgagor died in December 1872. In January 1873 the legislature changed the law so that a mortgage claim need not be presented where recourse against all other than the mortgaged property was expressly waived. The next month the administrator of the estate published notice to all creditors. In July 1874 the legislature again changed the law. Now a claim must be presented. If a claim arising upon a contract made before July 1874 was not presented within the time limits, the claim was "barred forever." The bank filed its foreclosure suit in 1877.

Justice E. M. Ross for the Court acknowledged all the legislative tinkering and found for the bank. Ross could find no legislative intent to apply the 1874 legislation retroactively. Absent retroactivity, the notice of February 1873 could not affect the bank's right to foreclose under the January 1873 statute. The majority viewed the right to a remedy as frozen in time in January 1873 regardless of the 1874 statutory change, the mortgage's maturity in March 1875, and the bank's foreclosure in 1877.

Justice Samuel B. McKee caustically dissented.[130] The California codes went into effect on January 1, 1873, McKee pointed out, and required the presentation of a claim within the ten-month period of publication of notice to creditors, or if the debt were not then due, ten months after it was due. Thereafter the claim was lost, forever barred by statute. The 1873 law gave the mortgagee the options of presentation of a claim against the estate or foreclosure after the debt was due but before barred by the Statute of Limitations. When the latter option was repealed by the 1874 amendment of the code, the remedy was repealed as well. Here McKee parted company with the majority, heaping corrosive precedents on Ross' opinion and attempting to burn holes in his reasoning. Most tellingly, he decanted *Ogden v. Saunders* (1827) and poured the Marshall Court's weighty language into the fray. "The right to a particular remedy [was] not a vested right," McKee declared, citing *Ogden*.[131] If the remedy was repealed, the right no longer existed, he continued. In the situation facing the Court, the remedy had been repealed by the legislature. McKee concluded that the creditor's failure to avail himself of the remedy in a timely manner barred him forever.[132] Justice John R. Sharpstein concurred in McKee's dissent, but the bank had its foreclosure. The year before, the Supreme Court had denied the Hibernia Savings and Loan a remedy because it had waited too long to foreclose and was barred by the Statute of Limitations.[133] Creditors had to be diligent to enforce their rights.

The California Supreme Court early had established and continued to maintain that the mortgage contract was "manifestly one of the written contracts" described by the statute limiting actions to four years from accrual.[134] If the instrument did not contain a due date, the Court presumed that it was due immediately or on demand, starting the running of the four-year limitation.[135] The exception to the running of the term was the creditor leaving the state. The Court made it clear in *Wood v. Goodfellow* (1872) that it did not favor devices prolonging the payment of a debt and forestalling actions even if based on "ingenious" arguments.[136] The Court favored quiet title and certainty in transactions rather than dormant interests.[137]

Although counsel's argument in *Wood* was "very able and ingenious," the Court displayed overt distress over counsel's actions in other cases. In *Christy v. Dana and Natoma Water and Mining Company* (1868), Justice Crockett angrily pointed out that the argument made by the defendant was "no longer an open question in this Court." Further, the Court was "strongly inclined to treat the appeal as frivolous and taken only for delay."[138] Chief Justice William T. Wallace echoed Crockett's concern four years later in *Wilber v. Sanderson* (1872). No briefs were filed. The defendant's appeal was "without merit," and Wallace tersely affirmed the judgment "with 20% damages."[139] Sloppy representation could also delay the process. Plaintiff's counsel in *Carpentier v. Brenham* (1875) had failed to properly file the complaint 15 years earlier, and when finally adjudicated, the plaintiff was dead and fortunately did not live to see the demise of his claim.[140] The pitfalls of the marketplace were only one hazard for creditors. Experienced and competent counsel was necessary to the process.

Although the legislature, the Court, and counsel gave some creditors reason for pause in the period, the rise of the Workingmen's Party and the constitution of 1879 gave most visions of disaster. The Workingmen's Party began in the fall of 1877 in San Francisco. Made up of the unemployed and the landless, the party grew dramatically under the leadership of Denis Kearney. Kearney aimed his inflammatory rhetoric against the railroads, the landed, the wealthy, and the Chinese. The Workingmen demanded the dismemberment of the railroad, land, and water monopolies. They wanted national control of the banks. Taxation required reform. Finally, the Chinese needed to be driven from the workplace and the land. To achieve these goals, the Workingmen sought and obtained the calling of a constitutional convention. In a frenzy, the conservative elements of both parties united against the Workingmen and prevented their domination of the convention.[141]

One convention proposal that sent shock waves through the financial community was the taxation of mortgages. The banks in 1878 and 1879 were emerging from the depression of 1876 with renewed confidence. The San Francisco *Evening Bulletin* reported on April 19, 1878, that "San Francisco has been measurably fortunate in her Savings Banks. Some of the earliest established still continue, notwithstanding all the violent fluctuations in values to which they have been exposed, and the senseless runs which have been made upon them."[142] But the confident optimism in the financial community was quickly shattered by the passage of a section in the taxation article taxing mortgages. Isaias Hellman wrote to Matthew Keller on April 22, 1879, that

> business is very dull here, the question whether the new Constitution is going to be adopted or rejected is the topic with everyone. If adopted business of all kinds will be paralyzed. The banks all over California are preparing for the worst and are calling in mature loans.[143]

The clear intent of the convention delegates to shift the burden of taxation was cause for concern.[144] The San Luis Obispo *Tribune* saw the provision as a blow to debtors and a deterrent to capital.[145]

The Santa Barbara *Daily Press* saw the provisions not only driving away capital,[146] but also as a windfall for the railroads. A May 5, 1879, editorial declared that "under the specious pretext of taxing mortgages, they have exempted every railroad in the state."[147] Many echoed this observation because the railroads were heavily mortgaged with New York creditors not subject to the tax. But it was uncertainty that troubled many. Matthew Keller wrote Isaias Hellman from New York on April 30, 1879:

> I see the new Constitution is agitating the whole state. It appears that it affects banking stocks, railroads, and mortgages. I hope the results will be for the general good.[148]

This view from New York was mirrored in a San Luis Obispo *Tribune* editorial stating that "the adoption of the new Constitution may so unsettle values that the savings banks and others loaning money may be compelled to foreclose mortgages."[149] Despite all the fears and trepidation, the Constitution passed by a vote of 77,959 to 67,134.[150]

For mortgage lenders the period ended as it had started. They were emerging from depression and uncertainty, but again the law and now the constitution itself created more uncertainty. The banking institutions of the state were more stable, more regulated. California was poised for the boom of the 1880s in which the ingenuity of counsel and the flexibility and craftsmanship of the judiciary would facilitate economic expansion despite the predictions of doom.

California's mortgage law and practice in the decade of the 1880s reflected the uncertainty of a boom-and-bust real estate market, the

problems of living with a new state constitution, and the eccentricities of
the State Supreme Court. With the uncertainty of the marketplace and the
growing complexity of law, lawyers came to play a greater role in the
mortgage field. With the professionalization of dealers in mortgage money,
California's mortgage law matured to meet the needs of the marketplace.

During the 1880s California experienced a real estate boom as well as the
increased commercialization of agriculture. Southern California land values
skyrocketed in this period.[151] Like wheat in the 1870s, crops like walnuts
expanded to commercial proportions.[152] Railroad promotions brought
thousands to California, resulting in Los Angeles' eightfold growth in the
period.[153] A key ingredient in the boom was, of course, the mortgage
money that fueled the boom and ultimately snuffed it out.

As California entered the decade, the 1879 constitution loomed as a
formidable barrier to expansive mortgage lending. The new organic act
placed a tax on mortgages.[154] In anticipation of the constitution's
ratification by the people in 1879, California banks severely curtailed
lending. As Frank Clough, a young San Francisco attorney, reported to his
mother in August 1879, "Nobody has any money here now. The banks won't
lend money on the best kind of real estate as security."[155] After the people
ratified the constitution, lawyers and lenders turned their immediate
attention to avoiding the constitution's provisions and maintaining the
burden of taxation with the borrower. Some merely increased the interest
rate to provide for the taxes. Jackson A. Graves, a Los Angeles attorney
and one of the founders of the powerful O'Melveny firm, wrote to Simon
Wallace in 1881 that "we will make the note 11 1/2% which will give you ten
percent and will allow 1 1/2% for taxes."[156] Others were direct and
explicit. David Jacks merely inserted the mortgage tax directly into the
mortgage instrument, and if not paid charged the debtor interest.[157] If the
tax assessor visited, John Reynolds, one of Jacks' real estate agents, "did
not say anything about the mortgage . . . as our contract was made before
the new constitution."[158] Lenders converted the mortgage tax from a
threat into a mere nuisance through artful drafting.

However, in the period 1867-1880, the California Supreme Court's record
on mortgage cases gave creditors greater reason for pause. Lenders won
only two of every three appellate decisions in the period.[159] Given the
existing value and potential appreciation of property, large sums of money
were at stake.[160] The state of the law in the decade of the 1870s caused
enough concern for David Jacks that he bought a personal law library and
kept several lawyers in business.[161] Professionals, such as Graves,
O'Melveny, and Shankland of Los Angeles, found the California Supreme
Court "eccentric" and proceeded cautiously in real estate foreclosures.[162]

One element of uncertainty, the mortgage tax, loomed large, and the
California Supreme Court gave lenders some indications of its reach early in
the decade. In *Beckman v. Skaggs* (1881), the Court made an *ex cathedra*
statement on the contract clause and mortgage taxation.[163] Applying the
long-standing federal constitutional doctrine of *Sturges v. Crowninshield*
without ever citing it or any other case,[164] the Court declared that
contracts made before the constitution were valid. Hence, an agreement
whereby the debtor paid any and all taxes must stand. John Reynolds'
restraint in 1880 was constitutionally correct. But would he be right in
1882? *McCoppin v. McCartney* (1882) took another position. As appellant's
attorney, Edward J. Pringle, observed, "The Constitution of 1879 made a
revolution in the revenue system of the State."[165] Amid the chaos of
revolution, the Court, again without citing a single case for

precedent, announced that "a mortgagee, prior to the adoption of the new Constitution, did not have a vested right or exemption from taxation." As to this 1872 mortgage, "the plain intent of the new Constitution [was] to subject to taxation classes of property previously exempt."[166] The state constitution apparently, in California at least, could wipe out precedent contractual expectations. Here the purchaser found, to his pocketbook's discomfort, not only that a satisfied mortgage made before the constitution could be assessed for taxation, but also that he must now pay again to maintain title.

In *Hay v. Hill* (1884), the constitutionality of the mortgage taxation provision again became a question. An 1879 mortgage for three years contained no covenants for the payment of taxes. In January 1883 the mortgagor paid off the note plus all interest excepting $395 he had paid in taxes on the mortgage interest. To Hill's surprise, George Hay foreclosed, apparently wanting his extra bale of $395. The Supreme Court, citing *McCoppin*, rejected windrows of precedents and tersely stated that "the mortgagor having paid an amount due from the mortgage to the third party--the State--is entitled to recover the amount so paid."[167] Although rejecting any unjust enrichment for Hay, the Court clearly identified the creditor as liable for the taxes.

Whereas Hay foraged for hundreds of dollars, the Sutter Street Railroad Company gang plowed for thousands in 1884. As corporations often found, they were in need of capital. To keep debt a profitable venture, the faceless company often turned to its directors for mutual benefit. So too here, as Julius Baum, corporate director, and Henry Shrier, his business partner, offered to advance capital to further the worthy goals of the Sutter Street Company at the same time collecting interest as well as dividends. But this was California in 1879. So with the specter of the constitution confounding profit, Baum's lawyer and the corporation's lawyer held a conclave. They drafted new corporate board resolutions and a new mortgage instrument. Before the constitution they had a $125,000 mortgage due in five years at 10 percent. After the conclave but before January 1, 1880, the effective date of the new constitution, the corporation had $125,000 in hand and Baum had corporate notes for $137,000. But all was not bliss on the board, as the corporation filed suit on June 26, 1880.[168]

Baum's attorney argued against the application of the constitution and unjust enrichment. The mortgage and notes predated the constitution. The constitution should not impair the agreement. Even if it did, Baum had paid out $5,436.43 in taxes and should be compensated. So went the litany.

Neither the trial court nor the Supreme Court was sympathetic. Not only was the mortgage found to be for $125,000 only, but it was also at the reasonable rate of nine percent less $158 expended in making and acknowledging it. Although the Supreme Court used corporation law for guidance, the locus of responsibility for taxes remained clear, and creditor Baum's attorney had not struck on any magic language.

The counselor's pen was without success until 1888 when, in *Marye v. Hart*, the Court discovered that the "taxes may be paid by either party."[169] The Court also uncovered the perfect exemption arrangement provided for by the constitution itself. In *People v. Board of Supervisors of the City and County of San Francisco* (1888), Mrs. C. L. Tams of San Francisco had a $63,000 mortgage on her property. The mortgage belonged to the Regents of the University of California. The tax collector, knowing he could not get a cent from the Regents, assessed Mrs. Tams for the full value of $142,845, refusing to deduct the $63,000. Mrs. Tams appealed to the supervisors, sitting as a board of equalization. The board agreed with Tams, but the attorney general intervened to overturn the board, claiming in lurid detail how the state's coffers would be depleted. Justice Thomas B. McFarland caustically reminded the attorney general that "the state should not expect to collect taxes on her own property--much less should she expect someone else to pay them." Finally, regarding the expected revenue shortfall, McFarland quipped that "the anticipated losses of the state will therefore simply be like the fancied losses of other people who fail to get what they ought not to have."[170] In sum, the Court left little room for legal maneuvering.[171] Of course, what creditors did, in fact, was take the advice of Jackson A. Graves and "allow 1 1/2% for taxes" when setting an interest rate.

Although the 1879 constitution posed a new challenge to lenders, many older problems plagued expectations. Transactions as well as the documents that evidenced the intent of the parties were not always clear, despite the increased use of form mortgages and deeds. California's homestead law exempting $5,000 in value from execution for debt snared the casual lender. Statutes also protected the property rights of married women, and the courts were firm in that protection even if a lender's expectations were dashed. Fraud as always was part of the risk. But mistakes were part of the legal record as well as the human condition. Lenders made mistakes in failing to check for a homestead or a senior mortgage, forgetting to have the wife sign and acknowledge the mortgage, and trusting the representations of debtors. Lawyers made mistakes, costing lenders their all, but this was the 1880s, before malpractice suits were entertained, and lenders could only shop for better practitioners of the trade. The system made mistakes. Trial court judges erred on occasion. Delay was a part of the system. Fate could strike the debtor down before his time (payment in full), and the lender or his lawyers could mistakenly interpret the Probate Code. Finally, as old and as chronic a problem as the boom-and-bust economy of the century, insolvency could intervene to deflate a lender's expectations. Although California law on these matters was relatively clear, the practice of lenders and their counselors-at-law did not avoid the age-old pitfalls.

Although the availability of form legal instruments was widespread in the decade, lenders and their lawyers still made mistakes. H. H. Bancroft and Company of San Francisco, among others, offered an extensive line of forms including mortgage, deed, lease, power of attorney, bond, bill of sale, assignment, and acknowledgment.[172] However, the boom of the 1880s made people scramble for property, and pens went awry in the process. "The people are getting the Los Angeles fever," William Warner reported in 1887; in fact, "Billy Minner was down 3 or 4 weeks and in that short time he made $5,000.00 speculating in property."[173] Although "some of the wildcat outside schemes, to wit: lots in the desert have fallen through," Jackson A. Graves reported that same year, Los Angeles property "will double in value in 12 months."[174] If the pen slipped in haste, then some blots were caught before resort to law. John D. Goodwin wrote to his "Friend Smith" in 1884 about a note and mortgage, "the former [being] all right but the latter [being] all wrong." It seems that the clerk "failed to copy either of the notes into the mortgage correctly. Nor did he copy your names to the notes."[175] William Pyburn wrote to David Jacks in 1887 that "in that mortgage made by Ford to you the other day you made yourself 'party of the first part' and Ford 'party of the second part'" and "it should be just the reverse."[176]

Lenders also failed to describe adequately the property in the mortgage. John Markey, Monterey County undersheriff and former county clerk, wrote David Jacks in 1881 that "it is hard to tell what is included in your descriptions, if anything. After some tracing back of original titles, I am almost certain that the lot on Alvarado St. known as the 'Zuick House' is in Wither's mortgage but not yours."[177] As often was the case, courts became the interpreters of the documents. The courts worked out doctrines and applied rules of construction that required a description sufficiently definite to identify the land, but allowed judges to interpret where doubt remained.[178] For example, the number of acres was an essential part of the description.[179] Land described in metes and bounds or with specific references to records was sufficiently definite.[180] Sometimes boundaries were lines between "an oak standing on the east and in contact with rocks forming the first rocky point on the south side of the Meadow Valley" and "the Rocky Hall at the San Jose Indian Village."[181] Despite the willingness of the Court to find a definite description, some instruments were "too indefinite and uncertain to support a judgment for specific performance." In *Burnett* v. *Kullak* (1888), the Court found a mortgage for $2,500 with no stated term, no rate of interest, and no default language.[182] The haste of transactions as well as the geography made description of the property a problem for some California lenders.

Lenders also neglected to check the homestead books before advancing funds secured by a mortgage on real estate. The result under statute was that $5,000 was exempt from execution for debt. As late as 1888 such an experienced lender as David Jacks still needed to inquire regarding the effect of a homestead declaration. William Pyburn told Jacks that

> a mortgage given or made subsequent to the filing of a declaration of a Homestead by a single person, does away with such declaration only so far as the mortgage is concerned. When the mortgage has been satisfied and satisfaction recorded, the declaration of Homestead before filed holds good. In a declaration of homestead by a married person, a mortgage if made must then be signed by both husband and wife. The effect of a satisfaction of mortgage is the same.
>
> In other words a Homestead declaration is to save the property from execution and unless it is encumbered afterwards it cannot be levied on only for the encumbrance placed upon it after homestead declaration.[183]

Other lenders inquired too late. The law firm of Graves and Chapman in Los Angeles tersely replied to J. H. Elwood in 1884: "Enclosed find Br . . .'s note. We can't collect it. He . . . has a house and lot, but when we came to look it up found a homestead on it."[184] Similarly, when the firm of Graves and O'Melveny requested an investigation, "The first question issued [was] is that property subject to a homestead?"[185] If it was, only the excess over $5,000 could be obtained. For the small farmer, merchant, and entrepreneur, this gave the debtor great leverage. As Graves, O'Melveny, and Shankland reported to a client in 1889, "If we hadn't accepted this settlement, he would undoubtedly have gone into insolvency and none of you would have gotten anything. The real estate not covered by the homestead would not bring $50, so it looked very much as if we would have gotten nothing if we hadn't accepted his proposition."[186] In this particular case, the creditor happily accepted 32 cents on the dollar.

The defense of a statutory homestead was a potent one, but the Court occasionally found that the declaration itself was invalid. In *Booth v. Galt* (1881), the Court found that the "declaration of homestead was clearly invalid" because the married woman failed to state that her husband had not made a homestead declaration when filing alone."[187] Further, Pyburn related to David Jacks and the Supreme Court declared in 1881, a subsequent declaration of homestead could have no effect on a precedent mortgage.[188] But in the main, the homestead declaration was an effective tool to preserve the $5,000 in value of the debtor's property and a stumbling block to the careless lender.[189] The law presumed that the lender knew of the homestead when the declaration had been properly filed.[190] Lending on such property was clearly at great risk. Fraud was a greater risk, but the Court would not allow it to stand defeating creditor interests. In *Shinn v. Macpherson* (1881), the defendant attempted to use the Homestead Act for diabolical purposes, but to no avail. The statute "was enacted for beneficent purposes," not as a cloak for fraud.[191] Equity would not allow the debtor to reap the fruits of his fraud.

If a lender was dealing with a married woman, then special care was needed as well. Although statute had eliminated the capacity problem of married women to make mortgages so prevalent in the 1850s and 1860s, the lender of the 1880s had to obtain a proper acknowledgment of the mortgage.[192] In 1850 the legislature passed a statute providing for the execution, acknowledgment, and certification of the acknowledgment of a conveyance of a married woman. Her acknowledgment had to be made to an officer qualified to take it and who personally knew the woman. The Supreme Court strictly construed the statute to provide the sole means for lawful conveyances. Reacting to the Court's construction, the legislature provided in 1860 that a county judge could correct defective acknowledgments made in good faith by husband and wife. On January 1, 1873, California adopted its Civil Code. The code changed the certification procedure, making execution, acknowledgment, and certification no longer necessary for the validity of a conveyance. Now execution and acknowledgment in accordance with the code were sufficient. Certification was simply a record proof of acknowledgment. Once obtained, the wife was bound by the contents of the deed on mortgage.[193] In sum, the legislature made the lender's task easier while continuing to protect the property interests of married women. The lender who failed to obtain the acknowledgment of the married woman to a mortgage had a mortgage that was "void."[194] But for the lender who proceeded carefully, obtaining the proper execution and acknowledgment, the Court would not later hear complaints about capacity or injustice.[195] It was the prudent lender, like David Jacks, who asked his lawyers in San Francisco, "Can a married woman living with her husband make a promissory note with mortgage to it acknowledging the mortgage before a notary public?" before he loaned money.[196]

Both lender and borrower had to be wary of sharp dealing. In *Hendy v. Kier* (1881), the lender induced the debtor to sign over a first mortgage in return for $400 and the release of a second mortgage. The lender then tried to foreclose the second mortgage, but the Court would hear none of it.[197] In *Rosenberg v. Ford* (1890), the Court used the doctrine of consideration to foil a foul machination grinding down the poor widow Ford. It seems that Jacob Rosenberg held a mortgage on the Ford homestead, but when the good Mr. Ford passed from this life, Jacob failed to present his claim to the widow Ford, administratrix, as required by statute. Jacob then went to widow Ford and obtained a second mortgage and notes, the poor widow not knowing that Jacob's tardiness had cut him off from ever collecting his money. When she learned of her ignorance of the law, she lost a degree of moral duty to pay and went to "Judge" Goodwin for advice. "Stop paying," said the judge, and after trial and appeal the Supreme Court agreed with the judge. The transaction lacked consideration, and Jacob Rosenberg lost his mortgage.[198]

A specter far more poignant appeared in *Randall v. Duff* (1889), with a widow and orphan pleading for justice. In 1863 William Duff departed California, leaving a power of attorney with his father, Richard. Dad fraudulently and without consideration conveyed the land to brother Robert Duff. Robert quickly mortgaged one parcel to William Ritchie and another to Charles Fiebig. William passed away in 1875. Suddenly, in 1881, William's widow and orphan learned of grandfather's dastardly deed, and they sued Robert and Frank Duff. Neither Ritchie nor Fiebig had any inkling that William had any interest in the property when they loaned out their money, but both foreclosed after William's untimely demise. A. W. Randall bought the parcel Ritchie loaned money on and happily received a sheriff's deed. Fiebig bought the other parcel and received his sheriff's deed. But the widow, Julia Duff, had filed her suit against Robert and Frank before the mortgages were foreclosed. *Duff v. Duff* (1886) resulted in a judgment for Julia, reversed on appeal and remanded for new trial. Meanwhile, *Randall v. Duff* was in trial.[199] The trial court ruled for the plaintiff and Julia appealed. In 1888 the Supreme Court reversed and remanded for a new trial. In 1889 the Court reheard the case. After sorting out all the litigational details, the Court simply stated that Robert acquired no title from William, and that Ritchie was an innocent mortgagee and acquired a valid lien by estoppel. Importantly, the Court applied equitable principles in arriving at its decision to avoid gross "injustice." The appellate cases dealing with fraud clearly established the Court's willingness to apply equity to avoid loss to an innocent lender.

Lenders had to be precise in following statutory provisions for foreclosure and redemption. Moreover, the interpretations of the Supreme Court could have impact upon practice. Witness Graves, O'Melveny, and Shankland's March 19, 1890, opinion to another law firm:

> As to the necessity of including the description of the mortgaged premises in the foreclosure summons, we refer you to People v. Greene, 52 Ca., p. 577. This was an action to foreclose the interest of the purchaser of lands from the State of California, holding under a certificate of purchase, and, while the point was not directly decided, still we think there is enough in the case to justify a Court as eccentric as the present Supreme Court of this State is in holding it to be conclusive of the proposition. However, as we agree that it is well to avoid all possible chances, we will insert description in the summons, irrespective of the law of the case.[200]

Not only did the Supreme Court's opinion sway practice, but the legal system's grindingly slow process impacted practice. Witness David Jacks writing to C. W. Gates on December 15, 1886:

> It is more than five years since judgment of foreclosure was rendered as you will see by the papers in the case.

But Judge Webb told me that Mr. Beeman made an application for a new trial in the case and that it was more than two years from that time until Judge Belden rendered a decision refusing to allow a new trial.

Judge Webb says that it will be all right to make an application to Judge Alexander for an order of sale to sell the property and that he will grant it on a reasonable showing. . . . If Beeman thinks that he can take advantage of the delay in getting the order of sale, he will be apt to do it.

If a deed from Mrs. Johnson will carry the legal title to the property by paying her some money to obtain it that will be the easiest and quickest way to end the matter.[201]

After foreclosure and sale, a sheriff's deed was issued to the purchaser.[202] The debtor was then allowed six months to redeem the property by settling up, under statute, with the purchaser.[203] The effect of the redemption period was, of course, to reduce the immediate marketability of the property.

If lenders blundered in their transactions, then the Court was not always sympathetic. In *Hibernia Savings and Loan Society v. Moore* (1885), the Court chided the lending institution for its failure to investigate the scope of a power of attorney. In this case, $57,000 was a hard lesson to learn, but clearly the lender had limited recourse, given its cavalier effusion of money.[204] The Court did come to the aid of the stumbling lender in *Weyant v. Murphy* (1889). In a sheriff's sale pursuant to a decree of foreclosure, the defendant failed, by what the Supreme Court characterized as "a stupid blunder," to bid the full amount of the judgment. He later increased his bid, which was accepted by the receiver. Weyant then tendered the original bid to Murphy. Murphy refused it, and Weyant sued. The Court would hear none of Weyant's argument and "assist him to profit by the defendant's mistake."[205] Again the Court applied equitable principles, avoided "the strict legal rights of the parties," and rendered "justice."[206]

The Supreme Court was not as charitable with the California bar. In nineteenth-century California, the creditor often put his interests at risk when he engaged legal counsel. As in most of the affairs of mankind, men were not perfect. Unfortunately for some lenders, their lawyers were sloppy, tardy, or incompetent. Lawyers were even critical of their brethren in the bar. For example, Creed Hammond, a successful Sacramento trial attorney, criticized John D. Goodwin, a Quincy attorney, in February 1869 for a failure to follow the Practice Act.[207]

The lender's attorney sometimes failed to bring all the parties before the bench. In *Brown v. Willis* (1855), the Supreme Court used the words of Chancellor Kent to remind the lender that "every person is bound to take care of his own rights, and to vindicate them in due season, and in proper order. This [is] a sound and salutary principle of law. Accordingly, if a defendant having the means of defense in his power, neglects to use them, and suffers a recovery to be had against him in a competent tribunal, he is forever precluded."[208] In *Brown* the lender's attorney failed in his original suit to include all the proper parties, and the litigation foreclosed any further opportunity to collect.

In the rough-and-tumble real estate market, a lawyer's mistake could be costly. David Jacks got involved in prolonged litigation over two lots in

Monterey. Lots worth only $5 per acre seldom inspired lengthy litigation, but when Jacks constructed a narrow-gauge railroad from Monterey to Salinas City, the lots soared to $50,000 each, and lawsuits began to fly. Three of the lawsuits ultimately reached the California Supreme Court.[209] Milton Little and his wife, Mary, borrowed money from David Jacks in 1874 and from James Withers in 1875. But the 1870s were hard times, and the lenders foreclosed. At the foreclosure sale, Withers purchased lots one and two, and Jacks bought lots three, four, five, and six. Jacks appealed from the trial court decree adjudging Withers' mortgage to be prior in right to Jacks' on the ground of the date of the filing of the mortgages.[210] However, in the notice of appeal dated July 21, 1879, Jacks' attorneys failed to stay the execution of the decree of foreclosure. Hence, the sheriff's sale was held, the property sold, and certificates issued. In 1887 the Supreme Court decided *Little v. Superior Court*, holding that when the Littles consented to judgment against them, fixing the amount due to Jacks, it would be an injustice to open the judgment against the Littles.[211] Soon after the decision, Jacks wrote to his Los Angeles attorney inquiring about a rehearing.[212] Jacks complained that he was out the $5,000 loan made over a decade ago, excepting two quarters' interest payment. Further, Withers knew of the mortgage to Jacks before he subsequently loaned money on Little's property.[213] Jacks also sought a second opinion on getting a rehearing, but a San Jose attorney gave him little hope.[214] The second shoe dropped in *Withers v. Jacks* (1889). When Jacks' attorneys failed to request the stay of execution of the foreclosure decree and subsequent sheriff's sale, the purchaser's title was final. Withers owned the land, and Jacks was a wiser man for the experience, although no richer.[215] It is hoped that the firm of Houghton and Reynolds in Los Angeles learned an equally useful lesson about California procedure.

On occasion, the Court was disposed to give a creditor a second chance before the bench. The Bank of Sonoma loaned George W. Charles and J. M. Charles $42,250 in 1886. Unfortunately, George passed away in 1889, leaving $38,069.58 in principal and $5,979.07 in interest unpaid. The bank made a presentation of the promissory note, but not of the mortgage of the administratrix. The probate judge rendered judgment, foreclosing the mortgage, awarding $500 in attorneys' fees, but refusing any deficiency judgment against the estate. On appeal in 1890 the Supreme Court found that the bank had failed to comply with the statutes providing for the presentation of mortgages. Hence, the demurrer refused at trial should have been sustained and the bank thrown out of court. On appeal the bank argued that another section of the California Civil Code allowed a holder of a mortgage to enforce the mortgage against a particular parcel of property "when all recourse against any other property of the estate is expressly waived in the complaint; but no counsel fees shall be recovered."[216] But the complaint contained "no such waiver, and such a plain statutory provision cannot be disregarded or explained away," Justice Thomas B. McFarland declared. However, with the sweep of the pen, McFarland proceeded to disregard the statute because "we do not think that the consequences of plaintiff's carelessness are so ruinous as to utterly preclude it from the benefit of the mortgage lien."[217] Further, McFarland stated, "the plaintiff certainly did not intend to waive or abandon its mortgage." Hence, to avoid injustice or inequity, the Court held that the bank could amend its complaint, waive all recovery against any property except the mortgaged parcel, and, of course, forego counsel fees so richly undeserved.

Here equity was applied to provide counsel opportunity to amend sloppy pleadings and practice, and the bank a foreclosure sale.

The Court was not sympathetic to the blatantly sloppy pleader. In *Bunnel v. Stockton* (1890), the trial court had decided a case against a homestead claimant for failure to comply with statute. The Supreme Court tersely held that the statement of homestead value was filed "too late," and the last application for extension to plead was "unauthorized."[218] As Justice John D. Works concisely stated, "The one extension of time beyond the thirty days did not give the judge any additional authority."[219] The case pointed out several imperfections in the legal system. The first trial in Lassen County, a rural jurisdiction, proceeded on a statutory theory that was incorrect. Neither lawyers nor the judge knew of the error. None of them had done their homework. On the motion for new trial, the judge exceeded his authority, and the respondent's lawyer was delinquent in making a timely filing.

The lender was often at the mercy of his attorney. In *Johnston v. McDuffee* (1890), the Court, in rendering judgment against him, commented that "though McDuffee's rights as a mortgagee might have been protected by taking the proper steps to bring them before the court, the record before us is not in a shape that presents them."[220] Other cases contained pleading error after pleading error.[221] Some cases were presented without documentary evidence; hence, the appellate court judges could collectively scratch their heads and observe that "it is somewhat uncertain who purchased at this foreclosure sale. No documents were introduced in evidence."[222] Still others evidenced the failure to serve the proper parties with required documents.[223] Competent counsel was clearly a factor in successful mortgage lending.

Even with effective representation, California's judicial system was far from perfect. Some trial court judges were far from precise in their findings of fact and conclusions of law. As the Supreme Court commented in *Bettis v. Townsend* (1882), "The decision of the Court below was somewhat informal."[224] On occasion, a trial court judge would order more land sold than was mortgaged.[225] On another, the trial judge would erroneously order a new trial, such as *Santa Marina v. Connolly* (1889), on "wholly immaterial" grounds.[226] Oftentimes, the errors led to considerable delay.

As was true across the country in the nineteenth century, the legal system could be used to delay foreclosure. Litigation could save clients money. Appeals could stop the legal process of foreclosure sale in its tracks. Sometimes it was a blatant practice. The Supreme Court was openly annoyed with counsel's strategems. In *Durkin v. Burr* (1882), the Court dismissed the suit for the third time in one sentence.[227] The Court often assessed costs or damages when appeals were brought for the obvious purpose of delay. In *Montgomery v. Robinson* (1888), the Court tersely dismissed the appeal as one "without merit" and assessed five percent damages.[228] Justice Thomas B. McFarland analyzed *Whitby v. Rowell* (1890) in two paragraphs, observing that "the appeal was evidently for delay," and assessed the debtor with $200 damages plus court costs.[229] Although debtors could use delay as an important tool to frustrate process, lenders who failed to exercise their right could lose their investment under the Statute of Limitations.[230] Regardless of whether one party or another used or failed to use the judicial system, the process was slow. John Wise loaned money in March 1876, received a judgment in August 1877, was forced to file an amended complaint in July 1880, and received finality in an affirmation of the decree of foreclosure by the Supreme Court in January 1889.[231] Collecting on a mortgage, where the debtor resisted the process, could be a long and complex process.

Even more complex was the collection of a mortgage after the debtor or spouse passed from this earth. The problem was complex because questions of homestead were often commingled with probate issues. The legislature attempted to preserve the homestead by having it set aside by the probate court (1860) and by having it vest absolutely in the survivor (1862).[232] However, debts acquired subsequent to the death of a spouse were not protected by the homestead declaration.[233] Clearly, those mortgages made after the declaration of a homestead had to be presented to the administrator of the estate and could not operate to dissolve the homestead exemption. The legislature had undoubtedly intended "to preserve the homestead if possible."[234] If the mortgage were not an incumbrance on a homestead, the lender could foreclose without presentment to the administrator if all recourse against all other property of the estate was expressly waived.[235]

The key analytical question for the attorney was statutory construction, but the California Supreme Court attempted to make clear that the presentment was necessary where a homestead was involved. Unfortunately, the lender and his counsel often read the statute book rather than the *Reports of the California Supreme Court*, and procedural error abounded.[236] Further, counsel often failed to bring the proper parties before the bench or the trial courts confused statutory issues, opening cases for appeal.[237] The process created confusion and delay. As Jackson A. Graves wrote to a client in 1880, "The mortgage has been foreclosed properly. At the sale the property bid in the name of yourself and the church as representatives of the estate of your husband and the deed was issued. This is bad for the reason that you individually own half of it."[238] Because of the blunder, the wife had to go to probate to liquidate her interests. To prevent procedural catastrophes, lenders had to be particularly aware of the obituary columns. David Jacks hurriedly telegraphed James A. Clayton in 1890, "If they are probating Shedaker estate, file sworn claim amount my note, mortgage immediately to prevent any bar of foreclosure. See recent decision Supreme Court."[239] Foreclosure was crucial to the lender to provide for the first mortgage gaining priority over other claims and avoiding a proportional distribution of estate assets where debts exceeded assets. The death of a debtor could signal the race to the courthouse. Significantly, David Jacks was reading the advance sheets of the California Supreme Court as well as the obituary columns.[240] Law was not the exclusive province of lawyers in California in the nineteenth-century nor could it be, given the uncertainty of mortgage law and practice.

Death was more certain than law, but bankruptcy certainly followed drought, credit constriction, or eastern financial panic. Here again the lender was caught in the intricate web of procedure, practice, and practicality. Collecting debts was a specialty of the lawyer's craft. Massillon Marsteller of Susanville told the world on his letterhead, "Collection of Debts a Specialty."[241] It must have been true.

One thing that was true was that collecting was a high-stakes game. For example, Graves and O'Melveny took great pains to map out a game plan for D. N. and E. Walter and Company in collecting on their mortgage. Their mortgage was "good against the assignment recently made by them (Barnhart and Kelly, debtors) for the benefit of their creditors." But if the other five creditors should "file a petition in insolvency against Barnhart and Kelly or should they voluntarily go into insolvency within thirty days after the date of your mortgage, there [was] some question as to whether your mortgage would have the preference." It was best to wait and let the 30 days run. If after 30 days, Barnhart and Kelly had failed to pay the interest due, then "immediately foreclose and sell the mortgaged property." Meanwhile, the creditor was not to sue on two small promissory notes then due because it might stampede the other creditors into filing insolvency proceedings. To make the point absolutely clear, Graves and O'Melveny pointed out that "you have too much at stake in the mortgage to risk for so small a consideration."[242] In other cases, the creditor would have to take what he could get to avoid insolvency. In 1889 Graves, O'Melveny, and Shankland reported that "the best terms of settlement we could get out of him was that he would turn over the liquor and give his note for $135 payable ten months after date with interest at one percent per month. If we hadn't accepted this settlement, he would have undoubtedly gone into insolvency and none of you would have gotten anything."[243]

Whether the settlement was a better shake than insolvency was sometimes questionable. As Jackson A. Graves reported to a client in 1881: "Enclosed you will find a deed from that bitch of a Johan Roberts to 500 acres in Rancho El Mission of San Diego. . . . I do not know whether the interest is worth a tinker's d. or not."[244] But the worst possible situation was, of course, the judgment-proof debtor. Such a person was one "Mr. Smart of Downey City," according to Graves. In fact, "he will promise payment with the same good grace that a worthy Friar does absolution and fail to pay on time with equal grace. To sue him comes to folly. If we can even catch him."[245]

On occasion, insolvency proceedings were advantageous to the creditor, but more often than not the problems outweighed the advantages. If interspousal transactions were raised as a defense to creditor interests, then insolvency was a means of negating such stratagems.[246] If the assignee could be controlled, prior interests could be advantaged.[247] But if the assignee failed in his duties, interests could be tied up for years. As George E. Bates, a San Francisco attorney, reported to David Jacks in 1890:

> [Peter] Heron filed his petition in bankruptcy July 12th, 1878. He was adjudicated a bankrupt July 13, 1878. Townsend Wood of Castroville was appointed assignee and a deed of assignment was made to him by the Register in Bankruptcy on March 8, 1879.
>
> The assignee has never filed any account, nor has the bankrupt ever applied for any discharge from his debts.
>
> These proceedings can not be dismissed, but they can be terminated. The debtor can apply for and obtain his discharge and (if necessary) the assignee can be required to account and thereupon the assignee can be discharged and the proceedings closed. The matter can be terminated in no other way.[248]

Insolvency proceedings clearly advantaged debtors and continued as a consideration in lending money in the decade.

Although lenders and borrowers operated in the marketplace, the California Supreme Court struggled with fact situations springing from the frenzied speculation of the decade. One continuing function of the Court was interpreting transactions to determine whether a mortgage had been intended. Here the work of Stephen J. Field played a significant role.

One of Field's major contributions of the 1850s, the parol evidence rule application to mortgages, was accepted as controlling in the 1880s. Field's opinion in *Pierce v. Robinson* (1859) and expanded upon in *Cunningham v. Hawkins* (1865) established that parol evidence was admissible to show that a deed absolute on its face was intended as a mortgage.[249] When California adopted its Civil Code in 1873, the code commissioners declared their intent, in two sections, to be to restore the rule of *Cunningham*.[250] With Field on the U. S. Supreme Court bench, the California Court also cited his similar holding in federal court.[251] The Court in the 1880s had continuing need to apply the rule. For example, in *J. S. Manasse v. Lazarus Dinkelspiel* (1886), the parties made an oral agreement to exchange a deed for property held by Manasse for an evidence of indebtedness held by Dinkelspiel of $1,800. In that Manasse's property might not bring at sale the $1,800 owed to Dinkelspiel, Manasse gave Lazarus a note for $500 to cover any deficiency. However, if the sale netted $1,800, Lazarus was to return any surplus land and the note. All seemed settled. Then the land boom shattered expectations, and Manasse wanted to raise up a mortgage from the deed, to pay it off, and reap a profit. But the Court simply went back to Field's test of "if there is no debt, there is no mortgage," and found that the $1,800 debt was satisfied by the deed and that no debt existed. In that Manasse could not raise a mortgage from the deed, Lazarus Dinkelspiel was left with the land to reap his harvest.[252]

The California Supreme Court also spent a great deal of energy exercising its equitable jurisdiction in superintending mortgages. This had become a substantial and a mainstream function of American state courts in the late nineteenth century.[253] Equity was a system of jurisprudence that focused upon the fairness or justice of dealings rather than strict legal rules. Naturally, equity gave courts greater latitude for decision, and the California experience was little different.

In *Wilhelmina Rumpp v. Jacob Gerkens* (1881), the Court applied equitable principles to decide the case. The plaintiff, Rumpp, had a mortgage from Jacob Gerkens and his wife, Isadora, dated July 18, 1876. Another defendant, Miguel Leonis, had a mortgage from the Gerkenses dated July 1, 1875. Leonis foreclosed on May 28, 1878, but did not make Rumpp a party, as he had no idea that the Gerkenses had mortgaged the place twice. The trial court granted the petition, entered a decree of foreclosure, and authorized the sale of the property. Leonis purchased at sale and received a sheriff's deed. But on December 19, 1878, Jacob and Isadora struck a bargain with Miguel to give him their deed in return for $3,973.25 and the cancellation of all debts Miguel held. For Miguel, it was a worthwhile bargain because the tyranny of the redemption period was thus slashed away from the execution sale and sheriff's deed. But all was not so clear in the brine in which transactions cured in Los Angeles during this period. Suddenly, Wilhelmina Rumpp appeared, and a trial court found that the Gerkenses owed her $1,039.32 in gold and that she now had the right of redemption that Miguel had just paid dear dollars to avoid. Parenthetically, the trial court ordered the Gerkenses to pay Wilhelmina $1,185.92 immediately or suffer a seven percent per year penalty. The Supreme Court placed its stamp of approval on the holding, citing equity. Equity protected Leonis by finding that he did not intend to give up his security by taking the deed or that his lien should be extinguished as against subsequent incumbrances.[254] Whether such a holding comforted a lender who had spent money to foreclose, paid out more money to avoid redemption, disbursed more to counsel to defend at trial and on appeal, and now faced an unknown creditor who could redeem for $2,800 is doubtful. Equity as well as debtors, litigation, and lawyers could leave lenders in a pickle.

Equity was generally beneficial to lenders' interests, but would not aid those that sat idly on their rights.[255] Debtors could not complain of a lender's lack of authority to loan money with the lucre in their hands attempting to avoid their obligation to pay.[256] Affirmatively, courts in equity could settle all accounts and grant damages for waste on rents and profits.[257] Clearly, the principles of equity favored the creditor. *Booth v. Hoskins* (1888) denied affirmative relief to the plaintiff until the money due the defendant was paid:

> Common honesty required a debtor to pay his just debts if he is able to do so, and the courts, when called upon, always enforce such payments if they can. The fact that a debt is barred by the statute of limitations in no way released the debtor from his moral obligation to pay it. Moreover, one of the maxims which courts of equity should always act upon is . . . that he who seeks equity must do equity.[258]

It was that "common honesty" that bound debtors to pay by whatever means that cemented the marketplace relations of many together on a continuing basis. David Jacks carried Jim Kee, a Salinas Valley farmer, for years, extending debts, signing new notes and mortgages, and taking crops in lieu of cash.[259] The great bulk of debtors paid on time and received the signed satisfaction of a mortgage document whether they paid in cash, kind, or land.[260] The principles of common honesty were very much a part of the marketplace.

Another institutional obligation of the California Supreme Court was considering the developing mortgage law of other states in formulating mortgage law for California.[261] Generally, the Supreme Court looked to New York cases for guidance.[262] The Court's reliance upon New York was not particularly surprising, given the state's adoption of the Field Code of New York and the influence of New York on law in that century in general.[263] Equally expected, California jurists and lawyers found some New York precedents not on point.[264] Unexpectedly, the California Court also ridiculed the New York Court. In *Brickell v. Batchelder* (1882), Justice James D. Thornton tore a New York opinion to shreds. After reciting the opinion of the New York Court, Thornton, attacking the ability of the New York Court to read plain English, asserted, given the mortgage language: "If such language does not authorize a party to proceed for a statutory foreclosure on failure to pay taxes by the mortgagor, it would be difficult to find any sufficient reason why." Thornton, looking at the same language, then declared that the "words could not make it plainer." How then could the New York judge make such a stupid reading of plain English? Thornton had the politic answer: "The Judge was surely mistaken." Even if he had not made a mistake, clearly the rule was "peculiar to the jurisprudence of New York."[265] The *Brickell* opinion was critical of the New York Court without jurisprudential cause because the mortgages could have been distinguished. However, the California Court, here as elsewhere, asserted its uniqueness and the rightness of its declaration as means of identification. Some found this eccentric. For the Court it was part of a more general process of asserting its judicial leadership in the developing law of the land.[266]

At the operational level, entrepreneurs sought money in every corner. Many borrowed from banks. Others borrowed from family. Prospective debtors deluged private lenders with requests for money on "good security."[267] Since many mortgages were short term, many debtors sought refinancing.[268] Other debtors requested extensions of existing loans.[269] Construction loans became a part of financing the expansion of rural enterprise.[270] Lenders adjusted interest rates to deal with the 1879 constitution's tax on mortgages.[271] As the economy changed, they also adjusted interest rates to market conditions, even if downward.[272] With flush times lenders introduced a prepayment penalty to ensure their return.[273] The prepayment penalty clause quickly became part of mortgage boilerplate. As James A. Clayton explained to David Jacks in 1890:

> The 3 months clause in the Welborn note is the customary method of making a note payable before due. This is found to be quite just as there are as many chances that it will be paid late in the year as it will be about the time of taxes--but it is figured that if it is paid shortly after the tax assessment the 3 months bonus will more than cover the amount of taxes. . . . As a whole you will find the rule of making a mortgagor pay 3 months bonus for paying before due a very satisfactory one to lender and borrower.[274]

Lenders also drafted around the deficiency judgment holdings of the Court. Debtors simply guaranteed by contract that they would pay any deficiency in a foreclosure sale.[275] The creditor as well as the debtor attempted to adjust practice to the market as best they could.

One such adjustment was the use of the deed of trust. It provided expedited sale and cut off the redemption period. In the twentieth century the deed of trust became virtually the sole instrument for security transactions in real estate.[276] In the decade of the 1880s, the California Supreme Court scrutinized such trust deeds carefully and required that debtors be treated equitably.[277] Further, although the redemption period was cut off, the purchaser had a difficult time dispossessing the debtor because the legal status of the trust deed and the debtor was uncertain.[278] In the next 40 years, the California Court and the legislature would enhance the trust deed's utility and make it the most desirable instrument.

The development of mortgage law in the period 1850-1890 evidenced a sometimes sketchy record of formal law fostering security and certainty in mortgage transactions. Clearly, the main thread of law encouraging the release of energy inherent in real estate transactions existed as Willard Hurst has often told us.[279] But in California there was more. Legal development followed social and economic change. But practitioners often found the law poorly suited to their goals. They drafted around problems where they could. However, as the California Supreme Court entered the 1870s without Stephen J. Field, the holdings oftentimes confounded the policies laid down in the 1850s and 1860s. Practitioners were not always certain of what the law was. This chief element of uncertainty was due both to the Court and to the practitioners.[280] Clearly, the Court was not always helpful in guiding entrepreneurs and their counsel, but equally clear, lawyers and lenders made egregious errors of omission and commission. The frontier nature of much of the marketplace as well as the frenzied bargaining in a boom and bust economy made mortgage law in California a challenge for jurists, legislators, lawyers, and lenders. As the law of mortgage developed, California's frontier economy and society made imprints in law and practice.

4
TORT LAW

The California courts in developing the law of torts for the state played an essential role in the social order. The responsiveness of the courts to social change in the period 1850-1890 laid a common-law foundation for what is today a leading jurisdiction and played a part in the process leading to workers' compensation.[1] Further, the developing law mirrored a basic tension of economic and social demands in a frontier situation. The values of entrepreneurial venture clashed with the social costs of a transportation revolution and industrialization. Although the history of the law of industrial accidents is well known,[2] the role of the California courts, although similar, demonstrates the vital role the judiciary played in the economic and social development of California.

Tort law in nineteenth-century America underwent rapid development. Broadly speaking, a tort is a civil wrong, other than a breach of contract, for which a court will provide a remedy in the form of action for damages.[3] The day-to-day complaints between and among California's bustling population sometimes matured into a lawsuit, but often they did not. John Whipple Dwinelle sued James Owen and Benjamin Cottle, San Jose newspapermen, on February 27, 1868, for $10,000 for printing allegedly libelous attacks on him using the terms "unmitigated scoundrelism," "trick demagogue," and other foul language.[4] Dr. B. H. Fairchild of Pomona wrote to John D. Bicknell, a Los Angeles attorney, in 1881 inquiring of his "legal redress" against a man who called him a "hard case" and alleged that he "left his wife [in the] east and married this woman." To make matters worse, "The man who is libeling me is as poor as you generally find men. Can I shut him up short of shooting him? I am sorry to say he is a Methodist minister and he uses his position to work me injury."[5] The judgment-proof were seldom taken to court. However, those with assets who were negligent found their way into the system. Actions for negligence came to outweigh all others in the late nineteenth century, while assault, battery, trespass to land, libel, and slander also were common on court dockets.[6]

The explosion of tort litigation based on negligence in the late nineteenth century was due to industrialization and the railroad. Industrial and railroad accidents grew with economic expansion. Tort law developed in response to the demands of industry and the broken bodies scattered about the workplace and the right-of-way. Fundamentally, courts created the law of tort to allow the injured party to recover despite the lack of a contractual relationship with the person or the thing causing the injury. Persons who, in the past, had been nonsuited for lack of a contractual relationship could now attempt to recover for their misery. Although the contract law concepts lingered into the twentieth century for consumers, the developing law of tort gave courts a major role in redistributing wealth. Given this proclivity to find a doctrinal means to compensate the injured victims of industrialization and the transportation revolution, it should not be surprising to find claimants succeeding in court.

The California Supreme Court in its first decade disposed of a variety of tort claims. If enterprise was at stake, then the Court's decisions protected venture through damages doctrines. However, litigation not involving enterprise received similar treatment. Throughout the decade the Court looked to a negligence standard, avoiding concepts of strict liability not then a part of tort doctrine. In fact, only with respect to the custody of animals known to be dangerous did the Court accept strict liability.[7] The judicial thinking of the times focused upon fault as the basis for liability. This fault emphasis necessarily involved a standard of conduct deemed to be the norm of society. The California Supreme Court was well aware that its decisions were helping to mold this standard of conduct. Further, the Court elaborated on the negligence standard to facilitate the plaintiff's ability to prove the case. The adoption of the *res ipsa* notion as early as 1859 was one significant edge the Court gave to plaintiffs. Another advantage was the Court's assignment to the lay jury to both ascertain the facts of defendant's conduct and evaluate the negligence significance of those facts.[8] Despite these advantages appellate cases reveal some contrary holdings of significance.

In *McDaniel v. Baca* (1852), a slander case, the Court recognized its crucial role. William McDaniel had purchased land from Manuel Baca. Subsequently, Baca had published in a newspaper a notice to all persons that they should not purchase any land from McDaniel because the land was obtained by false pretenses. The jury found for McDaniel in the amount of $17,711.50. Justice Alexander Anderson for the Court found the amount of damages "unexampled and unjustifiable." He noted that courts do not often disturb verdicts for that cause, but that they would if the verdict verged on "outrage." Here the Court would not disturb the verdict. Anderson went on to state:

> But by this, we do not mean to intimate that we should refuse for that cause under any circumstances, to disturb that verdict, if it were necessary to the end of justice. It is sufficient to say, that the facts in this case are of a novel and extraordinary character; and it is desirable for the sake of justice, that they should receive a full, fair, and impartial investigation. It is time in California, to begin in this respect a new era, and this Court is never better employed than when, by its decisions, it is pointing public attention, the public confidence, and the public judgment to that end.[9]

Anderson's words were expressive of the Court's basic concern that justice be done, that slander be discouraged, that land dealing be free of subsequent public attack outside of court, and that the Court be a primary exponent of these goals.[10]

If enterprise were visited by extraordinary damages, then the Court was more willing to intervene. In *Moody v. McDonald* (1854), a woman was injured by blasting in a rock quarry. Although 32 years later the Court would find the blaster strictly liable in tort, the Court in 1854 required that fault be established.[11] With negligence established, the rule was to allow actual damages only. Here the injury had found $2,500 actual damages and $2,500 "smart money" (punitive damages). Justice Solomon Heydenfeldt tersely noted that "in cases of negligence simply, the rule is to allow the actual damages" and that proof of malice was required for vindictive damages.[12] The holding was significant. The Court established a policy position that recognized that in a frontier situation, dangerous enterprises, involving a high degree of risk to others, were clearly indispensable to the development of the new land. The Court would not make enterprise the insurer of developmental activities. The interests of individuals had to give way to public interests in rapid development, but only to a certain extent. Negligent actions were still visited with actual damages. The nation's courts developed the law of tort to compensate the victims of negligent conduct, not to prevent those victims from recovering in a court of law. California's *Moody* decision was clearly part of this negligence-recovery philosophy. What is surprising and significant is that such a dangerous activity was accorded a negligence standard, allowing enterprise a defense to liability. This was both a frontier context decision and a refusal to go beyond a negligence standard in 1854.

Nuisance claims formed another area of concern for the Court. A private nuisance is a civil wrong based on some disturbance of rights in land. A public nuisance consists of some interference with the rights of the community. The Court's handling of flooding cases protected the property interests as well as enterprise. In two cases involving the flooding of agricultural and mining property, the Court held for the damaged property owner rather than the dam owner.[13] In both cases the Court looked to definitions of nuisance supplied by the English common law. The Court ordered the abatement of the nuisance, but not the elimination of the dams or works involved. In *Middleton v. Franklin* (1853), the Court explicitly favored enterprise. The defendant erected a steam boiler to run a grist mill in the cellar of a building occupied by the plaintiff. The plaintiff feared the explosion of the boiler and complained of noise and smoke. The Court found that the boiler did not constitute a sufficiently probable threat to warrant an injunction. Even if it did, damages were the appropriate remedy, not the termination of the enterprise.[14] *Surocco v. Geary* (1853) presented a prophetic case of public nuisance. The homeowner sued the mayor of San Francisco for blowing up his house to prevent the spread of a fire. The Court adopted the theory that a nearby blazing or adjoining house was a nuisance that the city had a duty to abate. Necessity provided adequate justification in this case leaving the plaintiff without compensation. The homeowner's plight was a matter for the legislature to remedy.[15] Although such public nuisance cases were an exception to the enterprise-landowner tension in nuisance cases, they did establish the Court's position favoring paramount community interest.

The Court also confronted tort cases generated by transportation enterprises. In cases of stagecoaches overturning, the Court developed a presumption that the cause was the negligence of the coachman. But the presumption was rebuttable.[16] Further, damages were limited to actual damages, thus providing a measure of enterprise protection.[17] The Court was willing to impute the negligence of an employee to the employer, setting the stage for the fellow-servant developments of the latter part of the century.[18] In a case involving the burning of a grain field caused by steamboat sparks, the Court retained for its discretion the determination of the proper standard of care. In that particular case, the absence of catches on the chimney constituted negligence.[19] Although the cases were not extensive, the Court did display a general attitude favoring enterprise.

This attitude was one tempered by strong language in those cases going in other directions. In *Wilson v. Cunningham* (1853), the Court used strong language requiring "extraordinary care" where enterprise (a street railroad) involved "constant risk and danger."[20] Stagecoaches overturning and the sparks of enterprise became legal facts that gave the victims the opportunity to recover and enterprise the opportunity to rebut the legal inferences of negligence inherent in the calamity.[21] The California Supreme Court gave enterprise the opportunity to defend. What we find today, of course, is an opportunity to insure and for insurance defense attorneys to settle.

In the next 30 years, the torts docket expanded dramatically. The cases of the first decade constituted only 9.7 percent of the total for the period. The cases decided during 1860-1879 equaled 38.6 percent of the sum, and the cases of the decade of the 1880s were 51.7 percent of the whole. Although the second two decades were ones of expanding tort litigation, the Court attacked the problems in an inconsistent fashion. Fact situations rather than doctrine came to dominate opinions, but the skeleton features of doctrines of industrial accidents did appear. While the justices developed doctrine, juries handed down verdicts. In the period 1850-1900, the appellate reports reveal 248 verdicts for plaintiffs and 26 for defendants.[22] The fact that the law provided the victims of the industrial and transportation revolution to recover money damages for injuries challenged enterprise's attorneys to deal with a growing legal and financial challenge.

During the period 1860-1879, the California Supreme Court handled a more varied docket and began to deal with statutory remedies. One of the first statutory aids to tort claimants was the wrongful death statute. In English common law the cause of action for tort died with the plaintiff. State legislatures adopted, in altered fashion, the English Fatal Accidents Act of 1846, preserving to surviving relatives a cause of action against the person or entity causing the death of kin. California enacted such a statute in 1862.[23] The statute contained a prophetic section that declared that death by falling through the sidewalks, streets, alleys, or wharf of any city or incorporated town was deemed "caused by the wrongful neglect and default" of the entity having a duty to repair such thoroughfares. In *Gay v. Winter* (1867), the Court was confronted with just such a case as a five-year-old child fell through a two-foot-square hole in a San Francisco street and drowned in the bay. In holding for the plaintiff, the Court also maintained that it was for the jury to decide whether the plaintiff was contributorily negligent and hence barred from recovery.[24] In another case out of San Francisco, a seven year old was crushed by a steam fire engine. Justice Royal T. Sprague noted for the Court that the statute was more liberal than other state statutes in terms of allowable damages.[25] The statute preserved the cause of action for the surviving kin and allowed more extensive recoveries than other state statutes. Although the statute provided a means of recovery, the issues of liability still remained. As Harvey S. Brown, an attorney for the Southern Pacific Company, wrote to John D. Bicknell, a Los Angeles attorney, in 1889 regarding the allegedly "negligent killing" of John Rand, "We cannot settle, because we think that we are not liable."[26] The statute allowed the lawsuit. The proof of facts remained, whether settlement or trial resulted from the negotiations of attorneys.

The Court also confronted torts arising from the bustling mining, mercantile, and construction enterprises. Hydraulic mining revolutionized the industry, but destroyed agricultural lands in the process.[27] Some farmers went to court and sued in trespass.[28] The courts looked at both the physical trespass of the mine tailings and the negligence of the miner in causing the trespass.[29] In these cases the Court found negligence and tersely found for the claimants. But in two construction industry cases, the Court found against the claimants. In *McNamara v. North Pacific Railroad Company* (1875), a railroad contractor left blasting caps near the plaintiff's well, and her children began playing with them. The mother took them away from her children, but the caps exploded in her hand, resulting in the amputation of her thumb and a finger. The contractor did not pay, however, because the mother was found contributorily negligent.[30] However, of almost 90 cases involving contributory negligence in the nineteenth century, only eight stood after appellate scrutiny. In 23 cases the Supreme Court held the plaintiff contributorily negligent as a matter of law.[31] Hence, the defense was apparently useful in approximately one case of every three where the defense presented the factual grounding. In another case a painter used a cornice as support for scaffolding. The cornice collapsed, and the painter fell 30 feet, necessitating the amputation of an arm. The Court held that the homeowner was not liable as he had taken the house complete and the subcontractors who had erected the cornice were not under his direction.[32] The Court seemed to indicate that it was unfair for the homeowner to be responsible for a latent defect. In a later age of homeowner's insurance and workers' compensation, the equities would be more clearly in favor of the injured party.

Just as mine tailings could destroy agricultural lands, so too could overflow from irrigation ditches damage crops. The Court consistently held ditch owners to a standard of ordinary care that prudent persons exercised in the management of their property.[33] This excluded natural overflow and acts of God.[34] Further, if a plaintiff, as in *Maumus v. Champion* (1870), was contributorily negligent, then he was barred from recovery. The Court indicated that the plaintiff got what he deserved in that "the plaintiff was in the habit of opening this notch while the defendant was using the water, and helping himself to what water he desired."[35] In this area of enterprise, the Court applied the standard approach to liability--fault; but the standard of care was not the most stringent that could be applied.

The Court also gave attention to torts arising from the cattle industry. These personal injuries often occurred in cities as the cattle moved to market. In an early case the Court held that the drovers in a city were governed by the law of common carriers, but the drovers had to be allowed to prove care and diligence to the jury.[36] Absolute liability would not be imposed. Other cases involved cattle maiming children. Although defendants argued that allowing children to roam at large was contributory negligence, the Court would not agree as a matter of law.[37] But the Court did impose a limit to damages. In *Karr v. Parks* (1872), the Court limited damages to healing original wounds. Justice Addison C. Niles argued that "there would be practically no limit to the liability of the defendant if the father could pursue, at pleasure, a series of expensive surgical operations for the purpose of removing every trace of the injury and charge the defendant with the entire cost."[38] These were the days before personal liability insurance, and the Court was reluctant to make the defendant an insurer of costs that were not foreseeable. This was, of course, at the expense of making a ten-year-old girl, without an eye and with horrid goring marks, whole again by surgery.

The law of common carriers underwent change in the period. Both the English common law and eastern precedent provided guidance for the California Supreme Court.[39] Accompanying the tort law changes were changes in the law of bailments. A bailment involves a delivery of personal property by one party to another in trust for a specific purpose with an express or implied contract that the trust be executed and the property returned or accounted for when the specified purpose is accomplished or upon demand. The law held the common carrier to be an insurer of goods placed in its control (bailment) and bound to deliver those goods in the same condition or pay for losses. The carriers attempted to limit their liability, but the California Court held them to a notice requirement. In *Griffith v. Cave* (1863), the Court held that a ferryman had the duty of providing a suitable boat and all the conveniences required for safe transportation. Further, the rules of ferries were inadmissible. Justice Edwin B. Crocker firmly stated that it was "essential in all such cases that the notice of any rule upon such subject . . . be brought home to the person employing the carrier, either directly or constructively."[40] The case was significant in that it laid the groundwork for limiting liability for the railroads and other carriers. But the common carrier could not be excused from its negligence particularly where neither an act of God nor actions beyond the control of the carrier were involved. In *Agnew v. Steamer Contra Costa* (1865), a boiler explosion caused by a steamboat race was not such a defense.[41] Absent such reckless conduct, common carriers were able to limit their liability by contract with proper notice. This was significant because the concept of the common carrier as insurer increased enterprise costs at a time when capital was dear.

Railroads began generating the bulk of tort cases after 1869 by causing damage to property, livestock, and persons. Within two decades the California Supreme Court changed its position on several basic legal doctrines, affording enterprise substantial insulation from tort claims. For example, railroads were responsible for numerous claims for starting prairie fires. As late as 1870 the Court found that a farmer leaving his pasture dry was not contributorily negligent barring recovery.[42] However, by 1875 the Court found that while permitting dry grass to remain was not negligence *per se*, it was evidence from which negligence might or might not be inferred by the jury.[43] Significantly, the Court placed the burden of care upon the victim of the sparks that voluminously spewed from the locomotives as they crossed California. Hence, the burden of capital expenditure to prevent fire was upon the farmer, not the railroad.[44] This trend was tempered by the Court in *Henry v. Southern Pacific Railroad* (1875): "Considering the long dry season of California and the prevalence of certain winds in our valleys, that it may be left to a jury to determine whether the spreading of a fire from one field to another is not the natural, direct or proximate consequence of the original firing."[45] The two 1875 cases clearly left major issues to local juries. This reality would play a significant role in the 1880s.

Livestock running on the open range posed another problem for the Court. Lacking a duty to fence livestock, the Court reasoned that the cattlemen's contributory negligence would have to be that which directly caused the injury.[46] By the 1870s the Court changed its position and found that allowing livestock to run at large was contributory negligence under most circumstances.[47] If persons crossed the tracks without stopping, looking, or listening, then the Court found that such contributory negligence barred recovery.[48] The problem of livestock was one of economics because fencing the tracks involved capital investment, and the Court was not the appropriate forum for the public policy decision.

Rolling stock also injured pedestrians. Here the Court applied the doctrine of contributory negligence, but allowed recovery for negligence on the part of the railroad. One area of particular interest was the Court's interpretation of children running at large in the street. In *Karr v. Parks* (1870), the Court held that parents were not contributorily negligent in allowing a ten-year-old girl to play in the street. In that case it was a cow roaming at large that caused the injury. The Court depicted the cow as presenting an "imminent danger."[49] But in *Schierhold v. North Beach and Mission Railroad Company* (1871), the Court found that a child playing in a San Francisco street was contributorily negligent. The Court reasoned by analogy that municipalities were afforded the "narrowest possible" liability because the public duty extended only to providing roads for particular purposes. Streets were not playgrounds for children.[50] The Court, most likely, also took notice of the fact that the child in *Karr* was playing in a street in Marysville, not in San Francisco. But the most significant policy factor was the fact that railroad enterprise liability required a narrower interpretation than that for livestock owners. Remembering the language of *Wilson v. Cunningham*, the railroad was a hazardous enterprise on urban streets whether drawn by horses or iron horses. If the railroad was negligent, then the Court let stand verdicts that in other cases it considered excessive.[51]

The liability of the railroad for injuries suffered by passengers was somewhat different. Generally, railroads were not insurers of the safety of the passengers, but they were responsible for a high degree of care. This care involved reasonable and proper precautions and actions under the circumstances of a particular case. Hence, the railroad had the duty to provide roadbeds, rails, engines, cars, and other accoutrements in accordance with the standards of the times. Passengers assumed the risk of accidents that such precautions and equipment could not prevent. Further, contributory negligence could bar recovery for a passenger.[52]

The Court provided enterprise substantial insulation from liability for tort claims by employees. Using the fellow-servant doctrine, the Court uncritically denied recovery to employees injured by the negligence of fellow employees.[53] In other situations the Court found that employees assumed the risks of their employment.[54] Late in the period the legislature committed the fellow servant rule to statute, and the Court merely repeated the legislative litany in denying recovery to injured workmen.[55]

In applying the doctrines of assumption of risk, contributory negligence, and fellow servant, the California Supreme Court was socializing the costs of rapid economic development. The legislature's approval of the fellow-servant doctrine affirmed the belief that social progress was inextricably linked to enterprise expansion. Limiting enterprise liability for industrial accidents was necessary to preserve capital and was the legal system's subsidy to business. In the 1870s lawmakers had yet to perceive the social and economic dislocation that industrial accidents would cause. This fellow-servant exception to general enterprise liability for negligence would soon fall to doctrinal tinkering by the courts and legislative assaults leading to workers' compensation statutes.

The decade of the 1880s was a time of legal consolidation of doctrine and a time for the Court to question some of its basic assumptions. The bulk of the cases arose from railroad accidents, but the number of cases generated by industry also increased. In many instances the Court split on doctrine or the merits of the case, and on similar facts the Court reached different results through the doctrine of proximate cause. Although the differing results caused some legal confusion for the bar, the Court's behavior evidenced a concern for the consequences of its developing concept of enterprise liability.

The Court's position on blasting demonstrated both a consolidation of doctrine and a growing concern for social interests amid a bustling economy. In *Colton v. Onderdonk* (1886), the Court changed its position from that taken in *Moody v. McDonald* (1854). In the case a property owner used gunpowder to blast rocks in a lot adjoining a private residence. In holding for the plaintiff, Commissioner H. S. Foote asserted the state's position clearly:

> The defendant seems by his contention to claim that he had a right to blast rocks with gunpowder on his own lot in San Francisco, even if he had shaken Mrs. Cotton's house to ruins, provided he used care and skill in so doing, and although he ought to have known that by such act, which was intrinsically dangerous, the damage would be a necessary, probable, or natural consequence. But in this he is mistaken.[56]

Hence, where an activity was inherently dangerous, the Court would hold the actor to a standard of strict liability. This position also recognized that the frontier conditions that necessitated the use of such instrumentalities had passed and that the reason for lessening the burden of liability to promote enterprise was no longer as compelling.[57] However, what constituted such a dangerous activity was still a matter of interpretation for the Court to decide.

Locomotives spewing sparks about the countryside were not such dangerous instrumentalities. In the 1880s the Court took the position that "by showing that the railroad had used all reasonable care and diligence in securing a proper engine, and in the management of it to prevent the happening of fires," a defendant had created an adequate defense.[58] The Court noted that several New England states had imposed strict liability by statute and California had not. The Court would not do so, but if evidence of negligence were circumstantial, then a jury could decide the issue.[59] The practical result was that the jury could establish such a standard if there was any evidence of negligence.[60] This reasoning was legally akin to *res ipsa*, reasoning that would hold that sparks igniting anything alongside was a *prima facie* proof of negligence.[61]

For the practicing bar, locomotive fires called for settlement unless cause in fact was at issue. John D. Bicknell regularly settled grass fire cases examining only the amount of damages absent a causation question.[62] Bicknell also recommended prevention. In 1889 he wrote to George C. Fabens, a claims adjuster for the Southern Pacific Company in San Francisco, that "the grasses growing upon the land of Watson in the neighborhood of Cerritos are about as inflammable as gunpowder and it would be well for our section men to put the right-of-way in the very best condition through his premises to prevent fires."[63] When Bicknell thought others, such as "tramps cooking over a fire near the track," started the fire, he litigated. But all never goes well in litigation. Bicknell "proved that our locomotives were in good condition and equipped with the best possible appliances to prevent sparks escaping." But the plaintiffs proved that dry grass was growing within three feet of the tracks and had a witness that was "positive that the fire started something near three hundred feet from the [tramps'] campfires." With a verdict of $1,256.45 plus $98.15 in costs, Bicknell recommended to Creed Hammond, the Southern Pacific Company general counsel, that they pay. After all, "the amount of damage award is low enough."[64] The trial was without a jury. The problems of proof were significant, and the railroad had the money. The tramps were unavailable to testify or pay.

John Bicknell did little better when ranchers drove their cattle on the tracks to collect from the railroad rather than at the slaughterhouse. On March 27, 1890, Bicknell told Creed Haymond that he had "a fighting chance on appeal, but like all cases of this class it [is] doubtful about our ever getting a verdict. Upon the whole, I consider it the best business policy to pay the judgment [of $300 plus $100 costs]."[65] Haymond agreed. On April 2 he wrote, "I think that under the circumstances you did pretty well. . . . The verdict was a small one . . . I have found it almost impossible to defend any of these cases successfully and have generally advised settling them."[66] So settle they did, and as would be expected, few cases went to appellate courts. Although Bicknell continued to seek out evidence of contributory negligence and the railroad created an accident form with the legend "Great care should be taken to prevent the killing of stock. Come to a full stop, if necessary, to avoid the accident," cattle, horses, and other livestock died on the tracks, and the railroad settled.[67]

The status of persons continued to play a large role in tort law. In cases of children wandering onto railroad tracks and being injured or run down in the street by horses, the Court's attention focused upon the possible contributory negligence of the parents.[68] The issue of supervisorial negligence by parents was one for the jury and increased the jury's role in distributing the costs of the transportation revolution and urban growth. That role was dramatically brought home to John D. Bicknell in 1890 in a case involving an eight-year-old boy playing on a railroad turntable in the sleepy little town of Santa Ana. In July 1890 the railroad lost a lawsuit for $300 to the boy's mother, but the boy's guardian brought a second suit. Bicknell reported to Creed Haymond that the second claim was "a dangerous suit."[69] When the jury came in in August, Bicknell did not have good news for Hammond. He wrote on August 9 that

> this case . . . falls in line of the long list of cases known in the books as "Turntable cases." I have always considered the case a dangerous one but did not deem it possible that a jury would award so high a verdict as they did, to-wit, the sum of $12,500.

The jury verdict had "surprised" Bicknell, but beyond the surprise he had good risk management advice.

> In view of the tendency of the courts in the various states in this class of cases, I feel disposed to call your attention again, as I did some months ago, to the necessity of some means of locking or fastening the turntables in the country towns, such as Santa Ana, where children pass near them upon the public highway and

the table is not guarded by the presence of any of our
employees.[70]

As an experienced attorney, Bicknell wanted to reduce the risk created by
the turntable, the courts, and the juries. A little boy with a leg amputated
between the hip and knee was a victim of industrialization and a dangerous
plaintiff before a local jury in a country town.

Passengers had a favored legal position, but the Court frequently found
that contributory negligence was a bar to recovery. The litany of common
carriers having a high standard of care was part of most opinions. But
passengers who got off the wrong side of a train, alighted when the train
was in motion, or jumped from overturning vehicles simply gave rise to a
question of contributory negligence.[71] The result was a diminished position
for the passenger. Although the Court applied a prudent man test to such
cases, what was prudent in a given situation was often a matter of judgment.

Employees continued to face the doctrine of contributory negligence as
a bar to recovery for injury on the job. As the *Reports* reveal, employees
guilty of some degree of contributory negligence were left disfigured,
maimed, or dead without compensation.[72] The Court retained a strict
adherence to the doctrine as a means of insulating enterprise from excessive
liability. This did not, however, create any general immunity for employers
from liability. In nineteenth-century California, the employee prevailed in
37 Supreme Court opinions, the employer in 43.[73] Further, the defense of
contributory negligence seldom stood alone.

Although contributory negligence gave juries and judges an issue to
examine, the doctrine of assumption of the risk proved more deleterious to
employees. For example, in *Sweeney v. Central Pacific Railroad
Company* (1880), the Court held that an engineer assumed the risk of
derailment due to collision with livestock because he knew the tracks were
not fenced.[74] But in *Trask v. California Southern Railroad Company*
(1883), the Court held that an employee did not assume the risk of a
negligently constructed road.[75] The Court found no conflict between the
cases. However, in *Magee v. Northern Pacific Coast Railroad Company*
(1889), the Court found for a brakeman thrown from a train when it hit a
bull on the tracks.[76] Finally, in *Vaugh v. California Central Railroad
Company* (1890), the Court decided that an employee on a construction train
did assume the risk of washouts.[77] The widow would have to bear the loss.
For the Court the doctrines of contributory negligence and assumption of
the risk overlapped to a degree. By assuming that an employee made a
choice in accepting employment with known hazards, the Court tacitly
recognized that with injury or death the employee had been contributorily
negligent in either making a wrong choice or voluntarily encountering a
known but arguably unreasonable risk. The result of the doctrines was, of
course, a defense to enterprise liability, particularly for the railroads. In
finding an assumption of risk, the Court made a choice that denied recovery
based on a perception of the employee's range of choice. That range of
choice became narrower in the late nineteenth century with the expansion
of enterprise.

The California Court did take the position that an employer had a duty to
provide reasonably safe machinery and to keep it in repair. In several cases
the Court found that an employer's failure to provide reasonably safe
machinery was a breach of duty to the employee.[78] But there were limits.
In *Madden v. Occidental and Oriental Steamship Company* (1890),

a laborer was squashed by cotton bales in the hold of a ship. The ship's sling broke, cascading the bales down upon the decedent. Justice John D. Works cast doubt on the element of negligence in such a case, stating that

> when it is said in some of the cases that the occurrence of an accident is *prima facie* evidence of insufficiency of the machinery or appliance being used, it must be confined to cases, if the rule is conceded to be the correct one, where the machinery or appliance is shown to have been used in the usual and proper way, at least where the same is being used by the party injured, or his co-employees.[79]

Taking this position the Court encouraged an evidentiary attack by defense attorneys upon the mode of use and reserved to itself interpretative authority. The employer's duty could be narrowly defined if enterprise liability required such protection.

Finally, the fellow-servant rule proved a bar to recovery for injuries sustained on the job caused by another employee. The Court in the 1880s consolidated its position on the rule, finding most injuries caused by an employee legally considered to be a fellow servant. In fact, if workers' claims were disallowed, the Supreme Court usually applied the fellow-servant rule.[80] On occasion, however, a member of the Court would question the appropriateness of the doctrine in its application.[81] The process of questioning the doctrine's assumptions had only begun. The well-known conclusion was the development of workers' compensation statutes.

The development of tort law in frontier California evidenced a recognition of the need to protect entrepreneurial venture in a frontier situation. The Court, on numerous occasions, decided cases, used doctrines, or interpreted fact situations favorably to enterprise and against plaintiff employees. The fact that the Supreme Court did develop employer defenses to tort liability and did apply those defenses to fact situations uncontrovertibly relieved enterprise of some of the costs of industrialization. The fact that the application of the defenses was not universal does not infer a judicial desire to burden enterprise. Industrial subsidy was not the goal or the result of judicial lawmaking. Victim welfare was not the goal or the result of appellate craftsmanship. Rather the California law of torts involved both industrial subsidy and victim welfare. The tension of appellate pronouncement and practitioner practicalities before juries in country towns revealed both in action. What the Supreme Court could give in the fellow-servant rule, the local jury could take away with awards unprofitable to appeal. Outside the employer-employee relationship, the Court was more prone to favoring plaintiffs. Cases like *Colton* explicitly recognized the end of the frontier conditions necessitating law favoring enterprise. But this was not an employer-employee fact situation. The recognition that the social costs of industrialization and transportation would have to be spread to enterprise and society as a whole was yet to come. As the Supreme Court developed exceptions to the fellow-servant rule and the legislature crafted a workers' compensation program, the social cost spreading and social consciousness of employer liability slowly withdrew from the tort law judicial system and more closely approximated the developing victim welfare conceptualizations that have come to dominate twentieth-century tort practice.

5
FINANCING COMMERCE

The period 1850-1890 was a time of testing for California lawmakers. California's statehood, the gold rush, and the demands of a thriving commercial community required immediate legal action to legitimize business dealings and structure credit transactions. Moreover, the frontier banking institutions failed to provide financial stability for almost two decades. In this context, California lawmakers sought rationalized legal systems for credit transactions.

The California Supreme Court considered significant chattel credit issues in 393 cases. Topics included bills and notes, pledges, chattel mortgages, and mechanics' liens. Although the data on appellate litigants are incomplete, the types of transactions, their value, and the results indicate that this 40-year period was one of relative legal confusion. Both the state legislature and the Supreme Court sought legal devices to lend certainty and security to transactions (particularly the banking and construction businesses), amid the fluctuations of a frontier economy.

California's banking history, until 1862, was one of instability and unstructured practices. Saloon keepers, express companies, and businessmen performed crude banking functions. Wells, Fargo, and Company, insurance companies, and local banks added their funds to the credit picture. However, in the financial panic of 1855, their haphazard business methods aided general economic collapse.[1] Besides, the panic of 1855 left a general distrust of both banks and paper currency. The California legislature of 1855 struck at an apparent abuse and prohibited the exercising of banking privileges or "creating paper to circulate as money."[2] This, of course, was not new in American history. The eastern states had experimented with such legislation for decades. In the 1860s the legislature revised its banking laws, and bankers contemporaneously reformed their procedures. Thereafter, banking institutions provided their traditional financial services to farmers and merchants with greater confidence.

Although paper currency was somewhat tainted, commercial paper was a necessity. The first state legislature provided dealers with a general statute on bills and notes. The 1850 statute declared that all written promises were due as expressed and were negotiable "in like manner as inland bills of exchange, according to the custom of merchants." Importantly, the statute provided a rate structure for damages. Damages were in lieu of interest and were set at 15 percent on paper drawn east of the Rockies and 20 percent if foreign. Further, "if the contents of such bill" were expressed "in money of account of the United States," the amount due and damages for nonpayment had to be "ascertained and determined without any reference to the rate of exchange existing between" California and the place on which the bill had been drawn. If the transaction stipulated payment in a foreign currency, the rate of exchange prevailed.[3] The statute was significant because merchants engaged in interstate and foreign commerce had some certainty in transactions. Even with this statute, many merchants used barter of goods in transactions.

California merchants found credit where they could and regularly had dealings in bills, notes, and barter, particularly in the first two decades. Rodman Price established substantial interests in Monterey and San Francisco in the period 1846-1850. Thereafter, he and his partner, Samuel Ward, ran their California affairs from a New York office dealing in sight bills, bills of exchange, and promissory notes to support California transactions.[4] Matthew Keller, a Los Angeles merchant, winemaker, and rancher, transacted business in cash, promissory notes, and sight bills on English and Australian banks.[5] When money, notes, or bills were unavailable, goods changed hands. George S. Beers of Sawpit Flat reported in 1865 to John D. Goodwin that there was "not a dollar of money in circulation."[6] John Hume wrote his sister in 1858 that in Placerville they had "no paper currency; a bank bill [was] seldom seen, and [was] of no possible use."[7] Although currency and notes circulated in San Francisco in 1864, Fletcher Haight paid in potatoes, hoping to sell his greenbacks "near the close of the campaign."[8] As late as 1880, Ellen Blood of Greenville pondered payment in "grain or vegetables" on small bills.[9]

Promissory note litigation evidenced a judicial concern for adherence to commercial practice and security in transactions. Although gaming contracts were illegal, the California Court recognized that in the hands of a third party, they were enforceable. Chief Justice Hugh C. Murray, speaking for the Court in *Carrier v. Brannan* (1853), argued that

> it needs no authority or arguments to satisfy this court that the practice of gaming is vicious and immoral in its nature, and ruinous to the harmony and well-being of society. Neither do we think that gaming debts have been legalized by the operation of the act of the legislature licensing gaming houses.[10]

The house could not use the courts to collect from its patrons. However, Murray recognized in *Haight v. Joyce* (1852) that a promissory note in the hands of a third party had to be enforced even if originally made to satisfy a gambling debt. "These contracts," Murray said, "can only be held void in the hands of third persons when made so by express statute." The consequences of deciding differently were too grave, the Court reasoned. "Any other decision would destroy confidence in commercial transactions, and open a wide door to fraud and perjury."[11] The underlying assumptions of negotiability and reliance, of crucial importance to the commercial community, would otherwise be undercut. This was explicit instrumentalist reasoning.

Adherence to commercial practice was often an explicit ground for decision. The Court in *Backus v. Minor* (1853) followed mercantile practice in calculating interest. Justice Solomon Heydenfeldt noted that "a different mode of computing interest is common among merchants." Merchants calculated the interest at the contract rate upon both the debt and the payments, resulting in "a slight difference . . . in favor of the debtor."[12] This, Heydenfeldt found, was "a deliberate, methodical plan of doing business, according to a well-comprehended rule." So stating, he continued that there was no authority or reason in "law or in equity" to disturb the method.[13] At a rate of six percent per month, the debtor probably needed such relief. But, more importantly, mercantile practice prevailed. Similarly, settled rules for bills and notes often received the corroborative aid of business practice. The California Court, in stating a rule on holders of negotiable paper endorsed before maturity, reminded the litigants that "the safety and convenience of the commercial community depended on this rule."[14] Similarly, the rule concerning the loss or destruction of negotiable paper "was established for the protection and safety of the commercial community."[15] The liability of an endorser in like manner paralleled "the universal understanding of business men."[16] These statements of business practice were, of course, recognized in the doctrines,[17] but mercantile practice could not supersede a positive rule of law.[18] These jurisprudential positions evidence a strong instrumentalist approach to lawmaking. Commercial practices were important aspects of bills and notes, but the symmetry of legal rules was also a goal of the Court.

The English common law was another source of guidance for the Court, but cases of a commercial nature seldom deviated from mercantile needs. The 1850 legislature adopted the English common law as the rule of decision for the California courts. In several cases English rules determined California law, but always with the aid of a public policy favoring mercantile requirements. For example, in *Wild v. Van Valkenburgh* (1857), the Court adopted the English rule on the place of payment named in a bill or note. Chief Justice Murray rejected American precedents, arguing that Joseph Story and Chancellor Kent both agreed that the English rule was correct. Moreover, American precedents were not based on adequate reasoning and "high authority." Public policy also supported the rule. "This state," Murray argued, "is so far removed from the commercial world, and the rates of exchange so largely against our merchants and citizens, that it would be more proper to adopt a rule which, we think, is founded on some logic, and calculated to protect the interests of our people."[19] Here the Court combined instrumentalist and formalist approaches to decision making.

The Court's care in protecting the security of commercial transactions was more manifest a year later in the case of *Aud v. Magruder* (1858). The case involved the obligation of a surety and the problems of overturning a California precedent only two years old, *Bryan v. Berry* (1856). The Court in *Bryan* had adopted a minority rule that the *Aud* Court felt had an "injurious import." Justice Joseph G. Baldwin for the Court argued that "principles of commercial law, long established and maintained by a consistent course of decision in other States, should not be disturbed." The consequences were too grave. Baldwin saw a tendency "to confusion and uncertainty," giving rise to "perplexing litigation" and doubts in the public mind. Moreover, new rules confused businessmen.

> Men knowing how the law has been generally received and repeatedly adjudged, govern themselves accordingly; but if Courts establish new rules whenever they are dissatisfied with the reasons upon which the old ones rest, the standards of

commercial transactions would be destroyed, and commercial business regulated by a mere guess at what the opinion of Judges for the time might be.[20]

California's commercial intercourse with other states necessitated both security and certainty in "well-settled general rules which prevail in those States as the laws of trade." To further emphasize this point, Baldwin concluded,

> We repeat, the stability and certainty of these rules are of more importance than any fancied benefits which might accrue from any innovation upon the system. Innovation begets innovation, and we can not always see with clearness what is to be the consequence of the new rule established.[21]

The California Court carefully outlined the commercial policy considerations dealers needed. Security and certainty were a goal of contract law generally and of bills and notes particularly.

Promissory note litigation was statistically the largest part of the Court's chattel credit docket. The 203 cases considered constituted 51.7 percent of the docket. Because of the nature of the document, the general credit of individuals was usually the only security. Of the cases considered, 54.2 percent had only a signature as security. While suretyship developed in the period, many notes for a small amount were on the credit of an individual. Who these debtors were is seldom ascertainable from the data. All debtors fell in this "unknown" category, totaling 55 percent. This high percentage was due to the almost universal "unknown" categorization of debtors in promissory note cases.

The California Supreme Court and legislature attempted to provide security and certainty in transactions, but plaintiff-lenders did not do well on appeal. For promissory notes, plaintiffs won 54.7 percent of the time. From 1850 to 1873, 67 plaintiffs won 44 of 91 cases. Although there were fewer cases following the Field Code's adoption, the cases do not indicate that dealers used it successfully in securing their interests. In fact, quite the opposite was true. Error substantial enough to defeat the plaintiff's interests appears to have abounded. Even with the Field Code's multitudinous provisions, the highest one-year plaintiff success score in the period 1874-1882 was 57.1 percent. This, of course, may not indicate great impact in the economy because dealers often seek noncontractual resolution of business disputes. However, it does indicate that the state of the perceived law in books did not find fruition in law in action until at least the mid-1880s.

On the operational level, dealers concerned themselves with making the note and collecting interest and principal. Benjamin S. Eaton scrawled his 1855 note to Matthew Keller on a scrap of paper, agreeing to pay three percent per month.[22] Charles Wolter, a Monterey entrepreneur, made his 1853 note to José Abrego in Spanish.[23] Rodman Price gave his $8,000 note at six percent per month to Robert Rodgers of San Francisco in 1850, promising to pay interest "in advance."[24] Amos Parmalee Catlin wrote a $7,000 note at three percent per month on a half-sheet of blue lined paper and another for $1,500 at two percent on a printed form in 1855 to finance the operations of the American River Water and Mining Company.[25] With the note made, payment was another object of concern. S. F. Folger of San Francisco paid off one note with another.[26] William B. Grave of Castroville proposed to delay payment on one note, borrow money on his note, and pay a third party in hopes of a future potato crop.[27] J. R. Bucklee of San Francisco paid all judgments and bondsmen in greenbacks and interest in gold in 1871.[28] However, when payment was not forthcoming, creditors had to resort to other means.

Credit and collection agencies abounded and used local lawyers to pursue the recalcitrant debtor. Many who left the east to dig for gold or to escape debt or both disappeared in California.[29] Eastern collection agencies sought them through California's bar. John D. Bicknell received requests for collections from Chicago, Philadelphia, Cincinnati, Denver, and small towns in Iowa.[30] But debtors were elusive beings. The Los Angeles law firm of Graves and O'Melveny reported to the Merchants Protective and Collection Agency in 1885 that they could not find the debtor. Further, they added:

> This town and county attract a large immigration much of it floating and it is simply impossible to find strangers when there is no clue as a foundation. We are constantly in receipt of claims of the character of those last mentioned [small debtors from eastern states] and it is rare that we even find the parties and never do we succeed in making a collection.[31]

Commercial firms and lawyers across the state sought credit information and collections from the local bar. Cigar merchants in San Francisco wrote to local lawyers for credit references on local firms prior to shipping orders.[32] More often, they requested the collection of debts, lawyers' fees included.[33]

Individual dealers in the marketplace also went to lawyers to enforce their expectations. Ah Jake of Downieville wrote his countryman, Hai Loe of San Juan, in 1874 that "the lawyer can collect that bill easy."[34] Many saw the attorney as their representative and as an instrument of the system. W. G. Wood wanted J. M. Rothchild of Los Angeles "to bring [the debtor] to Justice."[35] The moral duty to pay had been breached, and the lawyer was to enforce that duty against "very dishonest" men, swindlers, artful dodgers, and liars.[36] Other creditors merely wanted their money back for economic reasons and found "no excuse for failing to pay a just claim."[37] Although law and justice implied a duty to pay to creditors, the debtor saw duty otherwise. C. D. Cushman told David Jacks in 1890 that

> our blessed Savior said (Luke 6-35), "Do good and lend, hoping for nothing again, and your reward shall be great, etc." I do not ask you "to lend hoping for nothing," but if my request borders at all on that line, and you grant it, let it be done with the assurance given by the Savior of a great and heavenly reward.[38]

California debtors may have wanted the Lord as a surety, but when the debtor could not be found, California lawyers did not attach holy assets.

Unfortunately for creditors and their lawyers, debtors and their assets often faded into the frontier landscape. R. E. Arick reported from Panamint that the debtors sought by McConnell, Bicknell, and Rothchild had "left our digging." One had "sold out last spring," and the other had "left but a few days since."[39] John D. Bicknell pursued one debtor to Oregon, but a Portland attorney wrote that "I do not think Farwell is worth much now." Further, "quite a number of Los Angeleans [are] here. We have several collections against Cal. breakdowns, in fact, this seems to be a sort of asylum for 'busted' men."[40] The Rock Island, Illinois, firm of Sweeney, Jackson, and Walker told Bicknell in 1881 that they found the debtor, but they considered him "as execution proof."[41] Jackson A. Graves reported to one client that he attempted to collect on the note, but the debtor said that he "will not pay a cent. He is also 'BUSTED'."[42] With such news, some creditors gave up.[43] Siter, Price, and Company of Philadelphia wrote to the San Francisco law firm of Wells and Haight in 1854 calling the notes back from collection to avoid "any unreasonable expense." The facts dictated the action. "Knorr and Fuller have dissolved, and E. M. Seller and Co. [is] out of business, worse than nothing--the expense would fall on us."[44] Although the promissory note provided a viable mechanism for bootstrap financing and a circulating medium, the underlying insecurity of collection limited the effectiveness of the instrument. Further, the fact of noncollection was a limitation of the legal system. Regardless of the obligation, marketplace reality controlled the range of the promissory note.

Bills and notes were a significant portion of the docket and valuable items in litigation. Notes before the Court varied in value from $100 to $32,000. Table 1 indicates the average value of notes in litigation as well as the maximum value in a given year. Case data without note values were not included in the calculations. No data years simply indicates that notes litigated in those years did not have their values reported in the *California Reporter*.

The California Supreme Court also outlined the law of another credit form, the pledge. A pledge transaction involved an agreement whereby a lender or party extending credit took or retained possession of an asset of the debtor as security.[45] Reported court decisions on pledge transactions date to the Middle Ages, but even in nineteenth-century California, the pledge transaction could be a risky venture. The problem was that pledge assets were often bulky commodities like wheat or readily negotiable intangibles like securities. Both were fungible and rapidly convertible to cash. Pledging assets was a rapid but risky means of mobilizing capital.

The California Court attempted to protect debtor interests, but often both creditor and debtor were left without assets or recourse. "The object of the law," Justice Erskine M. Ross stated in *Hill v. Finigan* (1882), was "for the purpose of guarding against the greed and rapicity of money-lenders and those who deal in securities of this mining stock character."[46] But too often securities got lost in the shuffle of frontier transactions. *Ambrose v. Evans* (1884) involved such a situation.[47] W. G. Miller endorsed and delivered railroad stock to Henry Toomey "for safe-keeping." Toomey delivered the stock to Gomer Evans "as security for a loan of $350.00." Miller also assigned the stock to Samuel Ambrose, who then gave notice to Evans and demanded delivery. Evans refused. Justice Samuel B. McKee for the Court analyzed the problem.

> The indorsement and delivery of the stock by Miller to Toomey
> clothed the latter with the indicia of the legal ownership of the
> stock, so as to enable him to deal with it as his own; and when
> he, as owner, pledged the twenty shares as security for the
> payment of a debt which he owed to Evans, the transaction was
> legal, and the transfer of the stock for that purpose vested the
> pledgee with a right to it as security for the money advanced.[48]

TABLE 1

PROMISSORY NOTE LITIGATION VALUE

Year	Average	Maximum
1850	2,250.00	2,250
1851	1,498.00	1,498
1852	2,135.00	3,900
1853	9,111.75	17,000
1854	551.00	602
1855	2,660.00	4,320
1856	15,044.50	25,089
1857	1,010.00	1,500
1858	8,427.80	32,000
1859	1,119.25	3,000
1860	1,583.33	4,000
1861	493.29	828
1862	7,271.00	7,271
1863	399.00	500
1864	1,229.00	3,000
1865	4,031.33	5,000
1866	1,447.00	1,447
1867	5,655.71	20,000
1868	4,815.00	10,425
1869	1,608.33	2,100
1870	no data	no data
1871	3,233.33	6,500
1872	2,473.80	3,591
1873	999.25	2,500
1874	1,290.00	2,500
1875	4,434.33	12,691
1876	2,201.67	3,205
1877	4,500.00	4,500
1878	1,500.00	1,500
1879	no data	no data
1880	3,731.00	19,000
1881	7,066.00	14,957
1882	2,000.00	2,000
1883	2,731.83	6,750
1884	814.75	1,384
1885	8,375.00	16,000
1886	no data	no data
1887	3,126.33	8,154
1888	3,040.00	10,000
1889	3,700.88	12,000
1890	588.67	1,000

Not only did small transactions fall prey to the intricacies of the pledge, but also large investments were lost when creditors allowed obvious bankrupts too much latitude.[49] Pledge cases on the appellate docket broke 50/50 on the plaintiff-defendant success scores, but pledges constituted only 5.1 percent of the docket. Although the pledge was a simple security device with few formal requisites, the nature of the security often caused parties legal difficulty.

The chattel mortgage was a legal invention of the nineteenth century, and the California Court faced problems current in the nation. In working through the legal web, the Court was hampered by legislative work that frustrated the device itself.

The chattel mortgage was a creature of statute. Statutes typically validated mortgages of personal property without immediate delivery and possession by the lender if the mortgage were recorded. California adopted such a statute in 1853 after rejecting the concept in 1850.[50] In 1857 the legislators listed property that could be mortgaged, thus giving birth to a series of trouble cases and of session laws.

The Chattel Mortgage Act of 1857 listed personal property that could be mortgaged, stated the required contents of the instrument, and provided for its recording.[51] The list included numerous personal items as well as commercial property, but even within the list certain commodities had limits as assets. Hotel furniture and upholstery could be mortgaged only "when for purchase money." Watercraft had to be over five tons. But more seriously, prompted by the panic atmosphere following 1855, the legislature's listing implied exclusion of unlisted goods, limiting the line of credit of many entrepreneurs.

The California Supreme Court narrowly construed the legislature's handiwork. In *Gassner v. Patterson and Timson* (1863), the Court found that billiard tables were not included in chattel mortgage statutes. Justice Edwin B. Crocker for the Court gave the statute a strict construction.[52] For the Court to act as a legislature, Crocker reasoned, would deny the benefits of the statute. Further, the present case was "perhaps one of hardship upon the plaintiff"; it was a consequence of "his own oversight and neglect."[53] Lenders had to pay close attention to the items listed or, as in the case of the railroads, go to the legislature to change the law to include railroad equipment.[54] But with an ever expanding list of items and compliance with statutory recording provisions, lenders did have a reliable security interest.

The chattel mortgage was, in fact, the most reliable security interest. The plaintiff-defendant success score broke 70.8/29.2. However, the chattel mortgage constituted only 6.1 percent of the docket. This low proportion suggests that the reliability of this type of transaction resulted in settlement rather than litigation as a rule. The value of the chattel mortgages ranged from $550 to $90,000. The cases were bunched in the mid-1860s and late 1880s. The types of security included crops, hotel furniture, machinery, general merchandise, and a railroad.

Although mechanics' liens differed from other credit devices, they were nonetheless important financial devices. Lien statutes provided a broader lien than conveyed by common law to those who worked on various structures. This was crucial to wage security and thereby gave entrepreneurs a line of credit for the building of California.

The legislative history of lien law was one of institutional inertia, inept draftsmanship, and technical confusion. In this context the California Supreme Court enjoyed an instrumental position, adding to the coherence and orientation of session laws. By pointing out the logical inconsistencies, inequities, and plain mistakes in session laws, the Court aided the legislators in providing a remedy for artisans, laborers, and suppliers.

The first legislature passed a general statute, but soon found its terms too narrow. The 1850 session produced a lien law giving to "all masterbuilders, mechanics, lumber merchants," and others performing labor or providing materials "for the construction or repair of any building or wharf" a lien "to the extent of the labor done or materials furnished or both."[55] The act also supplied claimants with recording and enforcement procedure. This gave claimants a lien nonexistent in Mexican law and broader than the common law also adopted in 1850.[56] But in 1853 the legislature had to extend the 1850 statute's provisions to include "bridges, ditches, flumes, or aqueducts, constructed to create hydraulic power, or for mining purposes." Similarly, the legislature extended the class of claimants to "contractors, journeymen or laborers."[57]

In the brief interim before these changes, the California Court strictly construed the statute and limited its reach. Numerous dealers had attempted to use the mechanic's lien law as a creditor's catchall. In cases like *Bottomly v. Grace Church* (1852), the Court had limited the act's application.[58] Justice Heydenfeldt stated that the statute never contemplated that a lumbermerchant could follow materials sold under general terms, to obtain a lien. The language of the act, he said, was "sufficiently explicit, and must be strictly construed." The strict construction was necessitated because the statute gave rights in derogation of common law.[59] Similarly, the Court denied application of the statute to a lender whose loan was "expressly for the payment of materials and labor."[60] These cases illustrated a certain degree of confusion regarding the application of these statutes, but the Court also strictly construed application to work within the scope of the lien concept. For example, in *Burt v. Washington* (1853), the Court denied application of the lien law to labor on a bridge because a bridge was not a "building or wharf."[61] As noted above, the legislature did extend the lien's protection to such circumstances. Unfortunately for the plaintiff, the remedy came too late.

The Court in the 1850s also alerted legislators to problems of priority and notice. In *Rose v. Munie* (1854), a mechanic found that a prior unrecorded mortgage barred his recovery.[62] Chief Justice Murray outlined the problem.

> There is no obligation on the mortgagee to have his mortgage recorded, and that the same would only be void, as against subsequent purchasers or mortgagees without notice. Not only is the Mechanic's Lien Law defective, but also the Recording Act itself, and it may be safely said, that no provision is made for recording a numerous class of liens.[63]

In the absence of statutory guidance, the English common law prevailed. Since common law did not require recording, the law imposed the burden of ascertaining all outstanding titles and incumbrances upon all who would bargain with another. Although there was "some apparent hardship in the rule," it was for the legislature to act. Without such action an intolerable commercial situation existed, creating suspicion that in turn retarded construction. The financial panic of 1855, while identified with shoddy banking practices, had an accomplice in unstable and uncertain construction contracts.

The legislative session of 1856 produced a new mechanic's lien law, but it was filled with the flaws of the past. The act extended the lien to all artisans, builders, mechanics, and others working on buildings, wharves, or superstructures. This lien was to be recorded in a "Lien Book: at Recorder's office." The land on which a building was located was also subject to the lien. In addition, the legislators gave subcontractors a remedy against general contractors who were tardy in paying.[64] However, within a matter of months, the legislators were explaining and supplementing their statute. On April 19, 1856, they clarified the preference of mechanics' liens.[65] They later supplemented the act, extending it "to include . . . bridges, ditches, flumes or aqueducts."[66] But these failures of draftsmanship caused hardship.

The Court found that a claim on a canal had no statutory support. Stephen J. Field speaking for the Court in *Ellison v. Jackson Water Company* (1859), found that the repealer clause of the 1856 statute had carried with it the 1853 Supplementary Act, which included ditches. As a ditch was "not a building, or a wharf, and in no sense could be designated a superstructure," the $48,154 lien claim had no statutory basis.[67]

Priority concepts were little clearer. In *Crowell v. Gilmore* (1861), Justice Baldwin found that there was nothing in the statute giving priority to the mechanic who made the first contract or commenced work first. The act excluded this idea. With an intervening mortgage, problems increased. Baldwin reflected that it was possible "that some confusion might arise from the practical working of the statute," but the fault was with the law and the Court "had no power to remedy it."[68] Judicial restraint combined here with a lack of statutory specificity to further complicate transactions.

Legislative efforts to remedy statutory weakness often failed. The Mechanic's Lien Act of 1858 amended parts of the 1856 law. But, as the Court noted in *McAlpin v. Duncan* (1860), the act was "not a little confused and difficult of satisfactory construction." In fact, as Justice Baldwin maintained, "if it were designed to give to the sub-contractor and laborer a lien . . . for the entire amount of the last or sub-contract" without regard for the prime contract price, a "curious anomaly" existed whereby the whole property of the owner could be incumbered by the general contractor as he successively made subcontracts.[69] To avoid this, the Court rightly limited subcontractors' liens to the contract price and required them to follow statutory notice procedure.

The legislation of the 1850s demonstrated a lack of basic machinery designed to develop systematic definition of public policy. The value judgments were clear enough. It was in the public interest to confer a lien on those who labored or supplied materials to build California. The problem was with implementation. The legislature's tendency to enumerate in specific terms and the Court's tending to construe those terms strictly often defeated the practical goals that the legislature sought to fulfill. However, the Court's continuous efforts to promote coherent remedies did produce results.

The legal muddle created by California lien law had specific detrimental results in litigation. The Court handled lien claims of great value in its first decade. (See Table 2.)

TABLE 2

MECHANIC'S LIEN LITIGATION VALUE

Year	Average	Total of Cases	Maximum
1850	1,148.00	1,148.00	1,148
1852	2,481.67	7,445.00	5,000
1856	2,196.00	2,196.00	2,196
1857	3,920.00	11,760.00	10,000
1858	1,810.50	3,621.00	1,953
1859	25,027.00	50,054.00	48,1540
1860	4,464.67	13,396.00	11,850

Lien claimants did not find the statutory remedy of great value in a majority of the cases in the decade. Plaintiff-lenders did not get better than a 50/50 score until 1856 (Table 3).

TABLE 3

PLAINTIFF/DEFENDANT SUCCESS SCORES FOR MECHANIC'S LIEN CASES

Year	Plaintiff	Defendant
1850	0.0%	100.0%
1851	0.0%	100.0%
1852	33.3%	66.7%
1853	50.0%	50.0%
1854	50.0%	50.0%
1855	0.0%	100.0%
1856	66.7%	33.3%
1857	25.0%	75.0%
1858	66.7%	33.3%
1859	66.7%	33.3%
1860	33.3%	66.7%

Table 4 indicates that most of the cases providing data concerned the construction trades, particularly residential and commercial buildings. The building of canals also concerned the lien and the Court in the last years of the decade.

TABLE 4

MECHANICS' LIENS: TYPES OF LENDERS AND DEBTORS
(unknówns suppressed)

Year	Lender	Debtor(type of security)
1850	lumbermerchant	building
1851	lumbermerchant	building
1852	lumbermerchant (2)	building (3)
1853	mechanic (2)	building (2)
1854	mechanic (2)	building (2)
1855	lumbermerchant	building
1856	mechanic (2)	dwelling house (2)
	materialman	lumber
1857	mechanic (3)	dwelling house (3)
	lumbermerchant	building
1858	mechanic (3)	machinery
		dwelling house
		canal
1859	mechanic (5)	building (2)
		land
		canal (2)
1860	mechanic (3)	dwelling house (2)

The term "mechanic" covers all artisans including carpenters, plumbers, and the like. Numbers in parentheses indicate the number of cases involved for the lender-debtor in the given year. Building designation indicates that the data did not specifically distinguish the structure from a dwelling house, that the word "building" was used in the report, or that the report indicated that a commercial building was involved. Tables 2 to 4 indicate that the mechanic's lien litigation of the decade was extremely important. Not only the problems of doctrine, legislative draftsmanship, but also the security for large sums of money were involved. Moreover, as Table 3 demonstrates, the plaintiff-lender was not secure. That this insecurity contributed to a generally unstable financial climate is certain.

The California Supreme Court contributed to a more workable policy as it began to view the mechanic's lien laws as remedial legislation, subject to liberal rather than strict construction. However, the Court did continue to demand a substantial compliance with statutory procedures. For example, the Court stated in 1873:

The lien provided by the statute can be maintained only by a substantial observance of its provisions, and though we are certainly not disposed to defeat the lien by a nice criticism of the language in which the claim is set forth, we are not at liberty to uphold it in the face of the total omission to comply with a plain requirement of the Act.[70]

Here plaintiff failed to state the name of the employer in the lien claim and lost. Through 1890 others lost, and generally for the same reasons.[71]

The fact that no pattern develops from the 1870s can be attributed in large part to the procedural errors committed by claimants. The 1889-1890 period, however, is a reliable indicator of relative success, in that 23 cases were decided in the two year period with high plaintiff-lender success scores. (See Table 5.)

The Court also included service as part of the lien concept. In *McCormick v. Los Angeles Water Company* (1870), the Court found that a cook was not entitled to a lien for his wages. Justice Joseph B. Crockett found the consequences too horrifying.

If every one who contributed indirectly and remotely to the work is entitled to a lien, no reason is perceived why a surgeon called to set a broken limb of one of the laborers, whereby he will be enabled at an early day to resume work on the building, might not assert a lien; but services of this character, not performed on the building, are not within the provinces of the statute.[72]

Although the Court found a cook not a mechanic, the legislature was contemporaneously expanding the lien concept to include ranchers, stablekeepers, loggers, logging camp personnel, and farm laborers working at threshing.[73] With this legislative indication of intent and the Court's remedial view of the statutes, the justices shifted away from the *McCormick* position. When lawyers argued for the mechanic's lien concept of benefit to property, the Court simply cited statute "sufficiently comprehensive to include a case like this."[74] With the legislature the judges had come to recognize that liberal provision for wage security was in the public interest. Moreover, such care for the worker's interests ensured more stable transactions and in effect provided entrepreneurs with a line of credit for obtaining their labor supply, even if the terms of credit were still technical and involved.

At the operational level, lawyers negotiated first and litigated when negotiation failed. For example, John D. Bicknell of Los Angeles first sent a letter on behalf of the claimant, notifying the debtor of the mechanic's lien and advising settlement "to relieve me of the painful duty of foreclosing."[75] When negotiation failed, Bicknell proceeded to foreclose the lien.[76] The advantage to client and lawyer alike was the operational fact that there was usually real estate to foreclose upon, sell, and distribute to clients for the lien interest and to attorneys for fees.

The problems of collecting a debt in California were a limitation at the operational level of the legal system. The law presumed that when a contract had been consummated, the persons were obligated to perform or pay damages. Performance was commonly the payment of interest and principal when due or wages when due. Whenever the behavior of debtors did not meet the expectations of creditors, the latter resorted to the legal

TABLE 5

PLAINTIFF/DEFENDANT SUCCESS SCORES

Year	Plaintiff	Defendant
1850	0.0%	100.0%
1860	33.3%	66.7%
1861	100.0%	0.0%
1862	100.0%	0.0%
1863	66.7%	33.3%
1864	no data	no data
1865	50.0%	50.0%
1866	100.0%	0.0%
1867	100.0%	0.0%
1868	100.0%	0.0%
1869	33.3%	66.7%
1870	66.7%	33.3%
1871	100.0%	0.0%
1872	66.7%	33.3%
1873	66.7%	33.3%
1874	60.0%	40.0%
1875	no data	no data
1876	0.0%	100.0%
1877	no data	no data
1878	0.0%	100.0%
1879	no data	no data
1880	44.4%	55.6%
1881	100.0%	0.0%
1882	60.0%	40.0%
1883	60.0%	40.0%
1884	33.3%	66.7%
1885	66.7%	33.3%
1886	25.0%	75.0%
1887	33.3%	66.7%
1888	60.0%	40.0%
1889	81.8%	18.2%
1890	58.3%	41.7%
	56.6%	43.4%

TOTAL 1850-1890, 122 Cases

system. First, creditors made personal demands for timely performance. Then they went to lawyers, who sent letters of demand, spied out assets, parried debtor delay mindful of the Statute of Limitations, filed lawsuits including attachments and foreclosures, and worried about the judgment-proof debtor, insolvency proceedings, and reasonable attorney's fees. The process was often complex and frustrating.

The creditor's letter of demand could have mixed results. Many paid. Others did not. Matthew Keller, a Los Angeles businessman, wrote to Thomas J. Gentry in 1860 demanding that payment be made immediately to his account at Wells, Fargo, and Company.[77] Mrs. W. H. Harrison made similar demands, but "so far I have not been able to collect a dollar, possibly I never shall."[78] The creditor left with paper and no money often turned to the California bar for help.

Creditors saw the law as far more effective in collecting debts than lawyers. James T. Jenkins of Spanish Ranch told his lawyer to "attach and make my account good with whatever you can find attachable."[79] Charles Chapelain of Rich Bar sent a promissory note to John D. Goodwin in Quincy for collection through "suits and attachments."[80] Mere referral to an attorney was sometimes effective in motivating debtors. Hugh McCutcheon of Genesse Mine wrote to Goodwin on August 7, 1875, to collect from Angus McIntyre on a note. "I want you to go after any property you can get hold of," he demanded. Further, "he has not done as he agreed to and I don't rely upon his word anymore." Seven weeks later Hugh wrote again, reporting a "different arrangement" with Angus and directing Goodwin to stop the lawsuit and send his bill for services.[81]

Lawyers started their pursuit of debtor performance with the threat of a lawsuit. Jackson A. Graves sent form letters to debtors that concluded with "please call and adjust and save me the unpleasant task of suing you and yourself the costs of suit."[82] Graves also used the soft-sell approach. In 1879 he wrote one debtor informing him of three notes he had for collecting, asking whether he could "pay them now," and concluding that he did not "want to sue."[83] In 1885 Graves asked John R. Egan to "come in . . . and try and fix something up" because "we do not wish to wrong you in any manner and will give you time to pay."[84] John D. Bicknell used similar letters of demand, advising payment to "save all costs."[85] When several debtors inscribed their names to notes, Bicknell pursued each to satisfy the debt. In 1874 he wrote John Rumpp regarding an overdue note of his, C. Henry and Jacob F. Gerkens. Gerkens had failed to pay, and Bicknell instructed John to settle up to avoid the costs of litigation.[86] Letters led to payment in some cases. In others the creditor could decide to drop the matter. In 1888 the law firm of Graves, O'Melveny, and Shankland informed the Fairview Development Company that their client Isaias Hellman declined "to bring an action, saying that he does not care to make your fight in the name of his bank (Farmers and Merchants Bank of Los Angeles), as the bank is not seeking Court notoriety, and as a matter of business, of course, desires to avoid all litigation."[87] However, the bulk of the unfulfilled demands led to lawsuits.

Prior to filing the lawsuit, lawyers as well as creditors sought assets, for without assets, attachment, lawsuits, and the like were generators of frustration rather than recovery. One creditor executed on beans, potatoes, and pumpkins.[88] Another looked to hay and cattle for repayment.[89] But even if assets were found, too often other creditors joined the race to the courthouse. John W. Forbes of Montserrate reported that the affairs of Stewart and McKenzie of Julian were "in very bad order"; so bad, in fact, that "various attachments have been served on them." Then he advised the Los Angeles attorney representing a creditor "to make an attachment of their whole stock at once as people up there are tired of waiting and many talk of attaching."[90] But with assets, attorneys could "squeeze the amount out of [the debtor] by threatening attachment" as well as by attachment itself.[91]

The process of collecting was not without delay, particularly when threats were parried with promises. Many debtors asked for mercy and promised to pay "after the harvest," "as soon as the money can be spared," "until I can see my cattle [sold]," until "I can get them [hogs] in good order [for sale]," or when "I can market my butter and stock."[92] Promises often delayed lawsuits, but even with suit and judgment, lawyers still had to collect on the judgment. Granville H. Oury, a Phoenix, Arizona, attorney formerly of Missouri, California, and Tucson, wrote to John Bicknell and his client George Hanson in 1875 and told them that his client would pay "from time to time . . . such sums as he may be able to get hold of."[93] But even with time, assets, and promises, circumstance could crush the hopes of creditors. John Mohler Studebaker obviously knew wagons better than land prices in Los Angeles, and was the victim of "a very foolish deal." The transaction involved John rolling $8,000 into the Los Angeles boom blocks of the late 1880s, getting caught short and selling for $3,000, and in 1888 wanting the buyer to pay or give security, as Studebaker did "not consider the property worth the amount he owes us."[94] The notes that helped the boom of the 1880s were hard to collect when the boom was over.

Notes were even harder to collect when the creditor allowed too much time to pass. California's Statute of Limitations barred actions "in this state on any note made in another state, or any judgment rendered in another state, two years after the maturity of the note or the entry of the judgment."[95] For some it was too late. Harriet E. Cain of Warsaw, Missouri, loaned money to a Mr. Parkinson "nearly 20 years" ago, and wanted John Bicknell of Los Angeles to help.[96] The law was of no help. Notes made in California had a five-year statute, but lawyers could not help clients who had waited one month or one year too long.[97] Prudent creditors saw the statute's deadline nearing and wrote their attorneys to "put the matter in such shape as will render us secure."[98] Attorneys would negotiate new notes or new notes with a mortgage, or they would proceed to judgment.[99]

Despite these efforts, insolvency could thwart creditor expectations. In the 1850s there was a near universal complaint that the state bankruptcy laws made it ludicrously easy to defraud creditors and still come out rich.[100] In particular, many of the San Francisco merchants left heavy debt behind them in the east.[101] Between 1855 and 1860, there were 692 bankruptcy cases involving over $17.5 million.[102] Large numbers of others made settlements of outstanding debts at 30 to 50 cents on the dollar.[103] The bank failures of the period combined with the incredible uncertainty in the financial and mercantile community produced substantial anxiety for businessmen and work for lawyers.

The depression of 1854 that triggered the bank failures of 1855 sent smaller institutions and many San Francisco merchants into bankruptcy. Bankrupts as well as creditors needed lawyers to work through the intricacies of statute, judicial decision, and prudent negotiations. Alvin Adams found himself in such need in 1855 when Adams and Company, an express and banking firm, suspended business. His lawyers, "after as thorough and anxious a consideration . . . as the urgency of the occasion allowed," filed suits to dissolve the partnership, settle accounts, and liquidate debts."[104] Twenty years later lawyers still worked to put some parties into bankruptcy. Some made assignments for the benefit of creditors; others were involuntarily put into bankruptcy; and still others obtained "the consent of a number of creditors to compromise at 25%."[105] Others tried valiantly to avoid insolvency. John B. McGee told his attorney, John D. Goodwin, in 1875 that he wanted to avoid bankruptcy because "it would place [his] friends . . . in [a] bad position."[106] Another client, J. S. Bransford of Taylorsville, instructed Goodwin "to assign all partnership property for benefit of creditors rather than bankruptcy." It would "be better for us and much better for the creditors as much expense will be avoided."[107] Other clients wanted advice on action for other reasons. B. F. Seibert of Anaheim asked John Bicknell about insolvency and whether his creditors could levy against "the colt." "If it can be taken," Seibert probed, "can I make a bill of sale to any one who will, in future, return it to me?"[108] This type of paper transaction was fraud and would defeat a discharge in bankruptcy.[109] With creditors at the door, the debtor had a variety of statutory means of extinguishing debts and starting over. Creditors had the art of negotiation and the fast pen of their lawyers to attach goods prior to bankruptcy. Too often the race to the courthouse was part of an uncertain statutory game. Even by 1885, Graves and O'Melveny would confess to another attorney that "the machinery for discharge of an assignee for benefit of creditors is not very clearly laid down."[110] For creditors it was clear that hard times brought uncertainty about ever collecting their money at interest. Too often, the law was not functional at the operational level to enforce expectations.

California's legal problems with elemental credit devices demonstrated the limitations of the legal system and its eventual ability to function. Both the legislature and the Court floundered amid the turbulent economy of California's first decade. Exchange transactions suffered as a result. However, with experience, the Court and the legislature worked to provide dealers with the security and certainty they desired. But even here, as demonstrated by the lien cases, operatives in the frontier economy did not always follow statutory guidelines. In sum, the workings of law in action did not consistently approximate the design of the lawmakers. However, the design did provide dealers with the system needed for the commercial and industrial growth of the twentieth century.

6
ADMIRALTY LAW

California lawmakers in the period 1850-1890 attempted to provide accessible forums and legislation attuned to the state's commercial problems and developed admiralty law that conflicted with the U. S. Constitution. Although the leading cases are well known to constitutional historians and admiralty lawyers, the California cases and their struggle with issues of sovereignty and federalism are little known in state history. The cases demonstrate a vital sense of state sovereignty, encouraged by a confused federal admiralty law, and illustrate the continuing effort of California lawmakers to provide commerce with usable law in a frontier state.

The developing federal law of admiralty to 1850 provided state lawmakers with a confused jurisdictional jurisprudence. The law of admiralty in definition was relatively clear. It was the corpus of rules, concepts, and legal practices governing certain centrally important concerns of the business of carrying goods and passengers by water.[1] Exactly what these concerns were had been worked out in world maritime law and practice and in English legal history. The dual questions of what was received as the law of admiralty and which courts in a federal system should adjudicate the issues were unclear when our nation was formed.

The U. S. Supreme Court in dealing with jurisdictional questions necessarily struggled with federalism issues. In the early national period, the Court made strong nationalistic statements of exclusive federal admiralty jurisdiction.[2] However, in the face of increasing vehement attacks upon federal admiralty jurisdiction on the inland waterways, the Supreme Court retreated.[3] First, the Court found, in the *General Smith* (1819), that state law governed a vessel obtaining repairs and supplies in its home port.[4] Then, in the *Steamboat Thomas Jefferson* (1825), the Supreme Court yielded federal jurisdiction beyond the ebb and flow of the tide.[5] A quarter-century later, the Court reasserted federal authority on the nation's navigable waters in *Propeller Genesse Chief v. Fitzhugh* (1851).[6] Federal jurisdiction was again complete, including the rivers and lakes of the nation.

The California Supreme Court before and after *Propeller Genesse Chief* considered its admiralty jurisdiction to extend concurrently to all subjects of maritime commerce. In the Court's first decade, it presumed the state's sovereign power to extend state jurisdiction to interests of maritime commerce. It turned constitutional challenges aside with equal vigor. The California Court also construed federal statues involving maritime commerce. This vigorous states' rightism was briefly tempered by the Civil War and the U. S. Supreme Court, but the California Court's vigorous interpretation of state sovereignty perpetuated a confused jurisdictional situation well into the twentieth century. However mistaken the nineteenth-century California Court was concerning its admiralty jurisdiction, its concept of sovereignty was significant and helps explain both the development of general state jurisprudence and the leadership role of the California Court.

The California Supreme Court in the 1850s received maritime cases and law as if they were mere attributes of state business. For example, in *Innis v. the Steamer Senator* (1851), the Court considered and decided a case involving the collision of river steamers in San Francisco harbor. The Court never doubted nor questioned its jurisdiction, even though the maritime tort was within the ebb and flow of the tide and even though collision was a traditional part of admiralty jurisdiction. Further, since no custom of the harbor could be established by counsel, the Court decided the issue on general maritime law principles.

In the same session the Court considered the extent of its jurisdiction and found it complete. In *Pugh v. Gillam* (1851), the Court confronted the defendant's counsel arguments that it had no jurisdiction and that the plaintiff should sue in a British court.[8] The plaintiff was a British seaman discharged by the master of the vessel without any fault on the seaman's part. Left stranded in San Francisco without his wages for the 18-month voyage, the seaman went to court. The defense raised the jurisdiction issue, but the court would hear none of it. Justice Nathaniel Bennett, a New York Barnburner, replied for the Supreme Court that "in a case like the present, the state courts not only may, but ought to take cognizance of the action." Bennett continued citing international duty and a compelling state interest, the welfare rolls.[9] Bennett's argument was states' rightist in that it implyingly rejected the obvious exclusive federal jurisdiction in the case. As was well known, a seaman's wages were secured by a right in his ship. Maritime law gave the seaman a right conceived of as a property interest in the ship. This was a "sacred lien" enduring as long as a plank of the ship remained.[10] But the Court simply assumed that it had jurisdiction and acted accordingly.

The Court handled several other problems of maritime consequence in 1851. It construed charter parties (a contract by which a ship is let to a merchant for the conveyances of goods on a determined voyage to one or more places) by the general rules of maritime law. In the process the Court considered evidence of custom in San Francisco harbor and determined the rights of a coal merchant seeking to enforce a supply lien.[11, 12]

The Court also made a strong statement regarding control of state waters. In *Gunter v. Geary* (1851), Chief Justice S. C. Hastings, a former Iowa congressman and later California attorney general, asserted that "the absolute right of a state to control, regulate, and improve the navigable waters within its jurisdiction, as an attribute of sovereignty, cannot be in any manner disputed."[13] The case differed from the maritime cases in that the state opposed the rights of a private party and not federal jurisdiction. Further, the state interest in tidal lands was more firmly imbedded in American jurisprudence. But the statement by Hastings was nonetheless an affirmation of complete sovereignty over navigable waters.

In 1852 the Court went even further in asserting the state's authority over maritime law. In *Averill v. the Steamer Hartford* (1852), the Court defended the state statute granting it admiralty jurisdiction. Justice Solomon Heydenfeldt, a South Carolinian who practiced law in Alabama before coming to California, delivered the opinion of the Court. The sixth chapter of the Practice Act conferred admiralty jurisdiction on district courts, Heydenfeldt stated without hesitation. Further, their proceedings were governed by the principles and forms of admiralty courts except where governed by statute. Here a problem arose because California had altered a general admiralty rule.[14] To avoid the problem, the Court construed the act to mean that the first in time to serve process had jurisdiction.[15]

Although opposing counsel did not revive the jurisdiction issue until 1855, the Court continued to handle ordinary maritime business. The Court settled the relative liability of colliding vessels.[16] The state statute concerning wharfage gave the Court interpretative difficulties as it was "extremely awkward and ungainly," but the justices found its intent clear. At the operational level, law firms like Halleck, Peachy, and Billings handled admiralty cases in both state and federal courts without seeming contradiction.[17] It was business as usual until 1855.

In *Taylor v. the Steamer Columbia* (1855), the Court confronted a breach of a maritime contract involving a vessel that moved completely in interstate commerce and only on the high seas. The vessel's only contact with California was its incidental disembarking of passengers. But Justice Heydenfeldt would hear none of counsel's assertions of unconstitutionality. "The States are original sovereigns," he stated, "with all powers of sovereignty not expressly delegated by the Federal compact."[18] Hence, Congress had no authority to make the jurisdiction exclusively federal.[19] Heydenfeldt supported this conclusion with reference to the *Federalist* and two California Supreme Court cases including *Averill*.

The states' rightism overtones of the opinion were excruciatingly evident. Heydenfeldt adopted the compact theory of union. He also used strict constructionist theory to arrive at his conclusion. Although John Marshall had rejected these theories in several landmark cases, Marshall's interposition argument in maritime cases was not dissimilar. The important distinction was, of course, the international, nonconstitutional interrelationship of nations as opposed to the federal constitutional relationship of the states and the federal government. Heydenfeldt's constitutionalism was one the Confederates adopted in arguing for the constitutionality of civil war and states' rights.

With the Practice Act section conferring jurisdiction firmly enshrined in constitutionalism, the Court continued its maritime business. Issues involving freight paid in advance on a charter party and insurance on advance freight did not deter the Court. If difficulty of interpretation arose, then the Court looked to English maritime rules.[20] The justices also seemed comfortable handling a $10,000 insurance claim for a vessel lost in tow on the high seas.[21] But three cases in 1856 and 1857 caused the Court to strain to find jurisdiction.

In *Davidson v. Gorham* (1856), the Court construed two federal statutes to decide a case involving an $85,000 mortgage on a vessel. The parties sold the vessel while it was on the high seas, mortgaged it, and assigned the mortgage. The second owner's creditors were before the Court, attempting to have the mortgage set aside. The Court, in arriving at a decision, construed the federal Registry Act of 1792 and the Registration Act of 1850. Justice Heydenfeldt construed the 1792 act, strictly finding that only registered vessels were "vessels of the United States." Since the 1850 act referred to "vessels of the United States," and a sale with the failure to register also forfeited the status, the vessel involved was not a "vessel of the United States" under the 1850 act. The 1850 act provided that without the recording of the conveyance of "any vessel of the United States," the conveyance was not valid except against the "grantor or mortgagor."[22] The Court's decision obviously undercut congressional intent and weakened the certainty of secured interests in vessels. But the decision must have satisfied local merchants. Significantly, the Court willingly construed federal law with impunity and without citing any compelling state interest for doing so.

The Court also considered the possible conflict of the 1850 Registration Act with the California Statute of Frauds. In *Mitchell v. Steelman* (1857), the Court recognized the commerce clause authority for the federal act.[23] Justice Peter H. Burnett, a Tennessee attorney, Missouri merchant, and the first governor of California, argued for the Court:

> The act of Congress has established a uniform, plain practical and secure rule, for the sale and mortgage of vessels; and this regulation leaves the owners of these vessels of commerce, and all persons dealing with them, the means of protection without injury to either party. But if these vessels are still subject to the laws of the different States, after Congress has legislated upon the subject, then there can be no certain and uniform rule. From the rapid extension and increasing importance of our commerce, these provisions of the act of Congress become indispensable.[24]

This Burnett based on *Gibbons v. Ogden*, Chief Justice John Marshall's celebrated commerce clause decision. But Burnett went further. "Vessels completely engaged in the internal commerce of a State, and that never go beyond its limits, are admitted to be within the exclusive jurisdiction of the State."[25] Here Burnett read more into Marshall's opinion than existed. Marshall did not mention vessels, only "commerce." Burnett went on to distinguish ships in foreign commerce. "It is therefore necessary that Congress should have entire power over all vehicles of commerce in such cases."[26] The Court acknowledged Congress' power in this case, but the justices obviously did not consider admiralty jurisdiction exclusively vested in the federal courts.

In *Marziou v. Pioche* (1857), the Court violated the dicta on foreign vessels with impunity. In *Marziou* the captain of a French vessel engaged in the commerce between Bordeaux and Sydney had obtained a loan by pledging the ship and its cargo for security for the debt. Justice Burnett simply applied the general maritime law rules to the case and gave the plaintiff judgment.[27] Here, the case on diversity of citizenship and/or admiralty jurisdiction should have been in a federal court. On public policy grounds, the case should have been heard in admiralty in a federal court. It was not. One suspects that the local merchant wanted to use the state courts to achieve more rapid recovery in damages, and the local bar avoided the federal bench for similar reasons.

Until 1871 the California Supreme Court continued to handle ordinary admiralty business without questioning its jurisdiction. At the operational level, the bar carried on its admiralty work settling and litigating cases.[28] In 1867 the U. S. Supreme Court gave California practice a severe reprimand. In the *Moses Taylor*, Justice Stephen J. Field struck down the sixth chapter of the Practice Act giving district courts admiralty jurisdiction.[29] Field specifically considered *Averill v. the Steamship Hartford* (1852) and rejected its reasoning. Field found that a proceeding *in rem* was not a remedy afforded by the common law and was hence not saved to suitors.[30] In 1871 counsel confronted the California Supreme Court with the *Moses Taylor*.

In *Bohannan v. Hammond* (1871), counsel did raise the jurisdictional question, but Justice Jackson Temple made it clear that two decades of precedent were secure. The case involved 21 tons of damaged wheat loaded on a vessel to be carried from Stockton to San Francisco. The damage was due to the receding tide causing a piece of cordwood on the bottom to punch a hole in the boat. On jurisdiction, Justice Temple cited the saving to suitor's clause to validate state common-law jurisdiction.[31] Temple went on to apply the law of common carriers to the situation and give the plaintiff judgment. Temple neglected the admiralty's jurisdiction over waterborne traffic, the character of the vessel, and the nature of the legal relationship between the parties.

In *Crawford v. the Bark "Caroline Reed"* (1871), Temple was unable to avoid the jurisdictional question with distinctions. The case involved a Practice Act section 317 lien claim for equipment, repairs, and supplies provided a vessel in San Francisco. Since this was a statutory claim, Temple could not use the *Bohannan* device of distinction. Rather he followed the *Moses Taylor*. "A proceeding *in rem* is not a common law remedy, and the statute of this State, as far as it attempts to authorize proceedings *in rem* for causes of action cognizable in the admiralty, is unconstitutional and void."[32] Temple then faced the *General Smith* exception, allowing state proceedings where supplies and necessaries were provided in the vessel's home port. Temple retorted that the action was to recover materials and supplies upon a maritime contract, not to enforce a lien. Finally, Temple considered the constitutionality of the statute.

> I see no reason to doubt the constitutionality of the statute, so far as it may be made applicable to causes of action which are not cognizable in Courts of admiralty. There is no objection to the law merely because it authorizes a suit against the vessel itself, except so far as the suit is upon a marine contract.[33]

Temple's analysis was flawed in several ways. First, the maritime contract gave rise to the maritime lien, which required the *in rem* process, not the contract. Second, the *General Smith* precedent seemed applicable although not clearly so on the facts available in the appellate report. Third, Temple was clearly wrong regarding the constitutionality of the statute. For a state court to have jurisdiction, it must be enforcing or securing enforcement of its judgment by a levy on or attachment of a vessel as part of defendant's goods with a view to compelling appearance or to subjecting the defendant's interest therein to sale to satisfy the judgment. Moreover, the exception Temple cited was not valid because the statute also extended to marine torts.[34] Whatever the quality of analysis, the two decades of admiralty practice seemed substantially closed.

But two years later the Court was again deciding cases as if nothing had happened. In *Oakland Cotton Manufacturing Company v. Jennings* (1873), the plaintiff sued for recovery for breach of contract of affreightment. The case involved a charter party under which the plaintiff's machinery had been negligently stowed, causing the capsizing of the vessel and the resulting loss. The Court merely recited the law and gave judgment as if *Crawford* had not occurred.[35] In *Tomlinson v. Holt* (1874), the Court followed *Oakland Cotton* without hesitation or question.[36] So it went on into the twentieth century.[37] But the decisions were scattered and infrequent. Several factors account for the shift to the federal courts. First, both bench and bar came to recognize that the *Moses Taylor* severely limited state jurisdiction. Second, the federal courts implemented the *Moses Taylor* to clarify jurisdiction.[38] Finally, the public policy reasons for admiralty jurisdiction were more obvious to the legal community with the rise of international trade in the late nineteenth century.

Although admiralty business faded from the docket, the California Supreme Court's assertion of sovereignty did not lose its significance. Latent Confederates and southern sympathizers can be identified as perpetrators of state sovereignty concepts, but this general jurisprudential attitude of the California Court manifested itself in most areas of law. The heritage for the twentieth century has been an activist Court, which has led the nation in creative jurisprudence. This heritage stemmed in no small part from the Court's experience with admiralty law.

Finally, the operational level of admiralty law was little different from general civil practice in the need for the lawyer's skills. James A. Quinby, a prominent San Francisco admiralty lawyer, wrote a skit in 1930 entitled "Them Damaged Cargo Blues," which focused on the elements of daily practice.[39]

> As the curtain rises, the Cargo Owner is discovered downstage left, mournfully contemplating a pile of damaged merchandise. The Steamship Claims Agent rows up to the footlights in a leaky skiff. He carries a sheaf of form letters and begins to note a protest against heavy weather, singing happily as he works.

Claims Agent: - sing to Sweet Adeline

I

It is much to be regretted
That your goods are slightly wetted
But our lack of liability is plain,
For our latest bill of lading
Which is proof against evading
Bears exceptions for sea water, rust, and rain
Also sweat, contamination,
Fire, and all depreciation
That we've ever seen or heard of on a ship,
And our due examination
Which we made at destination
Shows your cargo much improved by the trip.

II

Furthermore, the protest shows
That the master blew his nose
And the hatches were demolished by the gale
Oh, we'll all stick together
To prove it's heavy weather
For we've got the cargo owner by the tail.
So, reserving all defenses
Alibis and false pretenses,
We suggest that your underwriter man
Is the guy that's out of luck
We always pass the buck
Yes--we always duck the issue if we can."

The admiralty attorney had to be as skilled in negotiation and litigation as his civil docket brethren. Although working in a very specialized field, the problems of parties defendant, often insurance companies, refusing to pay were frequently complicated by multiple insurers of multinational origins. The practice was predominantly in federal court despite the California State Supreme Court actions. At the operational level, California's bar had to exhibit the same skills but in a far more specialized realm. In the legal system some people wanted to avoid paying, to duck the issues, and to pass the buck.

CONCLUSION

This first volume detailing the development of law in frontier California has answered, in part, some of the questions about nineteenth-century legal history. Subsequent volumes pose different problems as well as alternative answers. But some things are clear.

The judicial behavior of the California Supreme Court was not uniformly instrumentalist or formalist. In the cases in which it was more instrumentalist, the Court portrayed a legal system that was not autonomous. In cases of a formalistic bent, the Court appeared to be announcing the found law of an autonomous legal system. The consensus position of concurrent modes of decision has a strong evidentiary basis in California. In cases without citation, and sometimes without apparent reasoning, the Court simply decided disputes with little clear indication of behavior.

The Supreme Court did not produce a record of consistent principled decision making. Rather it issued decisions that followed general principles and decisions that confounded precedents and principles. The latter type of decisions caused a degree of confusion for lawyers and clients at the operational level.

Legislators worked to channel behavior to productive transactional ends. The statutory products did not always achieve these goals. The interface with the judicial branch was productive of change at times. In other times and on other topics, the same judicial jostling was unheeded. The legislative product, like the judiciary's, was mixed in quality and timing.

Lawyers seeking certainty in law found a great deal of it, but also a great anxiety about the predictability of judicial behavior. They advised clients accordingly.

The people operating in the transactional society lived and worked in a law-based and directed society. The law they experienced was general and principled. It was certain, with grave exceptions, but it was functional. Finally, it had limits. The expectations for creditors were not always realized. Statutory expectations for artisans were varied and sometimes uncertain.

The role of law in society was pervasive and certain; yet there was that nagging anxiety about the certainty many relied upon in dealings. Certainty anxiety arose from human nature and behavior. Not every debtor intended to pay--hence the question, is the security adequate? Not every transaction of a technical nature could anticipate the behavior of the Supreme Court--hence the elaborate drafting of the legal community at the close of the period. But, in the main, the lawmakers facilitated the release of energy inherent in transactions in private property and supported the marketplace.

In law in books, California's experience was very much a part of the American legal experience. Law was the institutional bonding substance for social and economic relations. The formal law was little different, although the Court often cited California's peculiar circumstances in arriving at decision.

At the operational level, California's frontier marketplace, judicial ambiguity, and legislative waffling made the law's policy goals less certain. Law in action followed a less certain path to policy goals owing to the perceived uncertainty of both law and the frontier marketplace. As legal development at this level of behavior makes clear, legal history must encompass analysis of institutional as well as operational products and impacts.

NOTES

INTRODUCTION

1. See James Willard Hurst, *The Growth of American Law: The Law Makers* (Boston, Massachusetts, 1950); idem, *Law and the Conditions of Freedom in the Nineteenth Century United States* (Madison, Wisconsin, 1956); idem, *Law and Social Process in United States History* (Ann Arbor, Michigan, 1960); idem, *Law and Economic Growth* (Cambridge, Massachusetts, 1964); idem, *The Legitimacy of the Business Corporation in the Law of the United States, 1780-1970* (Charlottesville, Virginia, 1970); idem, *A Legal History of Money in the United States, 1774-1970* (Lincoln, Nebraska, 1973); idem, "Legal Elements in United States History," in *Law in American History*, edited by Thomas J. Fleming and Bernard Bailyn (Boston, Massachusetts, 1972), pp. 3-92; idem, *Law and the Social Order in the United States* (Ithaca, New York, 1977); Lawrence M. Friedman, *A History of American Law* (New York, New York 1973).

2. Robert S. Summers, *Instrumentalism and American Legal Theory* (Ithaca, New York, 1982).

3. The California Supreme Court consisted of a chief justice and two associate justices under the constitution of 1849. The first Court was elected by the legislature on December 22, 1849, and thereafter by popular election. The first legislature made S. C. Hastings, the founder of the Hastings Law School, chief justice. Henry Lyons and Nathaniel Bennett were the first associate justices. In 1862 the Court became a five-member Court pursuant to a constitutional amendment. The constitution of 1879 expanded the court to seven members. The new constitution also divided the Court into two divisions and increased the discretion of the chief justice in managing the business of the Court. During the nineteenth century, the Court's membership ranged from scholars of national reputation like Stephen J. Field to colorful western figures like David S. Terry.

CHAPTER 1

1. Lawrence M. Friedman, *Contract Law in America* (Madison, Wisconsin, 1965), p. 17.

2. Theophilius Parsons, *Law of Contract*, 2 vols. (Boston, Massachusetts, 1853), vol. 1, p. 3.

3. James Willard Hurst, *Law and Economic Growth* (Cambridge, Massachusetts, 1964), p. 285; also see idem, *Law and Markets in United States History* (Madison, Wisconsin, 1982).

4. William E. Nelson, *Americanization of the Common Law* (Cambridge, Massachusetts, 1975), pp. 154–59. Morton J. Horwitz, *The Transformation of American Law, 1780-1860* (Cambridge, Massachusetts, 1977), pp. 160–210 argued that this drive for certainty was so strong that it consumed equitable theories of contract and customary duties along the way to its triumph in doctrine. The attack on Horwitz was immediate and substantial. For a summation and defense, see Wythe Holt, "Morton Horwitz and the Transformation of American Legal History," 23 *William and Mary Law Review* 663–723 (Summer 1982).

5. *Angulo v. Sunol* (1859), 14 Cal. 402, 403.

6. *McDaniel v. Yuba County* (1850), 14 Cal. 444, 445.

7. *Webster v. Wade* (1861), 19 Cal. 291, 292.

8. *Grimes and Arthur v. Fall* (1860), 15 Cal. 63, 65.

9. *Doe v. Culverwell* (1868), 35 Cal. 291, 295.

10. *Morgan v. Stearns* (1871), 40 Cal. 434, 438; for similar statements regarding the clarity of the law stated without citation, see *Forbes v. McDonald* (1880), 54 Cal. 98, 99; *S.C.V. Peat Fuel Co. v. Tuck* (1878), 53 Cal. 304, 305.

11. 49 Cal. 665, 669.

12. 40 Cal. 378, 383; similarly, see *Crary v. Bowers* (1862), 20 Cal. 85; *Roysdon v. Carr* (1883), 63 Cal. 191.

13. 87 Cal. 249.

14. *Merehin v. Ball* (1885), 68 Cal. 205, 207.

15. *Jackson v. Beers and Davies* (1859), 14 Cal. 189.

16. *Blen v. Bear River and Auburn Water and Mining Co.* (1860), 15 Cal. 96, 99.

17. 72 Cal. 356.

18. *Ferrell v. Jones* (1870), 39 Cal. 655, 657.

19. See *Vance v. Dingley* (1859), 14 Cal. 53.

20. 82 Cal. 57.

21. 72 Cal. 1, 4.

22. 14 Cal. 146, 147–48.

23. *Kinney v. Osborne* (1859), 14 Cal. 112.

24. *Bohall v. Diller* (1871), 41 Cal. 532.

25. *Creighton v. Pragg* (1862), 21 Cal. 115, 119.

26. 38 Cal. 550, 553.

27. *White v. San Rafael and San Quentin Railroad Co.* (1875), 50 Cal. 417, 420.

28. *Bates v. Sierra Nevada Lake Water and Mining Co.* (1861), 18 Cal. 171, 175.

29. *Hewlett v. Owens and Moore* (1875), 50 Cal. 474.

30. Clough to Mother, May 23, 1883, Clough Collection, MSS, California State Library (Sacramento, California), California Section.

31. See Charles Fried, *Contract as Promise* (Cambridge, 1981).

32. Friedman, *Contract Law in America*, p. 28, found that land transactions constituted 26 percent of the contract law cases in the period 1836-1858. For the period 1850-1890 in California, land transactions constituted 24.6 percent of the California Supreme Court contract cases.

33. 1 Cal. 119; *Hoen* distinguished on the point of delivery of deed in *Tohler v. Folsom* (1850), 1 Cal. 207, 213.

34. *Tewksbury v. Laffan* (1850), 1 Cal. 129.

35. 2 Cal. 138, 143.

36. *Stafford v. Lick* (1858), 10 Cal. 12, 17.

37. *Tewksbury v. O'Connell* (1862), 21 Cal. 60.

38. *Boyd v. Brinckin* (1880), 55 Cal. 427.

39. See *Los Angeles Immigration and Land Co-Operative Association v. Phillips* (1880), 56 Cal. 539; *Breckinridge v. Crocker* (1889), 78 Cal. 529.

40. *Lawrence v. Gayetty* (1889), 78 Cal. 126; *McCarthy v. Pope* (1878), 52 Cal. 561; *People ex rel Ford v. Irwin* (1861), 18 Cal. 117.

41. 76 Cal. 535, 536-37; also see *Sere v. McGovern* (1884), 65 Cal. 244; *Booth v. Chapman* (1881), 59 Cal. 149; *Steele v. Branch* (1870), 40 Cal. 3; *Lewis v. Collvillaud* (1862), 21 Cal. 178, on pp. 189-91 for both the construction concepts and evidence of judicial restraint given the findings of the trial court below. The Court gave the parties great latitude in the use of contract language. As Justice Oscar L. Shafter stated in *Morrison v. Wilson* (1866), "If they see fit to agree that a mile shall stand for a league, or grant, bargain, and sell for quitclaim, or even black for white, however we might marvel at the caprice, we could not question the power" (see 30 Cal. 344, 348).

42. 79 Cal. 433.

43. 30 Cal. 138, 144.

44. 54 Cal. 41.

45. For examples, see Smith and Stephens (Los Angeles attorneys) to Fletcher, May 29, 1876, Bicknell Collection, MSS, Huntington Library (San Marino, California), Box 2; Yoch to Bicknell, June 14, 1882, ibid., Box 4; Hart to Bicknell, March 31, April 2, and April 5, 1887, ibid., Box 5.

46. Gleason to Bicknell, October 18, 1876, ibid., Box 2; also see Rosecrans to Schneider, August 29, 1873, ibid., Box 1; Rosecrans to Bicknell, September 30, 1873, and February 20, 1874, ibid.; William Hickman to Bicknell, June 30, 1878, ibid.; T. K. McDowell to Bicknell, May 2, 1887, ibid., Box 5; Graves to Easton, December 15, 1883, Jackson A. Graves Collection, MSS, Huntington Library, 1883-85 Letterbook.

47. H. A. Thomas contract with David Jacks, November 13, 1873 (fencing), David Jacks Collection, MSS, Huntington Library, Box B(V)(I)(10); Francis Doud to Methodist Encampment Association, July 21, 1875, ibid., Box B(V)(10); R. W. Roberson contract (Watsonville, August 27, 1869--pickets), ibid., Box B(II)(3);

L. Hafen-Matthew Keller contract to cultivate Rising Sun Vineyard, December 1, 1879, Matthew Keller Collection, MSS, Huntington Library, Box 3; Margaret Thomassen, John Bidwell, John Bruce contract to fence land, October 14, 1875, Bidwell Collection, MSS, California State Library, California Section, Box 136; Caspard Maurer to John D. Goodwin, May 23, 1874 (road building), John D. Goodwin Collection, MSS, California State Library, California Section, Box 733; Noah Greenwood, October 11, 1856, road-building solicitation (Contract No. 3), ibid., Box 730; E. A. Judkins-J. Kettle et al., contract to build quartz mill, May 21, 1862, ibid., Box 749; Jasper O'Farrell-William D. Farrand contract to erect stamping mill, September 22, 1862, Jasper O'Farrell Collection, MSS, Huntington Library, Box 1; San Francisco City Water Works-L. M. Hunt contract to build a tunnel, January 1, 1871, Albert Dressler Collection, MSS, California State Library, California Section, Box 759; Solicitation for bids . . . pumps, valves, etc., August 4, 1860, ibid.; Jerome Davis to L. F. Roussen, November 28, 1855 (cattle tending), Davis Collection, MSS, California State Library, California Section, Box 305; John Bidwell-James Dinning, William Luckett, Duncan Neel contracts for Wright's Ranch, March 1, 1853 (stock breeding), Bidwell Collection, Box 136; Bidwell-D. M. Doman, July 16, 1852, contract for stock breeding, ibid.; G. L. Grilley and S. D. Merchant-Natoma Water Co., May 13, 1852, contract to build flume, Amos P. Catlin Collection, MSS, Huntington Library, Box 1; John B. Chile-Thomas Ayers contract (tailoring), Davis Collection, Box 305; Bidwell-W. D. King et al., contract to manage Rancho Chico, Bidwell Collection, Box 136; J. A. Clark-Caroline E. Dwinelle contract to install a water well, July 23, 1889, Chipman and Dwinelle Papers, MSS, Huntington Library, Box 2; Charles Frances-David Jacks contract to paint the Cosmopolitan Hotel in Salinas City, March 22, 1883, Jacks Collection, Box B(II)(4); contract to build Abbott House Hotel, ibid., Box B(I)(2); Malcom Robertson to Jacks, October 14, 1889 (regarding contract for cook), ibid., Box C(7).

48. Sinclair to Jacks, February 9 and April 4, 1879, Jacks Collection, Box C(3).

49. Griffith to YMCA, November 3, 1887, and February 16, 1888, Graves Collection, 1885-88 Letterbook.

50. *Green v. Wells and Co.* (1852), 2 Cal. 548; *Whiting v. Heslep* (1854), 4 Cal. 327.

51. *White v. San Rafael and San Quentin RR.* (1875), 50 Cal. 417.

52. *Moore v. Kerr* (1884), 65 Cal. 519; *Katz v. Bedford* (1888), 77 Cal. 319.

53. *Harley v. Golden State and Miners Iron Works* (1884), 66 Cal. 238; *Wallace v. Ah Sam* (1886), 71 Cal. 197; *Nounnan v. Sutter County Land Co.* (1889), 81 Cal. 1

54. *Fisher v. Pearson* (1874), 48 Cal. 472; *Kendall v. Vallejo* (1851), 1 Cal. 371; *Hinkle v. S. F. and N. Railroad Co.* (1880), 55 Cal. 627.

55. *Lennard v. Vischer* (1852), 2 Cal. 37, 38.

56. *Hutchinson v. Wetmore* (1852), 2 Cal. 310, 312.

57. *Lassing v. Paige* (1877), 51 Cal. 575 and (1880), 56 Cal. 139.

58. *Harman v. Rogers* (1886), 69 Cal. 643; *Webster v. Wade* (1861), 19 Cal. 291; *Wallace v. Maples* (1887), 72 Cal. 356; also see *Nicholson v. Patchin* (1855), 5 Cal. 474.

59. *Williams v. Miller* (1855), 68 Cal. 290.

60. Sam Kee agency form, June 21, 1883, Jacks Collection, Box B(II)(4); also see Crosett and Co. Employment Agents (1878) advertisement, ibid., Box C(2); Empire Mill and Mining Co., Gold Hill, pay orders, Dressler Collection, Box 758; Wittenmyer-Gee Shoon contract, Goodwin Collection, Box 735.

61. *McDaniel v. Yuba Co.* (1859), 14 Cal. 444; *Canney v. South Pacific Coast RR. Co.* (1883), 63 Cal. 501.

62. 22 Cal. 86; see Friedman, *A History of American Law* (New York, New York, 1973), pp. 422-23.

63. *Hoffman v. Vallejo* (1873), 45 Cal. 564; *Ballard v. Carr* (1874), 48 Cal. 74.

64. *Drais v. Hogan* (1875), 50 Cal. 121, 127-28.

65. 80 Cal. 417, 419.

66. *Alpers v. Hunt* (1890), 86 Cal. 78, 88.

67. Friedman, *Contract Law in America*, pp. 47-49.

68. *Heyn v. Buon* (1869), 37 Cal. 529.

69. *Brown v. Pforr* (1869), 38 Cal. 550.

70. *Brown v. Central Land Co.* (1871), 42 Cal. 257.

71. *Phelan v. Gardner* (1872), 43 Cal. 306; *Neilson v. Lee* (1882), 60 Cal. 555; *Wilson v. Sturgis* (1886), 71 Cal. 226; *Phelps v. Prusch* (1890), 83 Cal. 626.

72. *Fuller v. Reed* (1869), 38 Cal. 99.

73. *Danielwitz v. Sheppard* (1882), 62 Cal. 339.

74. *McCarthy v. Loupe* (1882), 61 Cal. 299; *Myres v. Suryhne* (1885), 67 Cal. 657; *McPhail v. Buell* (1880), 87 Cal. 115.

75. David Jacks regularly bargained for lumber for construction and fencing. Price was often a major consideration, particularly in the 1880s. For example, see Amasa Pray to Jacks, September 16, 1872, Jacks Collection, Box C(1); A. Sanborn to Jacks, September 7, 1880, ibid., Box C(3); Jacks to C. W. Gates, June 22, 1886, ibid., Box C(5). On mining needs for timbering, the John Daggett Collection, MSS, California State Library, California Section, Box 437, contains numerous invoices as well as correspondence.

76. *Fitch v. Brockmon* (1853), 3 Cal. 348; *Helm v. Dumar and Williams* (1853), 3 Cal. 454; *Williams v. Lerch* (1880), 56 Cal. 330; *Humphreys v. Harkey* (1881), 59 Cal. 626; *Hogan v. Cowell* (1887), 73 Cal. 211. *Ruddle v. Givens* (1888), 76 Cal. 457, is another good example, but is also an example of the Court dealing with jury outlawry. In *John A. Watson v. John Rodgers* (1879), 53 Cal. 401, the father "sold" 213 sacks of barley, a threshing machine, 100 tons of hay, and 16 mules just ahead of the sheriff's attachment for his creditors. The Court cited the Civil Code, section 3440, that declared sales without delivery to be presumptively fraudulent and void against creditors. The Court still had to decide when delivery was complete. *Stewart v. Scannell* (1857), 8 Cal. 80, strictly construed the statute to require that a change of possession be actual and continuing.

Goldstein v. Nunan (1885), 66 Cal. 542, continued that line
of reasoning.

77. Manuscript examples are numerous. See Alfred Edmondson and
Charles Wolter, October 3, 1852, receipt, Charles Wolter
Collection, MSS, Huntington Library, Box 1; Josefa Wolter and Jose
Esmerigildo Montoya, October 9, 1865, contract and the March 12,
1867, purchase agreement, ibid., Box 2. William H. Quigley and
the Black Bear Quartz Mining Co. entered into a requirements
contract for beef on April 27, 1875 (Daggett Collection, Box
437). David Jacks bought and sold cattle, sheep, and horses
in substantial volume. The 1883 and 1887 folders in the Jacks
Collection, Box B(II)(4), contain dozens of such documents.

78. Even when enterprise required more complex arrangements,
the parties tried to express their objectives with some clarity.
In 1864 Gomez and Gomez agreed to sell cattle to J. W. Leigh and
Charles M. Blair. The cattle had several brands and were so
numerous that it would require "from four to six droves during the
months of June and July next" to deliver the cattle. Both parties
knew the objective of the agreement. They wrote it down: "the
object of this agreement being to sell all the cattle of the above
irons" (see contract of May 24, 1864, Wolter Collection, Box 2).

79. *Polhemus v. Heiman and George* (1873), 45 Cal. 573.

80. *Merehin v. Ball* (1885), 68 Cal. 205.

81. *Blackwood v. Cutting Packing Co.* (1888), 76 Cal. 212.

82. *Keller v. Ybarru* (1853), 3 Cal. 147.

83. *Verrkamp v. Hulburd Canning and Drying Co.* (1881),
58 Cal. 229-30.

84. *Brown v. Anderson* (1888), 77 Cal. 236.

85. *Gates v. Carquinez Packing Co.* (1889), 78 Cal. 439.

86. *La Rue v. Groeqinger* (1890), 84 Cal. 281.

87. Grass, stubble, and hay contracts are numerous in the Jacks
Collection. Commonly, Jacks received requests in letter form to
buy grass and followed the offers with a written contract [see
J. S. Young to David Jacks, April 27, 1869, Jacks Collection,
Box C(1)]. The arrangements were often so informal that they were
memorialized only by a receipt. Mrs. N. A. Thing made such
a receipt for $49.41 to John Center for hay on November 9, 1868
(see Dressler Collection, Box 755).

88. *Smith v. Friend* (1860), 15 Cal. 124.

89. Friedlander to Jacks, September 30, 1874, Jacks Collection,
Box C(2); also see, for example, Falkner, Bell, and Co. to M. C.
Ireland, August 19, 1874, and Friedlander to Jacks, August 24,
1874, ibid. The state prison manufactured grain bags, and this
form of state support of the agricultural sector was very
significant owing to the chronic shortage of bags. Jacks was
searching for bags on a seasonal basis. Albert Dressler bought
his bags at San Quentin (see Dressler receipt for bags, August 6,
1888, Dressler Collection, Box 755).

90. Connor Jacks contract of September 27, 1876 (barley), Jacks
Collection, Box (V)(I)(10).

91. Friedlander to Jacks, September 28, 1874, asking for the
sample, ibid., Box C(2); William B. Unruh to Jacks, July 17, 1878,
expressed concern about the grading due to barley (ibid.).

92. Roger W. Lotchin, *San Francisco, 1846-56, From Hamlet to City* (Lincoln, Nebraska, 1974), pp. 54-59.
93. 4 Cal. 355 and 4 Cal. 359, 361.
94. *Crosby v. Watkins* (1859), 12 Cal. 85.
95. 38 Cal. 659 and 43 Cal. 279, 284.
96. 50 Cal. 558, 560.
97. Fong Wo to Yu Wo and Yu Wo to Fong Wo, March 28, 1874 (both are telegrams), Dressler Collection, Box 756.
98. J. P. Sweeney to David Jacks, July 29, and August 4, 1871, Jacks Collection, Box C(1).
99. J. Glendening and Black Bear Mining Co. contract of May 31, 1878, Daggett Collection, Box 437.
100. Vulcan Iron Works, San Francisco, September 22, 1860, receipt, September 7, 1860, invoice, August 10 and 18 receipts, Dressler Collection, Box 755.
101. McElroy to Jacks, October 4 and 6, 1879, Jacks Collection, Box C(3).
102. Bicknell to J. M. Crawley, April 4, 1890, Bicknell Collection, Letterbook 6.
103. *Fitzgerald v. Gorham* (1854), 4 Cal. 289.
104. 8 Cal. 80, 83.
105. *Ross v. Sedgwick* (1886), 60 Cal. 247; *Schumacher v. Connolly* (1888), 75 Cal. 282.
106. Collins and Company Collection, MSS, Bancroft Library (Berkeley, California). See Account Book on p. 20 for loans.
107. L. B. Clark Ledger, MSS, Bancroft Library. The flow of business was irregular, but the problems with the formal legal system were few. See Baker and Hamilton Collection, MSS, Bancroft Library (Sacramento importers of agricultural implements); Wellman, Peck, and Company Collection, MSS, Bancroft Library (San Francisco mercantile); D. W. Earl Collection, MSS, Bancroft Library (San Francisco and Sacramento forwarding and commission merchants); Matthew Keller Collection, MSS, Huntington Library. (San Francisco Store Ledger contains entries for all types of merchandise with payment in money, labor, "by lumber," "by a bay horse," and "by chickens and eggs.") After 1876 the frequency of cash payment increased dramatically in Keller's store. Life in the country store was somewhat similar in transactions, but not in lifestyle. William Warner wrote to his son and wife on July 15, 1877, that "I have long since found out one fact which is as true as the gospel--and that is: a half day sometimes passes away without a customer--but the moment we set down to dinner a half dozen are sure to pop in and are in a great hurry for a can of oysters, a pound of crackers and a like quantity of cheese and crackers" (see Warner Collection, MSS, California State Library, California Section, Box 327).
108. *Correio v. Lynch* (1884), 65 Cal. 273.
109. 67 Cal. 610.
110. *Hoult v. Baldwin* (1889), 78 Cal. 410; cf. Friedman, *History of American Law*, p. 473.
111. *Bell v. McClellan* (1885), 67 Cal. 283; *Oro Mining v. Starr* (1888), 76 Cal. 166; *Joshua Hendy Machine Works v. Connolly* (1888), 76 Cal. 305.

112. Contract of December 30, 1853, Adams and Company Collection, MSS, Huntington Library, Box 1; also see correspondence of McAllister, Williams, and Rose with Woods, January 30, 1854, ibid., Box 1.

113. W. H. Hussey to Jacks, March 5, 1886, Jacks Collection, Box B(II)(4). Examples of business venture contracts are numerous: see H. J. Diggles and the Black Bear Quartz Mining Co., August 1, 1877, for freighting, Daggett Collection, Box 437; Keller-Mahoney partnership of 1876, Keller Collection, Box 3; Natoma Water and Mining Co. and Miners, Consumers, and Deer Creek Water and Mining Co. agreement of May 1854 to deliver water, Amos Catlin Collection, MSS, Huntington Library, Box 1.

114. Bicknell to J. M. Griffith, July 20, 1889, Bicknell Collection, Letterbook 5.

115. *Von Schmidt v. Huntington* (1850), 1 Cal. 55, 64.

116. 1 Cal. 55, 65.

117. 1 Cal. 55, 68.

118. 1 Cal. 55, 73.

119. *Tartar v. Finch* (1858), 9 Cal. 276.

120. *George v. Ransom* (1860), 14 Cal. 658; *Foulke v. San Diego and Gila Southern RR. Co.* (1876), 51 Cal. 365.

121. 54 Cal. 98.

122. 74 Cal. 46.

123. Arthur L. Corbin, *Corbin on Contracts* (St. Paul, Minnesota, 1962), vol. 6A, pp. 33-34.

124. 6 Cal. 258 and 8 Cal. 585, 591.

125. 36 Cal. 342, 357.

126. 36 Cal. 342, 361.

127. 36 Cal. 342, 362.

128. Warren A. Beck and David Williams, *California* (Garden City, New York, 1972), p. 214.

129. *Oregon Steam Navigation v. Winsor* (1873), 87 U.S. 64.

130. 10 N.Y. 241; Corbin, *Contracts*, pp. 62-63.

131. 40 Cal. 251.

132. *Prost v. More* (1870), 40 Cal. 347, 348.

133. 45 Cal. 152, 154.

134. 49 Cal. 665.

135. 76 Cal. 387.

136. James B. Hume Collection, MSS, Bancroft Library.

137. Philip T. Southworth Collection, MSS, California State Library, California Section, Box 309, contains financial correspondence and instruments dated 1851-1859 that typify the problems of mercantile financing for San Francisco-based enterprise dealing with New York and European suppliers.

138. Keller Collection, Box 1, contains such documents in substantial volume for the 1870s. Box 4 contains English sight bills as well as drafts on Australian banks. Also see Jacks Collection, Boxes C(1) and C(2).

139. See *Stearns v. Aguirre* (1856), 6 Cal. 176; *Palmer v. Tripp's Adm.* (1857), 8 Cal. 95; *Visher v. Webster* (1857), 8 Cal. 109; *Conner v. Clark* (1859), 12 Cal. 168; *Montgomery v. Kasson* (1860), 16 Cal. 189 (interesting constitutional law case involving impairment of contract). On the interpretation of

California's specific contract act, see Wesley C. Mitchell, *A History of the Greenbacks* (Chicago, Illinois, 1903), p. 144; William C. Frankhauser, *A Financial History of California, 1849-1910* (Berkeley, California, 1913), pp. 219-22; Ira B. Cross, *Financing an Empire*, 4 vols. (New York, New York, 1927), vol. 1, pp. 300-360; Joseph W. Ellison, *California and the Nation, 1849-1866* (Berkeley, California, 1927), pp. 216-27; Gordon M. Bakken, "Law and Legal Tender in California and the West," 62 *Southern California Quarterly* 239-59 (Fall 1980); *Ashley v. Vischer* (1864), 24 Cal. 322; *Gradwohl v. Harris* (1865), 29 Cal. 150; *Saunders v. Clark* (1865), 29 Cal. 299; *Smith v. Greer* (1866), 31 Cal. 476; *Wilbur v. Lynde* (1874), 49 Cal. 290; *Butler v. Baber* (1880), 54 Cal. 178; *Wolf v. March* (1880), 54 Cal. 228; *Lucas v. Pico* (1880), 55 Cal. 126; *Ferry v. Hammond* (1881), 59 Cal. 26; *McAfee v. Fisher* (1883), 64 Cal. 246; *Goad v. Moulton* (1885), 67 Cal. 536.

140. Peter R. Decker, *Fortunes and Failures* (Cambridge, Massachusetts, 1978), p. 91; Lotchin, *San Francisco*, p. 60.

141. The California Statute of Limitations provided that debt collection litigation had to be commenced within two years of the time of the accrual of the action. That statute was passed on April 2, 1855. See *Scarborough v. Dugan* (1858), 10 Cal. 305.

142. *Eck v. Hoffman* (1880), 55 Cal. 501.

143. 37 Cal. 670, 672.

144. 37 Cal. 670, 675.

145. 37 Cal. 670, 676.

146. 57 Cal. 78, 80; similarly, a contract amounting to graft, *Martin v. Wade* (1869), 37 Cal. 168, 174, 176.

147. *State v. McCauley and Tevis* (1860), 15 Cal. 429; *People ex rel McCauley and Tevis v. Brooks* (1860), 16 Cal. 11. The latter is a 55-page case with an exceptional opinion by Chief Justice Stephen J. Field.

148. *Zottman v. San Francisco* (1862), 20 Cal. 96.

149. 20 Cal. 497.

150. *Randall v. Yuba County* (1859), 14 Cal. 219; *Keller v. Hyde* (1862), 20 Cal. 593; also see *Wallace v. San Jose* (1865), 29 Cal. 180; *Sharp v. County of Contra Costa* (1867), 34 Cal. 284; *Rose v. Estidillo* (1870), 39 Cal. 270; *McCullough v. San Francisco Board of Education* (1876), 51 Cal. 418.

151. 28 Cal. 345, 364.

152. *Wetmore v. San Francisco* (1872), 44 Cal. 294; also see *Sloan v. Diggins* (1874), 49 Cal. 38; *Cochran v. Collins* (1865), 29 Cal. 129; *Taylor v. Palmer* (1866), 31 Cal. 240; *Nicolson Pavement Co. v. Painter* (1868), 35 Cal. 699; *Dougherty v. Miller* (1868), 36 Cal. 83.

153. Lotchin, *San Francisco*, pp. 174-81.

154. McLean and Fowler to Day, October 16, 1860, and January 9, 1861, Catlin Collection, Box 3.

155. See *Farnum v. Phoenix Insurance Co.* (1890), 83 Cal. 246; *Case v. Sun Insurance Co.* (1890), 83 Cal. 473.

156. Graves to Easton, December 15, 1883, Graves Collection, 1883-85 Letterbook.

157. Berwick to Jacks, October 27, 1887, Jacks Collection, Box C(6).

158. Cook to Goodwin, August 14, 1872, Goodwin Collection, Box 728.

CHAPTER 2

1. Gordon M. Bakken, "The Development of Landlord and Tenant Law in Frontier California, 1850-1865," 21 *The Pacific Historian* 374-83 (Winter 1977).

2. Joseph Lamson, "Nine Years Adventure in California from September, 1852 - September, 1866," MSS, Bancroft Library (Berkeley, California).

3. See Woods, Hale, Haskell, Hastings, Flint, Flint, and Peabody and Cohen and Company lease of the North Point Dock Warehouse, San Francisco, December 29, 1853, for one year; Adams and Company Collection, MSS, Huntington Library (San Marino, California), Box 1. By comparison, Jerome Davis leased the lower story and kitchen of a house in Sacramento for one year to T. Dassonville. The rent was $200 per month payable in advance. The lease also stipulated that if the tenant were two days in arrears on the rent, the landlord had the right to dispossess the tenant. Sacramento city lots were renting for four years at $25 per month in 1860 [see Jerome Davis Collection, MSS, California State Library (Sacramento, California), California Section, Box 305]. Bad times delayed the rent, but most saw good times ahead. E. S. Mumford of Mormon Island wrote to Amos P. Catlin in Benecia on April 22, 1853, that he was sorry for the delay in paying the rent, but "things are dull, but we live in anticipation" (Catlin Collection, MSS, Huntington Library, Box 1).

4. Adams and Company Scrapbook, vol. 1, p. 62. In flush times, the rent was high and the term shorter than a year. A store on the corner of Halleck and Battery in San Francisco was rented for six months at $850 per month (Philip T. Southworth Collection, MSS, California State Library, California Collection, Box 309).

5. Rodman M. Price Collection, MSS, Box 1, Huntington Library (July 30, 1850, lease); on the squatter problem see Roger W. Lotchin, *San Francisco* (London, 1974), pp. 144-48.

6. John Bidwell Collection, MSS, California State Library, California Collection, Box 136.

7. David Jacks Collection, MSS, Huntington Library, Box B(V)(4)(14).

8. Bidwell Collection, Box 136.

9. Lease of Juan Ramon of March 21, 1860, and Antonio Mays of July 2, 1863, Jacks Collection, Box B(V)(4)(14).

10. Thomson lease of January 19, 1860, and A. J. Wicker lease of November 1, 1862, ibid.

11. 33 Cal. 237.

12. 33 Cal. 237, 249.

13. 43 Cal. 299, 305.

14. *Abbey Homestead Association v. A. Willard* (1874), 48 Cal. 614; also see *Holloway v. Galliac* (1874), 47 Cal. 474; *Peralta v. Ginochio* (1874), 47 Cal. 459; *Ghiradelli v. Greene* (1880), 56 Cal. 629; *Lataillade v. Santa Barbara Gas Co.* (1881), 58 Cal. 4; *Standley v. Stephens* (1885), 66 Cal. 541; *Swift v. Goodrich* (1886), 70 Cal. 103; *Burgess v. Rice* (1888), 74 Cal. 590; *Davis v. McGrew* (1889), 82 Cal. 135.

15. O. H. Perry to Jacks, November 30, 1874, Jacks Collection, Box C(1).

16. Ibid., Box C(2).

17. 35 Cal. 558, 568.

18. 29 Cal. 577.

19. 46 Cal. 270–79.

20. *Skaggs v. Emerson* (1875), 50 Cal. 3; *The Opera House and Art Building Association v. Bert* (1877), 52 Cal. 471; *Potter v. Mercer* (1879), 53 Cal. 667; *Martin v. Splivalo* (1880), 56 Cal. 128; *Van Every v. Ogg* (1881), 59 Cal. 563; *Smith v. Hill* (1883), 63 Cal. 51; *Sauer v. Meyer* (1890), 87 Cal. 34.

21. 38 Cal. 677–78.

22. Also see on statutory construction *Walsh v. Fraser* (1869), 38 Cal. 481; *Shelby v. Houston* (1869), 38 Cal. 410; *Warburton v. Doble* (1869), 38 Cal. 619; *Bowers v. Cherokee Bob* (1870), 45 Cal. 495, and (1873) 46 Cal. 297.

23. 57 Cal. 189, 192; also see *Kower v. Gluck* (1867), 33 Cal. 401; *Hauxhurst v. Lobree* (1869), 38 Cal. 563; *Stoppelkamp v. Mangeot* (1871), 42 Cal. 316.

24. For example, see H. Hazen to Goodwin, September 23, 1883, Goodwin Collection, MSS, California State Library, California Section, Box 731.

25. J. F. Birlem to Jacks, November 29 and December 5, 1887, Jacks Collection, Box C(6).

26. F. Blackin to Jacks, August 23, 1888, ibid.

27. Lease of Jacks to Allen, July 13, 1864, ibid., Box B(V)(4)(14).

28. Kennedy, Hopkins, and Jacks to William M. R. Parker, March 1, 1871, ibid.

29. Jacks to Sam Kee, January 1, 1877, ibid.

30. Jacks to Grant Lease, May 3, 1870, ibid.

31. Graves to Thomas Bell, July 11, 1882, Graves Collection, MSS, Huntington Library, 1881–83 Letterbook.

32. Graves to Bell, October 11, 1880, ibid., 1879–80 Letterbook.

33. Delonay lease, February 24, 1866, Jacks Collection, Box B(V)(4)(14).

34. Olds lease, November 1, 1872, ibid.

35. Sniveley lease, January 25, 1876, ibid.

36. McFadden lease, December 15, 1879, ibid.

37. Ah Jim and Ah Kong lease, November 29, 1879, ibid.

38. P. Jorgensen lease, November 5, 1881, ibid.

39. Jacks to Samuel Cassidy, September 19, October 15, and November 16, 1870, and Cassidy to Jacks, October 3 and 22 and November 7, 1870, ibid., Box C(1). Jacks carried Cassidy on his ledger for $2,952.52 in 1869, and rent for 1870 was carried forward at 1.5 percent per month.

40. Iverson to Jacks, ibid.

41. Gondonin to Jacks, June 25 and October 15, 1887, ibid., Box C(6).

42. Harrison to Jacks, June 2, 1890, ibid., Box C(8).

43. Unruh to Jacks, August 27, 1880, ibid., Box C(3).

44. Romie to Jacks, March 11 and April 4, 1880, ibid.

45. Jacks carried tenants for years at a time. The account books reveal, for example, that as of 1881, O. H. Perry owed the garden rent for 1875 and 1876. The garden rent for 1877 was cancelled because there was "no crop for that season." The total carried forward was seven years totaling $420. The November 17, 1882, account showed $961 still on the books. The November 29, 1883, account had interest assessed at 1 percent per month of the total outstanding rentals from 1877–1883 of $867.36 [ibid., Box B(II)(4)]. The accounts of Jim Kee are similar despite Jacks' rental agents telling him year after year that Kee had paid little or nothing for a year or more [see Birlem to Jacks, November 29 and December 1, 1887, ibid., Box C(6)]. The accounts of Ingvard Lund of 1877 and 1878 reveal that Jacks carried Lund for wheat seed, rent, and interest on back rent at the rate of 1 percent per month to the extent of $418.09 for a one-year period [ibid., Box B(II)(3)].

46. Hines to Jenks, April 20, 1881, Goodwin Collection, Box 731.

47. Offers to David Jacks were numerous and varied, both large- and small-scale proposals. For example, see Wesley Burnett, June 6, 1873; J. O. Batcheller, June 12, 1873; John M. Cushing, October 27, 1873; Michael Kavanaugh, January 6, 1873; Preston Hodges, September 29, 1873; John G. Joy, June 7, 1873; Robert Kirk, June 6, 1873; Peter Matthews, February 15, 1873; John Chestnut, September 1 and 24, and October 18, 1874; J. J. Green, September 18, 1874; D. O. Hern, May 6 and October 16, 1874; Thomas Snyder, December 11, 1874; H. B. Howard, July 19, 1878; John Kalar, July 29, 1878; William B. Unruh, July 8 and August 4, 1878; John Whiteworth, August 5, 1878; C. Romie, August 21, 1879; William Dunphy, June 26, 1879; John Heinlen, March 20, 1879—all in Jacks Collection, Box C(2).

48. Holcomb to David Jacks, November 22, 1873, ibid.

49. O. H. Perry, George F. Carick, and Harrison Blim lease, August 12, 1876, read "from the time the grain is hauled off . . . up to the first of November" for a rent of $1,000. George F. Carrick lease, August 16, 1877, was for three months for $700 for a field abutting Carrick's property [ibid., Box B(V)(4)(14)].

50. Gigling lease, March 24, 1880, ibid., Box B(V)(4)(914). Jacks kept a separate stubble account for his records [Box B(II)(3)].

51. For example, Martin E. Ward wrote to Jacks on October 23, 1879, responding to an advertisement in the *Sacramento Union* [ibid., Box C(1)].

52. Richard Egan used Bancroft blank lease no. 729 in 1878–1880 (Evelyn Lionel Howell Collection, MSS, Huntington Library, Box 1). David Jacks also favored the blank forms after 1870 [Jacks Collection, Box B(V)(14)].

53. R. E. Bowen to Jacks, August 7, 1880, Jacks Collection, Box C(3). William B. Unruh wrote Jacks on August 3, 1878, that his "experience in customs pertaining to legal forms, notes, mortgages, etc. in this country, or elsewhere" was "rather limited and [he had] no blank forms to guide [him]."

54. John Chestnut to Jacks, October 21, 1874, ibid., Box C(2).

55. Charles T. Romie to Jacks, August 26, 1879, ibid., Box C(3).

56. Bodfish to Jacks, March 4, 1888, Jacks to C. W. Gates, March 21, 1888, Gates to Jacks, March 24, 1888, ibid., Box C(8).

57. Bodfish to Jacks, January 23, 1879, ibid., Box C(3).

58. Winham to Jacks, November 18, 1880, ibid.

59. Bauman to Jacks, November 23, 1886, ibid., Box C(5).

60. The best statement of the pioneer's respect for private property may be found in John Phillip Reid's *Law for the Elephant* (San Marino, California, 1980), pp. 335–52.

61. *Blythe v. Gately* (1876), 51 Cal. 236.

62. *Kelly v. Teague* (1883), 63 Cal. 68; also see *Salisbury v. Shirley* (1884), 66 Cal. 223.

63. Norris lease, May 22, 1851, Bidwell Collection, Box 136.

64. Manuel George lease, July 19, 1870, Jacks Collection, Box B(V)(4)(14); Theron R. Hopkins to Jacks, March 6, 1870, ibid., Box C(1); Jacks to Samuel Cassidy, September 19, October 4 and 15, and November 16, 1870, ibid.

65. David Jacks and D. R. Ashley lease to A. J. Rutherford, December 14, 1859, ibid., Box B(V)(4)(14).

66. The expectation in the rural setting was common that the tenant would not be able to pay on time or at all under certain circumstances. Further, the rural expectation was that the tenant would have little capital other than labor to contribute to the landlord's profit. Hence, leases would contain clauses that worked a forfeiture of improvements if there were a breach of a covenant in the lease. Lawyers often thought such a clause inconscionable, but it was more often a recognition of the realities of the husbandry on the frontier (see John W. Dwinelle, "Memorandum on points of law in Cassidy v. Jacks (1869)" and Cassidy to Dwinelle, June 29, 1872, Chipman-Dwinelle Papers, MSS, Huntington Library, Boxes 1 and 2). The reality of the Jacks–Cassidy landlord–tenant relationship was that, at the end of 1869, Jacks had carried Cassidy for almost three years to the extent of $2,952.52 [Accounts, Receipts of Samuel Cassidy Account Ledger, Jacks Collection, Box B(III)(3)].

67. 47 Cal. 56.

68. *Marks v. Ryan* (1883), 63 Cal. 107; *McNally v. Connolly* (1886), 70 Cal. 3.

69. 39 Cal. 151, 152.

70. *Savings and Loan Society v. Gerichten* (1884), 64 Cal. 520; *Sieber v. Blanc* (1888), 76 Cal. 173; *Willson v. Treadwell* (1889), 81 Cal. 58.

71. *Tatum v. Thompson* (1890), 86 Cal. 203.

72. *Dwyer v. Carroll* (1890), 86 Cal. 298.

73. *Polack v. Pioche* (1868), 35 Cal. 416.

74. 38 Cal. 89, 90.

75. 66 Cal. 114.

76. *Brewster v. De Fremery* (1867), 33 Cal. 341.
77. *Kalis v. Shattuck* (1886), 69 Cal. 593; *Riley v. Simpson* (1890), 83 Cal. 217.
78. 72 Cal. 498, 504.
79. This practice was common throughout the period. For example, the 1850 North Point Dock Warehouse lease to Cohen and Co. contained a covenant against subleasing except for "mercantile offices and stores" (Adams and Company Collection, Box 1). This type of modified covenant against subleasing was intended to control the type of subtenants and their use of the landlord's property.
80. Hendon to Jacks, March 3, 1879, Jacks Collection, Box C(3).
81. Daniel Leary to Jacks, September 4, 1889, ibid., Box C(7).
82. Kee to Jacks, October 30, 1886, ibid., Box C(5). Jim had paid $700 on account. Charles Louis to Jacks, September 4, 1886, ibid. The next year the routine was repeated. J. F. Birlem to Jacks, November 29, 1887, ibid., Box C(6).
83. T. Dassonville lease, January 30, 1852, contained a covenant to allow the landlord to dispossess if the rent were two days in arrears (Davis Collection, Box 305). This was an early example, but the practice continued more to create an expectation in the mind of the tenant than to give the landlord a legal tool.
84. For example, Thomas I. Talbot went to John Goodwin and had the notice drafted. In 1879 it was addressed to Montgomery Auble of Adin, Modoc County, and served on November 11, 1879, by Sheriff O. D. Weller for a fee of 90 cents. The notice was all handwritten (Goodwin Collection, Box 735).
85. Acknowledgment of Pancho Martinez, November 17, 1870, witness C. Romie, in handwriting of David Jacks, Jacks Collection, Box B(II)(3).
86. *Silva v. Campbell* (1890), 84 Cal. 420.
87. *Easton v. O'Reilly* (1883), 63 Cal. 305.
88. *Calderwood v. Pyser* (1866), 31 Cal. 333; *Levitzky v. Canning* (1867), 33 Cal. 299; *Salisbury v. Shirley* (1879), 53 Cal. 461; *Baughman v. Reed* (1888), 75 Cal. 319.
89. 49 Cal. 586.
90. 74 Cal. 287.
91. *McAlester v. Landus* (1886), 70 Cal. 79.
92. See *Hendy v. Dinkerhoff* (1880), 57 Cal. 3.
93. 54 Cal. 547, 555.
94. Of the 84 urban cases, San Francisco was the origin of 54 or 64.3 percent of the urban cases.
95. David Jacks regularly inserted detailed language directing his tenants in proper husbandry. For example, his lease with Antonil and Manuel Bodgers of November 1, 1880, contained the following: "The said lessees shall poison all squirrels that are on said premises, or that may come on said premises during the term of this lease, and shall clean up by the roots all Kuckle bur, Spanish Thistle or Chilanian Thistle, pig weeds, mustard and raddish, and all other noxious weeds that may be growing on said lands, and utterly destroy the same before or at the time it commences to blossom, so that it shall be an impossibility for any of the seeds to mature" [Jacks Collection, Box B(V)(4)(14)].

CHAPTER 3

1. Lawrence M. Friedman, *A History of American Law* (New York, New York, 1973), p. 216; Morton J. Horwitz, *The Transformation of American Law* (Cambridge, Massachusetts, 1977), pp. 265–66.

2. Friedman, *History of American Law*, p. 217.

3. Ibid.

4. Ibid., pp. 217–18.

5. 1 How. 311.

6. See Carl B. Swisher, *History of the Supreme Court of the United States: The Taney Period, 1836–1864* (New York, New York, 1974), pp. 148–51; Charles Warren, *The Supreme Court in United States History*, 2 vols., (Boston, Massachusetts, 1926), vol. 2, pp. 104–5; Gerald T. Dunne, *Justice Joseph Story* (New York, New York, 1970), p. 392; also see George L. Priest, "Law and Economic Distress," 2 *Journal of Legal Studies* 469–92 (June 1973), on the Illinois experience.

7. Friedman, *History of American Law*, p. 218.

8. Ibid., pp. 374–75.

9. Friedman, *Contract Law in America* (Madison, Wisconsin, 1965), pp. 144–45.

10. 2 Cal. 595, 596.

11. 2 Cal. 387, 407.

12. 1 Cal. 203, 205.

13. Ibid.

14. *Cal. Stats. 1850–53* (April 16, 1850), ch. 122, pp. 513–19.

15. *Cal. Stats. 1850–53* (April 29, 1851), Civil Procedure, Title 7, ch. 1, section 231, p. 562.

16. Couts to Stearns, July 12, 1852, Cave Johnson Couts Collection, MSS, Huntington Library (San Marino, California), Box 18.

17. March 18, 1857, deed and notes, John Center Collection, MSS, Huntington Library, Box 1.

18. Benjamin Davis Wilson Collection, MSS, Huntington Library, Boxes 2 and 3.

19. Banning Company Papers, MSS, Huntington Library, Boxes 2, 5A, 6, and 8.

20. See Robert Glass Cleland, *The Cattle on a Thousand Hills* (San Marino, California, 1941), pp. 102–16.

21. See Abel Stearns Collection, MSS, Huntington Library, Boxes 85 and 87.

22. See Los Alamitos Ranch Records, ibid., Box 84.

23. See Couts to Stearns, October 13, 1852, Couts Collection, Box 18.

24. John Center paid off a $20,000 mortgage in eight months in San Francisco selling bricks, while Stearns in Los Angeles frequently turned mortgages into real estate ownership within a year (see August 3, 1853, mortgage, Center Collection, Box 1, and Stearns Collection, Box 85.

25. See Indenture of September 2, 1854, Stearns Collection, Box 85.

26. January 27, 1854, note and mortgage, ibid.; also see January 11 and November 14, 1854, notes and quit claim deed ibid.; similarly, see Rancho Los Bolsas Collection, MSS, Huntington Library.

27. Bacon Collection, December 22, 1864 (HM 27622), MSS, Huntington Library.

28. See Charles Robinson Johnson to Abel Stearns, October 27, 1862, Stearns Collection, Box 27; Eagle Mills documents, June 13, 1864, ibid., Box 88.

29. See Drummer–Carrillo mortgage, 1851, Wilson Collection, Box 2.

30. 2 Cal. 489, 492; also see *Ord v. McKee* (1855), 5 Cal. 515, 516.

31. 6 Cal. 53, 54.

32. 9 Cal. 123, 125.

33. 9 Cal. 365, 405–21.

34. 9 Cal. 365, 407–8.

35. 9 Cal. 365, 411; on the common law of mortgages, see Theodore F. T. Pluncknett, *A Concise History of the Common Law* (Boston, Massachusetts, 1956), pp. 603–8; Max Radin, *Handbook of Anglo-American Legal History* (St. Paul, Minnesota, 1936), pp. 404–5; also see James Kent, *Commentaries on American Law* (New York, New York, 1830), vol. 4; Francis Hilliard, *The Law of Mortgages of Real and Personal Property* (Boston, Massachusetts, 1872); Charles T. Boone, *The Law of Mortgages of Real and Personal Property* (San Francisco, California, 1886).

36. See *Johnson v. Sherman* (1860), 15 Cal. 287, 293; *Goodenow v. Ever* (1860), 16 Cal. 461, 467–70; *Lent v. Morrill* (1864), 25 Cal. 492, 500.

37. *Swift v. Kraemer* (1859), 13 Cal. 526, 531; also see *Ferguson v. Miller* (1854), 4 Cal. 97, as an example of the rapid sale and resale of property evidenced by careless documentation.

38. 8 Cal. 424, 435–36.

39. 8 Cal. 424, 430.

40. 8 Cal. 424, 431.

41. 8 Cal. 424, 431.

42. 8 Cal. 424, 432–34.

43. 13 Cal. 116.

44. *Cunningham v. Hawkins* (1865), 27 Cal. 603, 606; also see *Johnson v. Sherman* (1860), 15 Cal. 291; *Lodge v. Turman* (1864), 24 Cal. 385; *Hooper v. Jones* (1865), 29 Cal. 18.

45. 10 Cal. 197, 206; also see *Ferguson v. Miller* (1856), 4 Cal. 97.

46. 10 Cal. 197, 207.

47. 17 Cal. 589, 593.

48. See *Fogarty v. Sawyer* (1863), 23 Cal. 570.

49. See *Green v. Butler* (1864), 26 Cal. 505.

50. 6 Cal. 99, 101.

51. 22 Cal. 116, 124.

52. 29 Cal. 253, 256; also see *Spring v. Hill and Carr* (1856), 6 Cal. 17; *Phelan v. Oleny* (1856), 6 Cal. 478; *Montgomery v. Tutt* (1858), 11 Cal. 307; *Tyler v. Yreka Water Co.* (1859), 14 Cal. 212; *Horn v. Volcano Water Co.* (1861), 18 Cal. 141;

Kearsing v. Kilian (1861), 18 Cal. 491; *Cook v. Guerra* (1864), 24 Cal. 237; *Doe v. Vallejo* (1866), 29 Cal. 385.

53. 23 Cal. 16, 31–34.

54. 26 Cal. 141, 145; also see *Lent v. Shear* (1864), 26 Cal. 361.

55. Cal. Code of Civil Proceedings (1851), sections 221–37.

56. Charles Walter purchased part of Rancho Lupyomi in 1852. On February 17, 1857, he completed his ownership of the rancho by sheriff's deed (David Alexander Collection, MSS, Huntington Library, Box 1). Also see Cleland, *Cattle on a Thousand Hills,* pp. 164–66.

57. *Sands v. Pfeiffer and Schleischer* (1858), 10 Cal. 258, 246–65.

58. *Montgomery v. Tutt, Wilson et al.* (1858), 111 Cal. 190; also see *Skinner v. Beatty* (1860), 16 Cal. 156.

59. 30 Cal. 367; also see *Brown v. Winter and Sherry* (1859), 14 Cal. 31; *The People v. Irwin* (1859), 14 Cal. 428; *Boggs v. Fowler and Hargrave* (1860), 16 Cal. 559; *Horn v. Jones* (1865), 28 Cal. 194; *Thomas v. Vanlieu* (1865), 28 Cal. 616.

60. *Benham v. Rowe* (1852), 2 Cal. 387; *Kent and Cahoon v. Laffan* (1852), 2 Cal. 595; *Allen v. Phelps* (1854), 4 Cal. 256; *Frink v. Murphy* (1862), 21 Cal. 108; *Blockley v. Fowler* (1863), 21 Cal. 326; *Daubenspeck v. Platt* (1863), 22 Cal. 330; *Green v. Butler* (1864), 26 Cal. 595; *Alexander v. Greenwood* (1864), 24 Cal. 505.

61. *Simpers and Craumer v. Sloan and Sloan* (1855), 5 Cal. 457; also see *Pfeiffer and Wife v. Riehn and Scannell* (1859), 13 Cal. 643.

62. 28 Cal. 37, 43. Lack of capacity was not limited to married women. One interesting case involved the Pueblo of San Jose and its efforts to become the state capital. To house the legislature, 17 citizens put up money to buy a facility. The city council, or Ayutamiento, purchased the land and building from the citizens' trustees. The city then sold the facility to the County of Santa Clara at a profit and refused to pay the trustees, who sued, purchased at the sheriff's sale, resold, and collected. But to their distress, the Court informed them that the city council lacked capacity and they were without effective remedy [*Branham v. Mayor and Common Council of San Jose* (1864), 24 Cal. 585].

63. 10 Cal. 296.

64. 12 Cal. 327, 329.

65. *Dillon v. Byrne and Byrne* (1855), 5 Cal. 455, 457; also see *Rix v. McHenry and Wife* (1857), 7 Cal. 89; *Dorsey v. McFarland* (1857), 7 Cal. 342; *Revalk v. Kraemer* (1857), 8 Cal. 66; *Cook v. Klink* (1857), 8 Cal. 347.

66. *Lunig v. Brady and Gilson* (1858), 10 Cal. 265.

67. *Dana v. Stanfords and Dietz* (1858), 10 Cal. 269. The debtor could die, creating other problems: see *Belloc v. Rogers* (1858), 9 Cal. 123; *Peachaud v. Rinquet* (1862), 21 Cal. 76; *Burton v. Lies* (1862), 21 Cal. 87; *Willis v. Farley* (1864), 24 Cal. 490; *Peck v. Brummagim* (1866), 31 Cal. 440.

68. 1 Cal. 203.

69. 4 Cal. 173, 174.

70. *Furguson v. Miller* (1854), 4 Cal. 97; *Peters v. Jamestown Bridge Co.* (1855), 5 Cal. 334; *Guy v. Carriere* (1855), 5 Cal. 511; *Borrell v. Schie* (1858), 9 Cal 104; *Raun v. Reynolds* (1858), 12 Cal. 190; *Daggett v. Rankin and Vischer* (1866), 31 Cal. 321. The priority questions were often clouded by the rapid and multiple transactions concerning the same property as well as sloppy legal work. See, as examples, *Ferguson* (1854), *Peters* (1855), and *Daggett* (1866). In *Daggett*, Chief Justice Currey caustically commented that "the pleadings in the suit are drawn in an extremely loose and careless manner" (31 Cal. 321, 326).

71. Average values of mortgage cases: 1850, $3,000.00; 1852, $3,675.30; 1853, $1,932.00; 1854, $7,828.55; 1855, $29,600.00; 1856, $2,513.70; 1857, $7,610.30; 1858, $11,211.50; 1859, $9,570.20; 1860, $21,257.40; 1861, $16,733.17; 1862, $4,431.40; 1863, $20,664.00; 1864, $7,402.40; 1865, $5,522.10; 1866, $8,350.00.

72. On instrumentalism, see Morton J. Horwitz, "The Emergence of an Instrumental Conception of American Law, 1780–1820," 5 *Perspectives in American History* 287–326 (1971); Harry N. Scheiber, "Instrumentalism and Property Rights: A Reconsideration of American 'Styles in Judicial Reasoning' in the 19th Century," 1975 *Wisconsin Law Review* 1–18 (1975); Lynda Sharp Paine, "Instrumentalism v. Formalism: Dissolving the Dichotomy," 1978 *Wisconsin Law Review* 997–1025 (1978).

73. See *Johnson v. Sherman* (1860), 15 Cal. 287; *Dana v. Stanfords and Deitz* (1858), 10 Cal. 269; *Hickox v. Lowe* (1858), 10 Cal. 197; Charles W. McCurdy, "Stephen J. Field and Public Land Law Development in California, 1850–1866," 10 *Law and Society Review* 235–66 (Winter 1976); idem, "Justice Field and the Jurisprudence of Government–Business Relations," 61 *Journal of American History* 970–1005 (1975).

74. Walton Bean, *California, An Interpretative History* (New York, New York, 1973), pp. 271–76; also see Hubert Howe Bancroft, *History of California*, 7 vols. (San Francisco, California, 1890), vol. 7, pp. 1–37; Gerald D. Nash, "Stages of California's Economic Growth, 1870–1970: An Interpretation," in *Essays and Assays: California History Reappraised*, edited by George H. Knoles (Los Angeles, California, 1973), pp. 41–43.

75. Bean, *California*, p. 276; Cleland, *Cattle on a Thousand Hills*, pp. 172–73; see Stearns Collection, Box 85, for some of the major transactions, including one for 55,523 acres.

76. Bean, *California*, pp. 271–72; Warren A. Beck and David A. Williams, *California* (Garden City, New York, 1972), pp. 278–79; David Lavender, *California: Land of New Beginnings* (New York, 1972), pp. 292–94.

77. See David Jacks Collection, MSS, Huntington Library.

78. Banning Co. Papers, Boxes 2, 5A, 6, and 8; also see Maymie Krythe, *Port Admiral, Phineas Banning, 1830–1855* (San Francisco, California, 1957).

79. Holmes to Jacks, May 16, 1866, Jacks Collection, Box C(1).

80. Lawton to Jacks, September 20, 1873, ibid., Box C(2).

81. Cf., for example, the handwritten deeds of the 1850s and 1860s with the printed form deeds of the 1870s. See deeds of

November 29, 1853, April 14, 1855, April 16, 1858, and April 23, 1861 (bargain and sale deed language), Gideon J. Carpenter Collection, MSS, Bancroft Library (Berkeley, California); deeds of June 15, 1872, and December 8, 1877 (Quitclaim), Campodonico Family Collection, MSS, California State Library (Sacramento, California),Box 146; John A. Sutter deed of June 1, 1849 (bargain and sale), George McKinstry, Jr., Collection, MSS, California State Library, Box 236; deeds of September 10, 1877,and October 10, 1885, for form deeds of period, John W. Snowball Collection, California State Library, Box 490.

82. Matthew Keller Collection, MSS, Huntington Library, Box 3: Lemmert mortgage of January 29, 1877, is a good example.

83. See J. Downey to Benjamin D. Wilson, July 20, 1866, Wilson Collection, Box 11. A deed was dropped off with two notes. Dealers in small transactions but high volume like David Jacks had several real estate agents and a bevy of attorneys to superintend the loaning of money on land.

84. For example, see Henry D. Bacon to Samuel L. M. Barlow, May 16, 1873, Barlow Collection, MSS, Huntington Library, Box 83; also see William Perry to Matthew Keller, May 18, 1868, bond for deed to portion of Rancho San Francisquito, William Wolfskill Collection, MSS, Huntington Library.

85. Keller Collection, Box 1.

86. 41 Cal. 22, 27.

87. 42 Cal. 169, 172.

88. 44 Cal. 100, 104.

89. Also see *Purdy v. Bullard* (1871), 41 Cal. 444; *Hall v. Yoell* (1873), 45 Cal. 584; *Hill v. Eldred* (1874), 49 Cal. 398.

90. See *Patterson v. Donner* (1874), 48 Cal. 369; particularly Rhodes' dissent, pp. 380-82.

91. *California Compiled Laws* (1853), ch. 122, pp. 513-19 (April 16, 1850); also see Friedman, *History of American Law*, p. 55.

92. *Cal. Laws 1865-66* (1866), ch. 349, p. 429.

93. *Cal. Laws 1865-66* (1866), ch. 636, p. 813.

94. *Cal. Laws 1865-66* (1866), ch. 620, p. 848.

95. See *Pio Pico v. Gallardo* (1877), 52 Cal. 206; *Frey v. Clifford* (1872), 44 Cal. 335.

96. John Reynolds to David Jacks, August 9, 1878 (also June 4, 1979), Jacks Collection, Box C(2).

97. James A. Clayton to Jacks, February 14 and 23, 1878, and January 10, 1879, ibid., Boxes C(2) and C(3).

98. See Henry D. Bacon to Samuel L. M. Barlow correspondence, July-December 1869, Barlow Collection, Box 69. Isaias Hellman to Matthew Keller, April 3 and September 11, 1878, Keller Collection, Box 1.

99. Hellman to Keller, August 12, 1879, Keller Collection, Box 1.

100. Clayton to Jacks, January 10, 1879, Jacks Collection, Box C(3).

101. Clayton to Jacks, January 25, 1879, ibid.

102. Clayton to Jacks, May 10, 1879, ibid.

103. Debtors often expressed personal regret that the action was necessary. For example, William Robson told Jacks in 1878

that his whole family was sick with "the idea of being attached"
(William Robson to Jacks, December 28, 1878, ibid.).

104. Jacks would lease property for six months to keep it up and
obtain some cash from the property [see W. H. Clark to Jacks,
April 2, July 30, 1879, ibid., Box C(2)]. Jacks even extended
redemption beyond six months [John Markley to Jacks, May 14, 1879,
ibid., Box C(3).

105. Soto to Jacks, December 30, 1879, ibid., Box C(1).

106. T. Wood to Jacks, December 17, 1878, ibid., Box C(2); also
see Notice of Warrant in Bankruptcy of Peter Heron, August 8,
1878, ibid.; Memorandum of Agreement of Creditors of W. B. Wells,
June 4, 1879, ibid., Box B(V)(I)(10); Charles Langley to Jacks,
June 24, 1879, ibid., Box C(3).

107. 59 Cal. 650.

108. 50 Cal. 650, 651.

109. *Cal. Laws 1873-74* (1874), ch. 474, p. 707.

110. *Cal. Laws 1860*, p. 311.

111. 33 Cal. 326, 331.

112. Also see *McLaughlin v. Hart* (1873), 46 Cal. 638.

113. 36 Cal. 11.

114. 36 Cal. 11, 22.

115. 36 Cal. 11, 23.

116. 52 Cal. 334.

117. 52 Cal. 334, 335.

118. 45 Cal. 580, 583-84; also see *Perkins v. Center* (1868),
35 Cal. 713.

119. 33 Cal. 668; also see *Remington v. Higgins* (1880),
54 Cal. 620.

120. 52 Cal. 644.

121. 52 Cal. 644, 650; also see *Bludworth v. Lake* (1867),
33 Cal. 255. Joining all parties was also necessary to avoid
losing part of an investment.

122. Clark to Jacks, April 2, 1879, Jacks Collection, Box C(3).
The workingmen paid six months in advance (Clarks to Jacks,
July 30, 1879, ibid.).

123. Jacks frequently carried debtors from year to year [see Soto
to Jacks, December 28, 1870, ibid., Box C(1); Albon to Jacks,
July 27, 1878, ibid., Box C(2); Abbott to Jacks, April 23, 1878,
ibid.]. Jacks even extended the statutory time of redemption
[John Markley to Jacks, May 14, 1879, ibid., Box C(3)]. See
generally on the late 1870s Robert Glass Cleland, *A History of
California: The American Period* (New York, New York, 1922),
pp. 402-23; Lavender, *California* pp. 295-310.

124. Bacon to Barlow, August 30, 1879, Barlow Collection, Box 125.

125. See Notice of Warrant of Bankruptcy of Peter Heron, August
8, 1878, Jacks Collection, Box C(2). Memorandum Agreement of
Creditors of W. B. Wells, June 4, 1879, ibid., Box B(V)(I)(10);
Charles Langley to Jacks, June 24, 1879, ibid., Box C(3).

126. Woods to Jacks, December 17, 1878, ibid., Box C(2).

127. 46 Cal. 603.

128. 46 Cal. 603, 607.

129. 56 Cal. 297.

130. 56 Cal. 297, 300-307.

131. 56 Cal. 297, 303; on *Ogden*, see Swisher, *History of Supreme Court*, pp. 152-54.

132. Also see *Pitte v. Shipley* (1873). Chief Justice Addison C. Niles declared similarly that "the failure to present the mortgage to the executrix and the Probate Judge in the manner required by the Probate Act, was fatal to plaintiff's recovery" (46 Cal. 154, 161). Statute of Limitations cases often presented similar problems [see *Wells v. Harter* (1880), 56 Cal. 342; *Biddel v. Brizzolara* (1880), 56 Cal. 374].

133. *Hibernia Savings and Loan v. Herbert* (1879), 53 Cal. 375.

134. *Low v. Allen* (1864), 26 Cal. 141.

135. *Espinosa v. Gregory* (1870), 40 Cal. 58, 62.

136. 43 Cal. 185, 187.

137. 43 Cal. 185, 187-88.

138. 34 Cal. 548, 553-54.

139. 43 Cal. 496, 497.

140. 50 Cal. 549.

141. See Beck and Williams, *California*, pp. 260-65; Bean, *California*, pp. 304-5; Zoeth Skinner Eldredge, *History of California*, 5 vols., (New York, New York, 1915), vol. 4, pp. 341-72.

142. First National Gold Bank Scrap Book, MSS, Santa Barbara Historical Society (Santa Barbara, California).

143. Hellman to Keller, April 22, 1879, Keller Collection, Box 1.

144. See Swisher, *Motivation and Political Technique in the California Constitutional Convention, 1878-79* (Claremont, California, 1930), pp. 84-85.

145. SLO *Tribune*, April 19, 1879, p. 4, col. 2.

146. Ibid., May 6, 1879, p. 1, col. 3; ibid., April 29, 1879, p. 4., col. 4.

147. Santa Barbara *Daily Press*, May 5, 1879, p. 3, col. 3.

148. Keller to Hellman, April 30, 1879, Keller Collection, Box 1.

149. SLO *Tribune*, April 28, 1879, p. 2, col. 1.

150. Bean, *California*, p. 305.

151. See Glenn S. Dumke, *The Boom of the Eighties in Southern California* (San Marino, California, 1944).

152. Beck and Williams, *California*, p. 290.

153. Ibid., pp. 299-303.

154. Swisher, *Motivation and Political Technique*, pp. 66-79.

155. Clough to Mother, August 18, 1879, Clough Collection, MSS, California State Library, California Section, Box 157.

156. Graves to Wallace, February 22, 1881, Graves Collection, MSS, Huntington Library, 1881-83 Letterbook.

157. Memorandum of McCarthy loan, February 23 and April 19, 1881, entries, Jacks Collection, Box B(II)4.

158. Reynolds to Jacks, May 10, 1880, ibid., Box C(3).

159. Ninety-one cases studied:

Year	Creditors won:
1867	71%
1868	60%
1869	50%
1870	43%
1871	90%
1872	71%
1873	67%
1874	67%
1875	75%
1876	100%
1877	100%
1878	60%
1879	40%
1880	62%
Average:	67%

160. Average by year of amount in controversy where noted in appellate case report.

1867	$24,732.50
1868	2,166.67
1869	9,581.79
1870	16,493.19
1871	3,040.14
1872	24,229.00
1873	2,950.67
1874	8,646.38
1875	17,927.67
1876	no data
1877	1,150.00 (single case with data)
1878	3,293.00
1879	17,833.33
1880	34,628.13

Range = $225,000 to $145.00

161. For example, see March 8, 1888, receipt for the W. A. Keany law library [Jacks Collection, Box B(V)(10)]; see James A. Clayton-Jacks correspondence, 1879-80, ibid., Box C(3).
162. Graves, O'Melveny, and Shankland to Jarboe, Harrison, and Goodfellow, March 19, 1890, Graves Collection, 1890-91 Letterbook.
163. 59 Cal. 541.
164. 4 Wheaton 122.
165. 60 Cal. 367, 368.
166. 60 Cal. 367, 371.
167. 65 Cal. 383, 384.

168. 66 Cal. 44, 45–46; for other corporation cases see *Granger v. Original Empire Mill and Mining Co.* (1881), 59 Cal. 678; *McLane v. Placerville and Sacramento Valley RR Co.* (1885), 66 Cal. 606; *Alta Silver Mining Co. v. Alta Placer Mining Co.* (1889), 78 Cal. 629. Mining companies were also in court: *Cornell v. Corbin* (1883), 64 Cal. 197; *Montgomery v. Keppeland Spring Valley Mining and Irrigating Co.* (1880), 75 Cal. 128; *McPherson v. Weston* (1890), 85 Cal. 90.

169. 76 Cal. 291. As late as 1887, the Court remained reluctant to so decide [see *Doland v. Mooney* (1887), 72 Cal. 34].

170. 77 Cal. 136, 139.

171. The Court did uphold the *Mayre v. Harte* rule in *Brown v. Clark* (1891), 89 Cal. 196. The issue did not go away until November 8, 1910, when the section was repealed. See *Knott v. Peden* (1890), 84 Cal. 199; *San Gabriel Co. v. Witmer Co.* (1892), 96 Cal. 623; *Mackay v. San Francisco* (1896), 113 Cal. 392; *Hibernia Savings & Loan Society v. Behnke* (1898), 121 Cal. 339; *Canadian Co. v. Boas* (1902), 136 Cal. 419; *Matthew v. Ormed* (1903), 140 Cal. 578; *William Ede Co. v. Heywood* (1908), 153 Cal. 615; *Bank of Willows v. County of Glenn* (1906), 155 Cal. 352.

172. H. H. Bancroft and Company to John D. Goodwin, September 15, 1869, Goodwin Collection, MSS, California State Library, California Section, Box 727; also see Couts Collection, Box 75; Blue Lake Water Company, BC 338, MSS, Huntington Library; Bancroft Blank No. 398–Declaration of Abandonment, Jacks Collection, Box B(III)(8); Barclay Collection, MSS, Huntington Library, Rancho Mascupiabe Section, Box 4.

173. Warner to George, Allice, and Elsie Warner, October 23, 1887, Warner Collection, California State Library, California Section, Box 327.

174. Graves to F. A. Hihn, November 10, 1887, Graves Collection, 1885–88 Letterbook.

175. Goodwin to Smith, November 2, 1884, Goodwin Collection, Box 730.

176. Pyburn to Jacks, December 15, 1887, Jacks Collection, Box C(6).

177. Markey to Jacks, April 13, 1881, ibid., Box C(4).

178. Arthur G. Bowman, *Ogden's Revised California Real Property Law* (Berkeley, California, 1974), vol. 1, pp. 587–88; also see Friedman, *History of American Law*, pp. 212–13.

179. *Hall v. Shotwell* (1885), 66 Cal. 379; also see *Pellier v. Gillespie* (1885), 67 Cal. 582.

180. *De Sepulveda v. Baugh* (1887), 74 Cal. 468.

181. *Gage v. Downey* (1889), 79 Cal. 140.

182. 76 Cal. 535, 536–37; also see *Borel v. Donahue* (1884), 64 Cal. 447.

183. Pyburn to Jacks, March 13, 1888, Jacks Collection, Box C(7).

184. January 21, 1884, Graves Collection, 1883–85 Letterbook.

185. Graves and O'Melveny to Klauber and Live, May 26, 1885, ibid.

186. Graves to Dalleman and Company, October 26, 1889, ibid., 1889–90 Letterbook.

187. 58 Cal. 254; also see *Grogan v. Thrift* (1881), 58 Cal. 378; *Fitzgerald v. Fernandez* (1886), 71 Cal. 504.

188. *Graham v. Oviatt* (1881), 58 Cal. 428.

189. See *Marbury v. Ruiz* (1881), 58 Cal. 11; *Orr v. Stewart* (1885), 67 Cal. 275.

190. *Grupe v. Byers* (1887), 73 Cal. 271; *Gleason v. Spray* (1889), 81 Cal. 217.

191. *Shinn v. Macpherson* (1881), 58 Cal. 596, 599.

192. See *Simpers and Craumer v. Sloan and Sloan* (1855), 5 Cal. 457; *Pfeiffer and Wife v. Riehn and Schannell* (1859), 13 Cal. 643; *Ramsdell v. Fuller and Summer* (1865), 28 Cal. 37.

193. *DeArnaz v. Escandon* (1881), 59 Cal. 486; *Joseph v. Dougherty* (1882), 60 Cal. 358; *California Civil Code* (1873), sections 158, 1093, 1186, 1187, 1191, 1202.

194. *Tolman v. Smith* (1887), 74 Cal. 345.

195. *Burkle v. Levy* (1886), 70 Cal. 250; *Bull v. Coe* (1888), 77 Cal. 54.

196. Jacks to Freeman and Bates, June 21, 1889, Jacks Collection, Box C(7).

197. 59 Cal. 138.

198. 85 Cal. 610.

199. 71 Cal. 513; 79 Cal. 115, 119.

200. Graves et al. to Jarboe, Harrison, and Goodfellow, March 19, 1890, Graves Collection, 1890-91 Letterbook.

201. Jacks Collection, Box C(5); also see Jacks to S. O. Houghton (L. A.), May 31, December 11, 12, and 14, 1887, and April 26, 1888, Box C(6), and April 26, 1888, Box C(7), for numerous complaints about delay and expense in foreclosure.

202. David Jacks had an agent in Salinas City dealing in sheriff's deeds for him [see F. F. Birlem to Jacks, January 7, 1888, ibid., Box C(6)].

203. See *Calkins v. Steinbach* (1884), 66 Cal. 117; *Watt v. Wright* (1884), 66 Cal. 202; *Hall v. Arnott* (1889), 80 Cal. 348.

204. 68 Cal. 156.

205. 78 Cal. 278, 282.

206. 78 Cal. 278, 283.

207. Hammond to Goodwin, February 28, 1869, Goodwin Collection, Box 731; on attorney's fees, see *Dean v. Applegarth* (1884), 65 Cal. 391; *Monroe v. Fohl* (1887), 72 Cal. 568. Hammond later changed the spelling of his surname to Haymond.

208. 67 Cal. 235, 236.

209. *Withers v. Little* (1880), 56 Cal. 219; *Little v. Superior Court* (1887), 74 Cal. 219; *Withers v. Jacks* (1889), 79 Cal. 297; also see *Little v. Jacks* (1885), 67 Cal. 165, and (1886), 68 Cal. 343. Jacks was often in court. See *Jacks v. Buell* (1873), 47 Cal. 162; *Jacks v. Baldez* (1892), 97 Cal. 91; *Jacks v. Estee* (1903), 139 Cal. 507; *Jacks v. Deering* (1907), 150 Cal. 272; *Jacks v. Johnston* (1890), 86 Cal. 384; *Swain v. Jacks* (1899), 125 Cal. 215 (on an 1877 foreclosure). Jacks went all the way to the U. S. Supreme Court to have title to lands he purchased on February 9, 1859, confirmed [*City of Monterey v. Jacks* (1906), 203 U.S. 360].

210. Jacks filed on June 2, 1876; Withers filed on December 12, 1875.
211. 74 Cal. 219.
212. Jacks to S. O. Houghton, December 11, 1887, Jacks Collection, Box C(6).
213. Jacks to Houghton, December 12 and 14, 1887, ibid.
214. S. F. Leib to Jacks, December 10, 1887, ibid.
215. 79 Cal. 297, 299–300.
216. *Bank of Sonoma v. Charles* (1890), 86 Cal. 322, 327.
217. 86 Cal. 322, 327.
218. 83 Cal. 319, 320–21.
219. 83 Cal. 319, 321; on works, see Leland G. Stanford, *Footprints of Justice in San Diego* (San Diego, California, 1960), pp. 38–40.
220. 83 Cal. 30, 32.
221. See *Glide v. Dwyer* (1890), 83 Cal. 477; *Campbell v. West* (1890), 86 Cal. 197; *McGurren v. Garrity* (1886), 68 Cal. 566; *Eaton v. Rocca* (1888), 75 Cal. 93.
222. *Wilson v. White* (1890), 84 Cal. 239, 241; also see *Leviston v. Henninger* (1888), 77 Cal. 461, where the plaintiff's attorney failed to introduce the judgment upon which the execution issued.
223. *White v. Patton* (1890), 87 Cal. 151.
224. 61 Cal. 333, 334.
225. *Schwartz v. Palm* (1884), 65 Cal. 54.
226. 79 Cal. 517, 523; also see *Schrivener v. Dietz* (1885), 68 Cal. 1, granting new trial for trial court error; for a case without substantial legal questions on appeal, see *Phelan v. DeMartin* (1890), 85 Cal. 365.
227. 60 Cal. 360; also see *Hamilton v. Jones* (1882), 62 Cal. 473; on *Burr*, also see *Grant v. Burr* (1880), 54 Cal. 298; *Bateman v. Burr* (1881), 57 Cal. 480.
228. 76 Cal. 229.
229. 82 Cal. 635.
230. See *Biddel v. Brizzolara* (1883), 64 Cal. 354; *Barnard v. Wilson* (1884), 66 Cal. 251; *Hibernia Savings and Loan Society v. Conlin* (1885), 67 Cal. 178.
231. *Wise v. Griffith* (1889), 78 Cal. 152.
232. *Cal. Stat.* (1860), p. 311, fourth section, amending the tenth section of the 1851 Homestead Act; *Cal. Stat.* (1862), p. 319; see *Herrold v. Rene* (1881), 58 Cal. 443.
233. *Watson v. His Creditors* (1881), 58 Cal. 556.
234. *Camp v. Grider* (1882), 62 Cal. 20, 27.
235. Ibid., 26; *Security Savings Bank v. Connell* (1884), 65 Cal. 574; *Barnard v. Wilson* (1887), 74 Cal. 512; *Moran v. Gardemeyer* (1889), 82 Cal. 96.
236. See *Harn v. Kennedy* (1890), 85 Cal. 55; *Perkins v. Onyett* (1890), 86 Cal. 348; *Building and Loan Association v. King* (1890), 83 Cal. 440.
237. See *Murdock v. Clarke* (1881), 59 Cal. 683; *Crosby v. Dowd* (1882), 61 Cal. 557; *Johnston v. San Francisco Savings Union* (1883), 63 Cal. 554; *Chambers v. Stockton Building and*

Loan Society (1883), 64 Cal. 77; *Bayly v. Muehe* (1884), 65 Cal. 345; *Goldtree v. McAlister* (1890), 86 Cal. 93.

238. Graves to Mrs. Kellogg, January 5, 1880, Graves Collection, 1879–80 Letterbook.

239. Jacks to Clayton, March 22, 1890, Jacks Collection, Box C(8).

240. In 1888, Jacks purchased W. A. Kearney's law library for $200 and moved his prior collection including "Judge Cutter's library" into Kearney's office [see bill of sale, ibid., Box (V)(10)].

241. Marsteller to Goodwin, May 21, 1883, Goodwin Collection, Box 733.

242. Graves and O'Melveny to D. N. and E. Walter and Co,. March 16 and May 10, 1888, Graves Collection, 1885–88 Letterbook.

243. Graves, O'Melveny, and Shankland to Dalleman and Company, October 26, 1889, ibid., 1889–90 Letterbook.

244. Graves to Leach, November 19, 1881, ibid., 1881–83 Letterbook.

245. Graves to Lilienthal and Company, December 27, 1881, ibid.

246. Graves and O'Melveny to Klauber and Live (law firm), May 26, 1885, ibid., 1883–85 Letterbook.

247. Graves to J. Naphtely, February 24 and March 1, 1880, ibid., 1879–80 Letterbook.

248. Bates to Jacks, April 15, 1890, Jacks Collection, Box C(8).

249. 13 Cal. 116; 27 Cal. 604.

250. See Friedman, *History of American Law*, p. 353; *Taylor v. McLain* (1884), 64 Cal. 513.

251. See *Husheon v. Husheon* (1886), 71 Cal. 407, 411–12.

252. 68 Cal. 404; also see *Scranton v. Begol* (1882), 60 Cal. 642; *Ross v. Brusie* (1886), 70 Cal. 465; *Dalton v. Leahey* (1889), 80 Cal. 446; *Smith v. Smith* (1889), 80 Cal. 323.

253. Friedman, *History of American Law*, pp. 374–75; Horwitz, *Transformation of American Law* , pp. 265–66; James Willard Hurst, *Law and Economic Growth* (Cambridge, Massachusetts, 1964), pp. 285–88. Edwin G. Gager, "Mortgages of Real Property," in *Two Centuries' Growth of American Law* (New York, New York, 1901), pp. 153–66.

254. 59 Cal. 496, 501–2; also see *Boughton v. Vasquez* (1887), 73 Cal. 325, where equity was applied, giving the creditor a mortgage interest in the property of an insolvent debtor.

255. *Persons v. Shaeffer* (1884), 65 Cal. 79; *Matzen v. Shaeffer* (1884), 65 Cal. 81.

256. *Grangers' Business Association of California v. Clark* (1885), 67 Cal. 634.

257. *Wise v. Walker* (1889), 81 Cal. 11; *Montgomery v. Merrill* (1884), 65 Cal. 432 (a 25–page opinion).

258. 75 Cal. 271; also see *Cazara v. Orena* (1889), 80 Cal. 132; *Rhorer v. Bila* (1890), 83 Cal. 51.

259. As F. Blackie (Castroville) reported to Jacks on August 26, 1890,

> Jim Kee promises verbally to bring all or nearly all of his crop here (Morocojo Warehouse) and instructs me to send you net proceeds thereof to be applied in paying off his mortgage. He seems to be quite honest in his intentions, but as his promise to haul

his crop here is only verbal, I would suggest the
better to secure yourself that you have some written
agreement whereby to bind him to deliver all here on
your account or until such time as the mortgage is
paid.

Jacks Collection, Box C(8). The prevalent need felt to have
a written contract was clearly evidenced here, as well as the
developing use of warehousemen as third-party receivers of goods
to pay outstanding debts. Jacks used the warehousemen and
warehouse receipts as part of his lending and collection system
throughout the decade [see W. P. L. Winham to Jacks, November 11,
1880, ibid., Box C(3)].

260. For example, see James A. Clayton to Jacks, June 2 and
October 13, 1887, ibid., Box C(6); John Markey to Jacks, October
19, 1881, ibid., Box C(4); John Chase Hall to John Goodwin, May 30
and June 16, 1883, Goodwin Collection, Box 731; "Deeds and
Mortgages given by W. B. Couts . . . 1887," Couts Collection,
Box 75.

261. The California Court was quite willing to follow its own
precedent as well as to overthrow it and make new law. The parol
evidence rule cases of decades earlier than the 1860s and the
deficiency judgment cases of the 1870s were examples of creating
new precedents. In the 1880s the Court avoided creating new law
by deference to the legislature or the code where convenient. See
Bollinger v. Manning (1889), 79 Cal. 7; *Barbieri v. Ramelli*
(1890), 84 Cal. 154, 158, in which Justice Thomas B. McFarland
tersely stated the general proposition that where "there is no
sufficient reason for overturning the line of decisions on the
subject," they should stand. However, "if the question were an
open one, I would come to a different conclusion." The Court's
reputation as eccentric stemmed from viewing too many questions
as "open ones."

262. See *Tapia v. Demartini* (1888), 77 Cal. 383; *Lavenson v.
Standard Soap* (1889), 80 Cal. 245; *Staples v. May* (1890), 87
Cal. 178; *Downing v. LeDu* (1890), 82 Cal. 471; *Wilson v. White*
((1890), 84 Cal. 239.

263. See Friedman, *History of American Law*, pp. 343-45; also
see, on the adoption of English common law, Edwin W. Young,
"The Adoption of Common Law in California," 4 *American Journal of
Legal History* 355-63 (1960); Leon R. Yankwich, "Social Attitudes
as Reflected in Early California Law," 10 *Hastings Law Review*
250-70 (1959).

264. See John C. Hall to John D. Goodwin, May 5, 1883, Goodwin
Collection, Box 731; *Brickell v. Batchelder* (1882), 62 Cal.
623. The Court also found a Pennsylvania precedent not to be
helpful [*Kelly v. Matlock* (1890), 85 Cal. 122].

265. 62 Cal. 623, 633-37.

266. Also see Gordon M. Bakken, "Admiralty Law in Nineteenth
Century California," 58 *Southern California Quarterly* 499-513
(Winter 1976).

267. See Deeds and Mortgages listing, Couts Collection, Box 75;
William H. Patterson (San Francisco) to David Jacks, April 26,
1880, Jacks Collection, Box C(3); James A. Clayton to Jacks,

September 12, 1883, ibid., Box C(4); J. S. Raine to John Goodwin, August 20, 1881, Goodwin Collection, Box 735. There are dozens of solicitations in the Jacks Collection for every year from 1880 to 1888. For 1879-1880, see Box C(3), especially James A. Clayton and R. D. McElroy correspondence.

268. For example, see Benjamin F. Jones (Buffalo, New York) to David Jacks, December 18, 1889, January 18, 1890, February 10 and 20, 1890, Jacks Collection, Boxes C(7) and C(8); H. S. Dunn to John Goodwin, March 25, 1882, Goodwin Collection, Box 729.

269. See Mary S. Salisbury to David Jacks, March 22, 1886, Jacks Collection, Box C(5); Lizzie L. Suedaker to Jacks, December 9, 1889, Jacks to Suedaker, December 13, 1889, ibid., Box C(7); J. A. Riley to Jacks, January 7, 1890, ibid., Box C(8).

270. For example, L. W. Pollard increased his mortgage indebtedness to David Jacks to finance the construction of ranch buildings [James A. Clayton to Jacks, April 3 and May 3, 1888, ibid., Box C(6)].

271. James B. Capip to Jacks, October 25, 1889, ibid., Box C(7).

272. Jacks adjusted his rates downward in the mid-1880s. See N. A. Dorn to Jacks, March 15, 1883, ibid., Box C(4); James A. Clayton to Jacks, June 28, 1884, ibid., Box C(5); William P. Hook to Jacks, July 21, 26, 28, 1887, ibid., Box C(6).

273. James A. Clayton to Jacks, October 29, 1888, ibid., Box C(6).

274. Clayton to Jacks, June 6, 1890, ibid., Box C(8).

275. Contract of Guarantee to Henry Cowell, December 31, 1875, ibid., Box (V)(I)(10).

276. John R. Hetland, *California Real Estate Secured Transactions* (Berkeley, California, 1970), p. 11.

277. *More v. Calkins* (1890), 85 Cal. 177.

278. A. M. Kidd, "Trust Deeds and Mortgages in California," 3 *California Law Review* 381, 390 (1915).

279. James Willard Hurst, *Law and the Conditions of Freedom in the Nineteenth-Century United States* (Madison, Wisconsin, 1956), pp. 3-32.

280. The appellate win-loss record for the decade was little different from the decade of the 1870s.

Year	Creditors won	Average value	Number of cases studied
1881	66.00%	$ 3,807.30	(10)
1882	87.00%	$ 8,874.68	(10)
1883	53.00%	$ 18,389.40	(5)
1884	72.00%	$ 16,662.14	(10)
1885	66.00%	$ 23,051.99	(8)
1886	73.00%	$ 7,781.63	(10)
1887	71.00%	$ 3,087.91	(7)
1888	57.00%	$ 116,006.22	(9)
1889	47.50%	$ 16,543.52	(10)
1890	78.00%	$ 11,608.07	(19)
Average:	68.47%	$ 11,322.79*	176 cases studied

*Average for period based on 97 cases, $11,3232.79, excluding one $1,000,000.00 case.

CHAPTER 4

1. As many students of the law realize, the California courts
have had a leadership role in tort law: See *Muskopf v. Corning
Hospital District* (1961), 55 Cal. 2d 211, sovereign immunity;
Williams v. Carr (1968), 68 Cal. 2d 579, guests; *Vanoni v.
Western Airlines* (1967), 247 Cal. App. 2d 793, emotional
distress; *Pike v. Hough Co.* (1970), 2 Cal. 3d 465, defective
products.
2. See Lawrence M. Friedman and Jack Ladinsky, "Social Change
and the Law of Industrial Accidents," 67 *Columbia Law Review* 50
(1967); Carl A. Auerbach, Lloyd K. Garrison, Willard Hurst, and
Samuel Mermin, *The Legal Process* (San Francisco, California,
1961); Philippe Nonet, *Administrative Justice* (New York, New
York, 1969), a history of the California Industrial Accident
Commission; Gary T. Schwartz, "Tort Law and the Economy in
Nineteenth-Century America: A Reinterpretation," 90 *Yale Law
Journal* 1717-75 (July 1981).
3. William L. Prosser, *The Law of Torts*, 3rd ed. (St. Paul,
Minnesota, 1964), p. 2.
4. *Dwinelle v. Owen* (1868), Chipman-Dwinelle Papers, MSS,
Huntington Library (San Marino, California), Box 1.
5. Fairchild to Bicknell, February 3, 1881, Bicknell
Collection, MSS, Huntington Library, Box 3.
6. Lawrence M. Friedman, *A History of American Law* (New York,
New York, 1973), p. 261.
7. Schwartz, "Tort Law," pp. 1732-33.
8. Ibid., pp. 1758-59.
9. 2 Cal. 326, 340.
10. Also see *Butler v. Howes* (1857), 7 Cal. 87; *Sears v.
Hathaway* (1859), 12 Cal. 277.
11. *Colton v. Onderdonk* (1886), 69 Cal. 155. Professor
Schwartz thinks the language is ambiguous regarding "whether [it]
is the language of negligence or of *Rylands* strict liability"
(Schwartz, "Tort Law," p. 1758, n. 301). The House of Lords used
the term "non-natural" in describing the activity, and English
courts adopted terms like "extraordinary," "exceptional," or
"abnormal" in describing *Rylands* strict liability. The *Colton*
Court used the terms "unreasonable, unusual, and unnatural."
I believe the terms to be those of strict liability. See Prosser,
Law of Torts, p. 520.
12. 4 Cal. 297, 299.
13. *Ramsay v. Chandler* (1853), 3 Cal. 90; *Stiles and Davis v.
Laird* (1855), 5 Cal. 121. Nuisance was a usual subject for early
law practice (see Holladay Family Papers, vol. 1: Notes, Legal
Cases, MSS, Huntington Library).
14. 3 Cal. 238, 241.
15. 3 Cal. 69, 73-74.
16. *Fairchild v. California Stage Co.* (1859), 13 Cal. 599.
17. *Wardrobe v. California Stage Co.* (1857), 7 Cal. 118.
18. *Finn v. Vallejo Street Wharf Co.* (1857), 7 Cal. 253.

19. *Gerke v. California Steam Navigation Co.* (1858), 9 Cal. 251; for comparison, see Gordon Morris Bakken, "Judicial Review in the Rocky Mountain Territorial Courts," 15 *American Journal of Legal History* 56, 63 (January 1971).

20. 3 Cal. 241, 243; see Schwartz, "Tort Law," p. 1751

21. See *Perry v. Malarin* (1895), 107 Cal. 363 as an example.

22. Schwartz, "Tort Law," p. 1764.

23. *Cal. Laws* (1862), ch. 330, pp. 447–48.

24. 34 Cal. 153.

25. *Myers v. San Francisco* (1871), 42 Cal. 215.

26. Brown to Bicknell, June 27, 1889, Bicknell Collection, Box 6.

27. See Robert L. Kelley, *Gold vs. Grain, The Hydraulic Mining Controversy in California's Sacramento Valley* (Glendale, California, 1959).

28. See *Robinson v. Black Diamond Coal Co.* (1875), 50 Cal. 460.

29. *Pastene v. Adams* (1874), 49 Cal. 87; *Graeber v. Derwin* (1872), 43 Cal. 495.

30. 50 Cal. 581.

31. Schwartz, "Tort Law," pp. 1762–63.

32. *Fanjoy v. Seales* (1865), 29 Cal. 243.

33. See, for example, *Todd v. Cochell* (1860), 17 Cal. 97; *Campbell v. B.R. and A.W. and M. Co.* (1868), 35 Cal. 679.

34. *Mathews v. Kinsell* (1871), 41 Cal. 512.

35. 40 Cal. 121, 124.

36. See *Ficken v. Jones* (1865), 28 Cal. 618.

37. *Karr v. Parks* (1870), 40 Cal. 188.

38. 44 Cal. 46, 50 (1872).

39. See Leonard Levy, *The Law of Commonwealth and Chief Justice Shaw* (New York, New York, 1957), pp. 140–65.

40. 22 Cal. 534, 537.

41. 27 Cal. 425; also see *Yeomans v. Contra Costa Steam Navigation Co.* (1872), 44 Cal. 71.

42. *Flynn v. San Francisco and San Jose RR Co.* (1870), 40 Cal. 14.

43. *Perry v. Southern Pacific RR Co.* (1875), 50 Cal. 578.

44. See Bakken, "Judicial Review," p. 63.

45. 50 Cal. 176, 183; see Schwartz, "Tort Law," p. 1748.

46. *Richmond v. Sacramento Valley RR Co.* (1861), 18 Cal. 351.

47. *Needham v. San Francisco and San Jose RR Co.* (1869), 37 Cal. 409; *Deville v. Southern Pacific RR Co.* (1875), 50 Cal. 383; cf. *McCoy v. California Pacific RR Co.* (1871), 40 Cal. 523; also Bakken, "Judicial Review," pp. 61–63.

48. *Flemming v. Western Pacific RR Co.* (1874), 49 Cal. 253. However, the bulk of appellate cases indicates an appellate willingness to support plaintiff claims against the railroads (Schwartz, "Tort Law," pp. 1752, 1756, 1761, 1770).

49. 40 Cal. 188.

50. 40 Cal. 447, 455–56.

51. *Robinson v. Western Pacific RR Co.* (1874), 48 Cal. 409. The Court also circumscribed the reach of the contributory negligence doctrine generally (see Schwartz, "Tort Law," pp. 1759–63).

52. See *Boyce v. California State Co.* (1864), 25 Cal. 460, on damages; for railroad liability cases, see *Wheaton v. N.B. and M.R.R. Co.* (1869), 36 Cal. 590; *Kline v. Central Pacific RR Co.* (1870), 39 Cal. 587; *Taylor v. Western Pacific RR Co.* (1873), 45 Cal. 323; *McQuilken v. Central Pacific RR Co.* (1875), 50 Cal. 7.

53. See *Conlin v. San Francisco and San Jose RR Co.* (1868), 36 Cal. 404; *Hogan v. Central Pacific RR Co.* (1874), 49 Cal. 128.

54. *McGlynn v. Brodie* (1866), 31 Cal. 376.

55. *Alexander McLean v. Blue Point Gravel M. Co.* (1876), 51 Cal. 255; *McDonald v. Hazeltine* (1878), 53 Cal. 35.

56. 69 Cal. 155, 159; also see Schwartz, "Tort Law," p. 1758, at footnote 301, finding the language in the case uncertain.

57. Cf. *Everett v. Hydraulic Flume Tunnel Co.* (1863), 23 Cal. 255; also see *Munroe v. Pacific Coast Dredging and Reclamation Co.* (1890), 84 Cal. 515. *Munroe* was a clear rejection of a commercial advantage argument.

58. *Butcher v. Vaca Valley and Clear Lake RR Co.* (1885), 67 Cal. 518, 525.

59. *McDermott v. San Francisco and North Pacific RR Co.* (1885), 68 Cal. 33.

60. See *Steel v. Pacific Coast RR Co.* (1887), 74 Cal. 323.

61. Schwartz, "Tort Law," p. 1746.

62. See Bicknell Collection, Letterbooks 4 and 5 and Box 6, for numerous documents involving such settlements.

63. Bicknell to Fabens, August 2, 1889, ibid., Letterbook 5.

64. Bicknell to Hammond, March 18, 1889, and March 27, 1890, Letterbook 6.

65. Ibid. Hammond changed the spelling of his name to Haymond.

66. Haymond to Bicknell, April 2, 1890, ibid., Box 6.

67. For example, see Bicknell to J. A. Muir, September 6, 1889, ibid., Box 6. Box 6 also contains the accident form that stated that "if the Engineer kills stock when it is apparent that he might avoid doing so, the value of the stock so killed will be deducted from his pay." An August 17, 1889, report alleges that 16 cattle died when "they were driven on [to the tracks] by owners." Settlements from George C. Fabens for 1889–1890 also grace Box 6. Also see Bicknell to Fabens, October 8, 1890, regarding a "runaway" mare that broke its neck when it crashed into a box car (ibid., Letterbook 6); Bicknell to Fabens, November 15, 1890, recommending settlement rather than appeal, ibid.; Bicknell to M. G. Watson, July 19, 1890, offering settlement, ibid.

68. See *Crowley v. City RR Co.* (1882), 60 Cal. 628; *Roller v. Sutter Street RR Co.* (1884), 66 Cal. 230; *Durkee v. Central Pacific RR Co.* (1886), 69 Cal. 533; *Higgins v. Deeney* (1889), 78 Cal. 578. Also see Schwartz, "Tort Law," p. 1752.

69. Bicknell to Haymond, July 7, 1890, and Bicknell to George C. Fabens, July 7, 1890, Bicknell Collection, Letterbook 6.

70. Bicknell to Haymond, August 9, 1890, ibid.

71. Cf. *Jamison v. San Jose and S.C. RR Co.* (1880), 55 Cal. 593; *Spearman v. California Street RR Co.* (1881), 57 Cal. 432; *MacDougall v. Central RR Co.* (1883), 63 Cal. 431; *McQuilken v.*

Central Pacific RR Co. (1884), 64 Cal. 463; *Lawrence v. Green* (1889), 70 Cal. 417; *Craven v. Central Pacific RR Co.* (1887), 72 Cal. 345; *Lewis v. Riverside Water Co.* (1888), 76 Cal. 249; *Kerrigan v. Southern Pacific RR Co.* (1889), 81 Cal. 248; *Treadwell v. Whittier* (1889), 80 Cal. 574; *Franklin v. Southern California Motor Road Co.* (1890), 85 Cal. 63.

72. See, for example, *Brown v. Central Pacific RR Co.* (1887), 72 Cal. 523; *Ryall v. Central Pacific RR Co.* (1888), 76 Cal. 474; *Taylor v. Baldwin* (1889), 78 Cal. 517.

73. Schwartz, "Tort Law," p. 1768.

74. 57 Cal. 15.

75. 63 Cal. 96.

76. 78 Cal. 430.

77. 83 Cal. 18.

78. *Beeson v. Green Mountain Gold Mining Co.* (1880), 57 Cal. 20; *Sanborn v. Madera Flume and Trading Co.* (1886), 70 Cal. 261; *Monaghan v. Pacific Rolling Mill Co.* (1889), 81 Cal. 190; also see *Colbert v. Rankin* (1887), 72 Cal. 197.

79. 86 Cal. 445, 448–49.

80. See *Kevern v. Providence Gold and Silver Mining Co.* (1886), 70 Cal. 392; *Stephens v. Doe* (1887), 73 Cal. 26; *Fisk v. Central Pacific RR Co.* (1887), 72 Cal. 38. Schwartz, "Tort Law," p. 1769.

81. See Paterson's dissent in *Fagendes v. Central Pacific RR Co.* (1889), 79 Cal. 97; for general treatments of tort, contract–tort relationships, and liability theories see Oliver Wendell Holmes, *The Common Law* (Boston, Massachusetts, 1881), pp. 145-63; John Phillip Reid, "Experience or Reason: The Tort Theories of Holmes and Doe," 18 *Vanderbilt Law Review* 405 (1965); idem, *Chief Justice: The Judicial World of Charles Doe* (Cambridge, Massachusetts, 1967), pp. 133-47; Grant Gilmore, *The Death of Contract* (Columbus, Ohio, 1974); Morton J. Horwitz, *The Transformation of American Law, 1780-1860* (Cambridge, Massachusetts, 1977), pp. 201-10; G. Edward White, *Tort Law in America* (New York, New York, 1980); Robert A. Silverman, *Law and Urban Growth* (Princeton, New Jersey, 1981), pp. 99-131; Philip J. Merkel, "The Origins of the Expanded Federal Court Jurisdiction: Railroad Development and the Ascendancy of the Federal Judiciary," 58 *Business History Review* 336-358 (1984).

CHAPTER 5

1. See generally Ira B. Cross, *Financing an Empire*, 4 vols. (Chicago, Illinois, 1937); Robert G. Cleland and Frank P. Putnam, *Isaias W. Hellman and the Farmers and Merchants Bank* (San Marino, California, 1965). Several textbook accounts are good: Andrew F. Rolle, *California* (New York, New York, 1969), pp. 297-99; John W. Caughey, *California*, 3rd ed. (Englewood Cliffs, New Jersey, 1970), pp. 205-6.

2. *Cal. Laws* (1855), ch. 150, p. 128.

3. *Cal. Laws* (1850), in *Comp. Laws* (1853), p. 146.

4. See Rodman M. Price Collection, MSS, Huntington Library (San Marino, California), Box 1.

5. See Matthew Keller Collection, MSS, Huntington Library, Box 4; for the San Francisco experience, see Peter R. Decker, *Fortunes and Failures* (Cambridge, Massachusetts, 1978), pp. 87-105; Roger W. Lotchin, *San Francisco* (Lincoln, Nebraska, 1974), pp. 45-82.

6. Beers to Goodwin, Goodwin Collection, MSS, California State Library (Sacramento, California), California Section, Box 727.

7. Hume to Jane, February 20, 1858, Hume Collection, MSS, Bancroft Library (Berkeley, California).

8. Haight to Henry H. Haight, August 9, 1864, Haight Collection, MSS, Huntington Library, Box 5.

9. Blood to John D. Goodwin, February 9, 1880, Goodwin Collection, Box 727.

10. 3 Cal. 328, 329.

11. 2 Cal. 64, 67.

12. 2 Cal. 231, 233.

13. 2 Cal. 231, 235.

14. *Palmer v. Goodwin* (1855), 5 Cal. 458, 459.

15. *Price v. Dunlap* (1855), 5 Cal. 483, 484.

16. *Beebe v. Brooks* (1859), 12 Cal. 308, 310.

17. For comment on similar rules without the commercial practice verbiage, see *Tevis v. Wood* (1855), 5 Cal. 393 on the liability of indorsers; *Smith v. Harper* (1855), 5 Cal. 329 on the effect of substitution of new security; and *Gregory v. Higgins* (1858), 10 Cal. 339 on attachment.

18. See, for example, *Langenberger v. Kroeger* (1874), 48 Cal. 147. The case has additional significance in that it involved the legal tender issue. In deciding the case, Justice Crockett said: "As the draft specified no particular kind of money which it was payable, it might have been paid in legal tender notes; and it was not competent for either of the parties to prove by parol, that it was understood and agreed that it should be paid either in gold or silver."

19. 7 Cal. 166, 168-69.

20. 10 Cal. 282, 291.

21. 10 Cal. 282, 291-92.

22. Eaton note, March 1, 1855, Keller Collection, Box 1.

23. Wolter note, March 3, 1853, Charles Wolter Collection, MSS, Huntington Library, Box 1.

24. Price note, October 3, 1850, Price Collection, Box 1.

25. D. Catlin notes, May 9 and November 5, 1855, Catlin Collection, MSS, Huntington Library, Box 2. Other examples are legion: See Jerome Davis Collection, MSS, California State Library, California Section, Box 305; Wolter Collection, Box 2 (1866-69 notes); Gideon J. Carpenter Collection, MSS, Bancroft Library; John W. Snowball Collection, MSS, California State Library, California Section, Box 490; Keller Collection, Box 3; John Bidwell Collection, MSS, California State Library, California Section, Box 136; John Daggett Collection, MSS, California State Library, California Section, Box 437; David Jacks Collection, MSS, Huntington Library, Box B(V)(I)(10).

26. S. M. Folger to Dear Friend, December 28, 1863, Goodwin Collection, Box 730.

27. Grave to M. C. Ireland, November 9, 1870, Jacks Collection, Box C(1).

28. G. Bucklee to Goodwin, February 8, 1871, Goodwin Collection, Box 727.

29. Decker, *Fortunes and Failures*, pp. 49–52, 95, 117–81.

30. Ellison and Sons to Bicknell, June 28, July 17, and September 14, 1876 (Philadelphia), Bicknell Collection, MSS, Huntington Library, Box 2; W. Cornell to Bicknell, October 16, 1876, and James C. Hopple and Co. to Bicknell, October 30, 1876 (Cincinnati), ibid.; Bromwell and Sleeth to Bicknell, July 31, 1877 (Denver), ibid.; also see Lake and Harmon to Bicknell, October 31, 1876 (Independence, Iowa), ibid.; G. A. Follansbee to Bicknell, January 30, 1877 (Chicago), ibid.; J. T. Beem to Bicknell, July 17, 1877 (Marengo, Iowa), ibid.

31. Graves and O'Melveny to Merchants P. and C. A., December 1, 1885, Jackson A. Graves Collection, MSS, Huntington Library, 1885–86 Letterbook.

32. Liebes Bros. and Co. to J. M. Rothchild, July 26, 1875, Bicknell Collection, Box 1; Joseph Bremer and Co. to John D. Goodwin, September 8, 1883, Goodwin Collection, Box 727.

33. Douglas and Co. (Visalia) to Bicknell, December 12, 1874, Bicknell Collection, Box 1; B. Brundage (Bakersfield) to Bicknell, May 21, 1879, ibid., Box 3; Boren and Curtis (San Bernardino) to Bicknell, February 20, 1874, ibid., Box 1; S. Z. Millard (Compton) to Bicknell, June 8, 1876, ibid., Box 2; J. Robertson (Rovena) to Bicknell, November 4, 1882, ibid., Box 4; Holladay, Saunders and Cary (San Francisco) to John Stuber (Sacramento), September 9, 1855, Holladay Family Papers, MSS, Huntington Library, Letterbook 5.

34. Jake to Loe, October 30, 1875, Albert Dressler Collection, MSS, California State Library, California Section, Box 756.

35. Wood to Rothchild, June 8, 1875, Bicknell Collection, Box 1.

36. W. Hoffman to P. O. Hundley, July 25, 1862, Goodwin Collection, Box 731; H. Goodman to Goodwin, December 21, 1883, ibid., Box 730; J. M. Eastman to Goodwin, May 28, 1868, ibid., Box 729; J. M. Richards to sheriff of Plumas Co., August 16, 1865, ibid., Box 735; R. Strahan to Bicknell, February 24, 1876, Bicknell Collection, Box 2; John B. Ellison to Bicknell, March 23, 1875, ibid., Box 1.

37. Harry Fiske to D. W. Jenks, February 24, 1883, Goodwin Collection, Box 730; also see Henry C. Biddle to Bicknell, February 10, 1875, Bicknell Collection, Box 1; E. A. Fargo to Bicknell, September 1, 1873, ibid; General Correspondence 1871–75, Goodwin Collection, Box 729.

38. Cushman to Jacks, September 1, 1890, Jacks Collection, Box C(8).

39. Arick to McConnell, July 14, 1875, Bicknell Collection, Box 1.

40. J. V. Beach to Bicknell, July 7, 1880, ibid., Box 3.

41. Sweeney et al. to Bicknell, March 28, 1881, ibid.

42. Graves to Howe and Hass, July 3, 1878, Graves Collection, 1878–79 Letterbook.

43. Graves to Dinkelspiel and Co., September 26, 1879, ibid., 1879-80 Letterbook.

44. Siter to Wells, June 19, 1854, Haight Collection, Box 3.

45. See Grant Gilmore, *Security Interests in Personal Property*, 2 vols. (Boston, Massachusetts, 1965), vol. 1, pp. 5-23.

46. 62 Cal. 426, 440.

47. 66 Cal. 74.

48. 66 Cal. 74, 75.

49. See, for example, *Salinas City Bank v. Graves* (1889), 79 Cal. 192. Here the bank failed to act with knowledge of an assignment and allowed pledged property to go into the hands of a third party, losing its interest valued at $17,640. Also see *Dodge v. Meyer* (1882), 61 Cal. 405, which involved $90,118.19 in wheat pledged by farmers to commission merchants. The legislature attempted to cover this entrusting situation in *Cal. Laws* (1878), ch. 535, pp. 835-37.

50. *Cal. Laws* (1853), in *Comp. Laws* (1853), ch. 193, p. 911, repealing *Cal. Laws* (1850), in *Comp. Laws* (1853), ch. 47, section 17, p. 201, which declared that chattel mortgages were invalid without delivery and possession by the mortgagee.

51. *Cal. Laws* (1857), ch. 264, pp. 347-50.

52. 23 Cal. 299, 300-301.

53. 23 Cal. 299, 301.

54. Note the problem in *Wilson v. Brannan* (1865), 27 Cal. 258. The legislature expanded the list of goods mortgageable. See *Cal. Laws* (1861), ch. 202, pp. 197-98; *Cal. Laws* (1863), ch. 257, pp. 331-32; *Cal. Laws* (1887), ch. 8, pp. 4-5. Recording in statutory form was also a necessary requisite to the creation of the chattel mortgage [*Beamer v. Freeman* (1890), 84 Cal. 554].

55. *Cal. Laws* (1850), in *Comp. Laws* (1853), pp. 808-11.

56. *Macondray v. Simmons* (1851), 1 Cal. 393. A lumbermerchant had no lien because in Mexican law there was no materialman's lien.

57. Supplementary Act of 1853, in *Comp. Laws* (1853), pp. 811-12.

58. 2 Cal. 90; also see *Houghton v. Blake* (1855), 5 Cal. 240.

59. 2 Cal. 90, 91.

60. *Godeffroy v. Caldwell* (1852), 2 Cal. 489.

61. 3 Cal. 236.

62. 4 Cal. 173. Filing deadlines also concerned both the Court and the legislature. The 1850 statute required a contractor to file his lien claim 60 days after completion of the building. Subcontractors, including materialmen, laborers, and the like, had 30 days after notice to the owner to file. The Court in *Walker v. Hauss-Hijo* (1850), 1 Cal. 183, strictly construed this filing deadline requirement. *Cal. Laws* (1855), p. 156. See *Cahoon v. Levy* (1856), 6 Cal. 295. On priority among lien claimants, see *Moxley v. Shepard* (1853), 3 Cal. 64.

63. 4 Cal. 173, 174; also see *Ferguson v. Miller* (1856), 6 Cal. 402.

64. *Cal. Laws* (1856), ch. 134, pp. 230-35; also see *Cal. Laws* (1855), ch. 130, p. 156.

65. *Cal. Laws* (1856), ch. 61, p. 58.

66. *Cal. Laws* (1857), ch. 87, p. 84. The process of addition and clarification continued in the 1858 session [*Cal. Laws* (1858), ch. 270, p. 225].

67. 12 Cal. 542, 554.

68. 18 Cal. 370, 372.

69. 16 Cal. 126, 127; also see *Bowen v. Aubrey* (1863), 22 Cal. 566. Crocker on p. 571 reiterated the fear of excessive general contractor authority.

70. *Wood v. Wrede* (1873), 46 Cal. 637, 638. The substantial compliance position was one dating to the 1850s. In *Hotaling v. Cronise* (1852), 2 Cal. 60, the Court held that "convenient certainty" in the description of the property was enough. Vagueness on omissions that failed to put a debtor on notice resulted in the defeat of the claim. Also see *McDonald v. Bacus* (1873), 45 Cal. 262; *Goss v. Strelitz* (1880), 54 Cal. 640.

71. See *Phelps v. C.G.M. Company* (1874), 49 Cal. 336; plaintiff failed to properly file the claim and include the name of the person receiving materials. *Rosenkranz v. Wagner* (1882), 62 Cal. 151. The complaint failed to state that the defendant owed the general contractor and failed to allege that defendant was notified of plaintiff's claims prior to payment to general contractor; *Harmon v. Ashmead* (1882), 60 Cal. 439. Lien claim was filed before debt became payable; *Penrose v. Calkins* (1888), 77 Cal. 396. Justice Works noted that "the courts have been very liberal upholding imperfect descriptions in this class of cases but here there is absolutely no description of the property." 77 Cal. 396, 397.

72. 40 Cal. 185, 188.

73. *Cal. Laws* (1870), p. 723 (stockman's lien); *Cal. Laws* (1878), ch. 484, pp. 747–48; *Cal. Laws* (1880), ch. 49, pp. 38–39 (logger's lien). *Cal. Laws* (1885), ch. 125, p. 109 (threshing machine worker's lien).

74. *Church v. Garrison* (1888), 75 Cal. 199. The case involved the threshing machine worker's lien. The shift was not complete. Note *Wilson v. Barnard* (1885), 67 Cal. 422, on loggers' liens. The majority retained the mechanic's lien law concept of possession, while McKee in dissent argued that "a construction possession" was sufficient (67 Cal. 422, 425–26).

75. Bicknell to John Robarts, March 21, 1889, Bicknell Collection, Letterbook 4.

76. See, for example, J. D. Boyer and W. M. Gregory to Bicknell, December 12, 1879, ibid., Box 3; also see Goodwin Collection, Box 746, for lien foreclosure litigation papers.

77. Keller to Gentry, July 30, 1860, Keller Collection, Box 1; also see, on prepayment of notes, Thomas H. O'Conner to Bicknell, January 31 and September 10, 1888, Bicknell Collection, Box 5.

78. Harrison to David Jacks, July 17, 1890, Jacks Collection, Box C(8).

79. James T. Jenkins to D. W. Jenks, September 19, 1884, Goodwin Collection, Box 732.

80. Chapelain to Goodwin, May 10, 1864, ibid., Box 728.

81. McCutcheon to Goodwin, August 7 and September 29, 1875, ibid., Box 733.

82. For example, see Graves to Orr, McCaige, McFadden, Rogers, Richardson, Thomas, Trask, Vance and Young (nine letters all dated July 3, 1878), Graves Collection, 1878-79 Letterbook.

83. Graves to J. M. Soto, July 21, 1879, ibid., 1879-80 Letterbook.

84. Graves and O'Melveny to Egan, February 24, 1885, ibid., 1883-85 Letterbook.

85. Bicknell to Machado and Cornell, October 15, 1874, Bicknell Collection, Letterbook 1.

86. Bicknell to Rumpp, December 7, 1874, ibid.

87. Graves et al. to Fairview, December 6, 1888, Graves Collection, 1888-90 Letterbook.

88. Certificate of execution against Stephen J. Worden, November 4, 1854, Dressler Collection, Box 759.

89. Leander Bushon to John Bicknell, July 8, 1883, May 11, 1884, March 15, 1885, Bicknell Collection, Box 4.

90. Forbes to H. S. Ledyard, November 10, 1875, ibid., Box 1.

91. Charles H. Larrobee to Bicknell, July 21, 1873, ibid.; E. A. Fargo and Co. to Bicknell, May 26, 1874, ibid.; Daniel E. Waldron to J. M. Rothchild, August 2, 1875, ibid. Jackson A. Graves of Los Angeles often obtained the writ of attachment and sent it to distant county sheriffs for action (Graves to sheriff, Inyo County, May 24, 1879, Graves Collection, 1879-80 Letterbook).

92. A. J. Ford to John D. Goodwin, May 29, 1883, Goodwin Collection, Box 730; W. C. Fairchild to A.L. Rhodes, December 18, 1889, ibid.; Ellen Callahan to Goodwin, May 28, 1883, ibid., Box 728; Fred Shulter to David Jacks, March 28, 1870, Jacks Collection, Box C(1); J. Bates to Goodwin, July 14, 1883, Goodwin Collection, Box 727.

93. Oury to Hanson, July 30, 1875, to Bicknell, August 25, 1875, Bicknell Collection, Box 1; on Oury, see C. L. Sonnichsen, *Tucson* (Norman, Oklahoma, 1982), pp. 48-49; Jay J. Wagoner, *Arizona Territory* (Tucson, Arizona, 1970), pp. 81, 83, 85, 89, 90-96, 115.

94. Studebaker to Bicknell, August 24, 1888, Bicknell Collection, Box 5.

95. Graves, O'Melveny, and Shankland to Mrs. L. D. Cook, May 7, 1889, and to Samuel Parks, December 6, 1888, Graves Collection, 1888-90 Letterbook.

96. Cain to Bicknell, July 19, 1887, Bicknell Collection, Box 5.

97. A. H. Loughborough to Bicknell, February 5, 1890, ibid., Box 6; Samuel A. Way to Henry Haight, January 2 and May 30, 1856, Haight Collection, Box 4; Frank O. Day to Haight, March 24, 1854, ibid., Box 2.

98. Thomas H. O'Connor to Bicknell, November 11, 1887, Bicknell Collection, Box 5.

99. Thomas H. O'Connor to Bicknell, June 8, 1889, ibid., Box 6; Bicknell to O'Connor, January 2, 1889, ibid., Letterbook 4; James A. Clayton to David Jacks, November 4 and 26, 1889, Jacks Collection, Box C(7); Thompson and Davis to Goodwin, September 12, 1874, Goodwin Collection, Box 735; Judgment of December 6, 1871, to Clough and Goodwin, October 16, 1871, ibid.

100. Lotchin, *San Francisco*, p. 249.

101. Decker, *Fortunes and Failures*, p. 16.

102. Ibid., p. 91.

103. Ibid., p. 92.

104. James, Doyle, Barber, Boyd, Hackett, and Casserly to Adams, Adams and Company Collection, MSS, Huntington Library, Box 2; also see Scrapbook, vol. 4, p. 108, and vol. 2, pp. 139–40; further, documents on the dissolution are in Box 4 and the transcripts of the litigation are in folders AM 26, 27, and 42; writs of attachment are in AM 17–22.

105. J. M. Rothchild to Bicknell, June 12, 1875, Bicknell Collection, Box 1; H. Behrendt and Co. to McConnell, Bicknell and Rothchild, July 30, 1875, ibid.; E. K. Chapin to Bicknell, December 4, 1878, ibid., Box 2; F. Butler to Bicknell, July 22, 1877, ibid.; George Roberts to Bicknell, August 18, 1881, ibid., Box 3; Charles H. Larrobee to Bicknell, July 18, 1873, ibid., Box 1; Robert Watt to Bicknell, February 27, 1877, ibid., Box 2; Watt to Bicknell, August 28, 1876, ibid.

106. McGee to Goodwin, November 16, 1875, Goodwin Collection, Box 733.

107. Bransford to Goodwin, November 3, 1875, ibid., Box 727.

108. Seibert to Bicknell, October 16, 1882, Bicknell Collection, Box 4.

109. Jackson A. Graves to J. Naptely, April 5, 1880, Graves Collection, 1879–80 Letterbook.

110. Graves and O'Melveny to J. H. Shankland, August 25, 1885, Graves Collection, 1883–85 Letterbook.

CHAPTER 6

1. Grant Gilmore and Charles Black, *The Law of Admiralty* (Brooklyn, New York, 1957), p. 1.

2. See John C. Miller, *The Federalist Era* (New York, New York, 1960), pp. 126–54; Noble E. Cunningham, Jr., *The Jeffersonian Republicans* (Chapel Hill, North Carolina, 1957), pp. 54–66; see Charles Warren, *The Supreme Court in the United States History*, 2 vols. (Boston, Massachusetts, 1926), vol. 1, pp. 106–115; *Glass v. Sloop Betsy* (1794), U.S. 74, 75; *Croudsen v. Leonard* (1808), 4 Cranch 434.

3. See Warren, *Supreme Court*, p. 634.

4. 17 U.S. 440; Gilmore and Black, *Law of Admiralty*, p. 526; *St. Jago de Cuba* (1824), 22 U.S. 110.

5. 23 U.S. 465.

6. 12 Howard 443 (1851).

7. 1 Cal. 459.

8. 1 Cal. 485.

9. 1 Cal. 485, 486.

10. *John G. Stevens* (1898), 170 U.S. 113, 119.

11. *Brooks v. Minturn* (1851), 1 Cal. 481.

12. *Brown v. Howard and Howard* (1851), 1 Cal. 423.

13. 1 Cal. 462, 469.

14. 2 Cal. 308, 309.

15. Also see "Comment: Admiralty: Power of the States and of Congress in Respect Thereto," 8 *California Law Review* 114, 116–17 (1919).

16. *Griswold v. Sharpe* (1852), 2 Cal. 17.

17. *Sacramento v. Steamer New World* (1854), 4 Cal. 41; also see *Sacramento v. Steamer Confidence* (1854), 4 Cal. 45. Admiralty practice documents are in Halleck, Peachy, and Billings Collection, MSS, Huntington Library (San Marino, California), Box 2.

18. 5 Cal. 268, 273; also see *Gordon v. Johnson* (1854), 4 Cal. 368.

19. 5 Cal 268, 274; also see *Warner v. Uncle Sam* (1858), 9 Cal. 710, 733.

20. *Reina v. Cross* (1856), 6 Cal. 29; *Lawson v. Worms* (1856), 6 Cal. 365.

21. *White v. Steam-Tug Mary Ann* (1856), 6 Cal. 462.

22. 6 Cal. 343.

23. 8 Cal. 363.

24. 8 Cal. 363, 374.

25. 8 Cal. 363, 374.

26. 8 Cal. 363, 375.

27. 8 Cal. 522, 534.

28. See *Hayden v. Davis* (1858), 9 Cal. 573; *Jones v. Steamship Cortes* (1861), 17 Cal. 487; *Sheldon v. Steamship Uncle Sam* (1861), 18 Cal. 526; *Edgerly v. Schooner San Lorenzo* (1866), 29 Cal. 418; see Neilson and Bleecker, "Ship Aquilla (General Average)," vol. 2, Holladay Family Papers, MSS, Huntington Library.

29. 71 U.S. 411 (1867).

30. Field redrafted the Practice Act, believing that he had saved it from his own decision, but it too was later overturned. See "Comment," pp. 114–119; also see Neal Gobar, "Note: Admiralty: Partition of Ships: Concurrent Jurisdiction of State and Admiralty Courts," 42 *California Law Review* 331–36 (1954).

31. 42 Cal. 227, 228–29; see to the contrary *Philadelphia W. and B.R.R. v. Philadelphia and H. de G.S. Towboat Co.* (1860), 64 U.S. 209.

32. 42 Cal. 469, 473.

33. 42 Cal. 469, 474.

34. See *Plymouth* (1866), 70 U.S. 20, 36.

35. 46 Cal. 175.

36. 49 Cal. 310.

37. See *Olsen v. Birch* (1901), 133 Cal. 479; *Madruga v. Superior Court* (1954), 346 U.S. 556.

38. See Gilmore and Black, *Law of Admiralty*, pp. 34–36; for the federal court experience, see Christian G. Fritz, "Judicial Style in California's Federal Admiralty Court, Ogden Hoffman and the First Ten Years, 1851–1861," 64 *Southern California Quarterly* 179–203 (Fall 1982).

39. Derby, Cook, Quinby, and Tweedt Scrapbook, private collection, law office at 333 Market Street, San Francisco.

BIBLIOGRAPHIC ESSAY

Histories of California are numerous. Although general in nature, the state histories are useful as context: John W. Caughey and Norris Hundley, Jr., *California*, Englewood Cliffs, New Jersey, 1982; Walton Bean, *California*, New York, New York, 1968; Warren Beck and David A. Williams, *California*, Garden City, New York, 1972.

The relationship of government and the economy is best covered by Gerald Nash, *State Government and Economic Development: A History of Administration Policies in California, 1849-1933*, Berkeley, California, 1964. Regarding land ownership and the transitions of the 1850s, Paul Gates, *California Ranchos and Farms, 1846-1862*, Madison, Wisconsin, 1968, and Leonard Pitt, *The Decline of the Californios*, Berkeley, California, 1966 analyze the process of social and economic change on the land.

The interface of law, policy, and socioeconomic change in urban California is best analyzed by Roger W. Lotchin, *San Francisco, 1846-1856*, New York, New York, 1974. With broader brush, Kevin Starr's *Americans and the California Dream, 1850-1915*, New York, New York, 1973, presents a masterful sociointellectual portrait of a state of mind.

Historians have given a great deal of attention to the California gold rush. Rodman Paul's work is clearly the most comprehensive: *California Gold*, Cambridge, Massachusetts, 1947; *The California Gold Discovery*, Georgetown, Washington, D.C., 1966; *Mining Frontiers of the Far West, 1848-1880*, New York, New York, 1963.

John Phillip Reid gave law and society on the Overland Trail masterful analysis in *Laws for the Elephant*, San Marino, California, 1980. For general history of law in California, see Richard R. Powell, *Compromises and Conflicting Claims: A Century of California Law, 1760-1860*, Dobbs Ferry, New York, 1977. Reid's study is an example of the significance of law in society and of the potential of legal history. As legal history of the western experience, it is clearly the most insightful.

The best contemporary account of California legal history is Jackson A. Graves, *My Seventy Years in California, 1857-1927*, Los Angeles, California, 1927.

INDEX

About the Author

GORDON MORRIS BAKKEN is Professor of History and Director of Faculty Affairs and Records at California State University, Fullerton. He is the author of *The Development of Law on the Rocky Mountain Frontier* published by Greenwood Press in 1983.